SIGNS OF AGNI YOGA

AGNI YOGA

AGNI
YOGA

1929

Agni Yoga Society
319 West 107th Street
New York NY 10025
www.agniyoga.org

The Blessed Mahatma who gave the books, *The Call, Illumination,* and *Community,* has given much counsel and the Signs of Agni Yoga. These practical indications were gathered by us for the use of those who seek knowledge.

Sanskrit and Senzar lend a special flavor to the exposition and do not always find their equivalent in other languages. Nevertheless the meaning of the expressions is preserved exactly. And those who take part in contemporary life will read attentively this wise Teaching which emanates from the experience of centuries.

PREFACE

Yoga—that supreme bridge to cosmic attainment—has existed through all ages. Each Teaching comprises its own Yoga, applicable to that step of evolution. The Yogas do not contradict each other. As the branches of one tree they spread their shade and refresh the traveler exhausted from heat.

His strength regained, the traveler continues on his way. He took naught that was not his, nor did he divert his striving. He embraced the manifested benevolence of space. He liberated the preordained forces. He mastered his single belonging.

Do not reject the forces of Yoga, but like light carry them into the twilight of labor unrealized.

For the future, we arise out of sleep. For the future, we renew our garments. For the future, we sustain ourselves. For the future, we strive in our thought. For the future, we gather strength.

First we shall apply the counsels of life. Then we shall pronounce the name of the Yoga of the time approaching. We shall hear the advancing footsteps of the element of fire, but we shall already be prepared to master the undulations of the flame.

Therefore, we hail the yoga of the past—the Raja Yoga. And we affirm that of the future—the Agni Yoga.

AGNI YOGA

1. They will ask, "Can the time of Maitreya create a New Era?"

Answer, "If the Crusades brought a new age, then truly the Era of Maitreya is a thousandfold more significant." In such consciousness should one proceed.

2. People do not realize the meaning of God or Bodhisattva. As though blind, they ask, "What is light?" But people even lack words to describe its properties, though daily they perceive light.

So wary are people of the unusual that they are confused about the boundaries of light and darkness. It is simpler for them to conceive of God inhabiting a palace upon the largest star. Otherwise their God would remain dwellingless. Their manifest lack of co-measurement impels them to demean what exists.

3. Often you wonder why I do not reply to a question. You must know that the arrows of thought often graze the subject of the answer. Imagine a traveler who is crossing an abyss upon a rope. Would it be wise to begin calling him? The call may disturb his balance. Therefore, one should pronounce names less often, reserving them for urgent need. The ability to use individual names is necessary, but uttering them should be like the blow of a hammer in space.

4. Regarding simpler words for simple people, one should remember that simple people need smaller doses of medicine. There is the identical law—as above, so below. Therefore simple people are the best disseminators.

5. The expansion of the blood vessels is characteristic of the growth of consciousness, and this process must be protected by physical means from the effect of the sun's pressure upon the solar plexus.

Let us not forget how the priestesses of antiquity were shielded from the sun. They wore breastplates of lithium, covered with wax, the melting of which indicated the danger line of temperature.

In addition to immersing the hands in water, immersing of the feet is permitted. But cold baths may be as harmful as the sun's rays.

6. One can visit different planets in one's mental body. Thus is indicated that future step when consciousness will not be confined to the one planet. As we now cross from one part of the world to another, the same principle will be applied in interplanetary crossings.

The Teacher bids you rejoice at each attainment of the spirit. The way to and from other planets is no more difficult than is the passage between the physical and astral bodies, no more complicated than understanding the process of thought and striving to the stars. Only in striving for the interplanetary can we be assured of the evolution of humanity.

7. The manifestation of new rays prompts beautiful additions to Our plans. The densification of the astral body is inconsequential in itself when compared with the conscious work of the mental body. For one's tasks on this planet the mental body need not be released from its shielded condition. But this highest body is needed for interplanetary activity.

The affirmation of new rays will permit one to retain consciousness in diverse spheres. Formerly only certain strata of the atmosphere permitted the retention of consciousness. But interceptions by gaseous currents were still possible. However, the new rays can penetrate these interceptions, creating open channels, and thus expanding the conscious activity.

Work on the utilization of these rays is underway at Our Community. Usually, they have no significant effect on the brain, but sometimes they can be quite dangerous.

8. One can point out why the Teachers of Knowledge experienced such suffering on departing Earth. Of course, this suffering was conscious and voluntarily chosen. Just as the host fills the guest's cup to the brim, so does the Teacher desire to impress this last sign of His Teaching.

The poisoning of Buddha spared Him from deification. The suffering and resurrection—or the transformation of matter—by Christ provided the attainment of the supreme earthly achievement. But no one knew about the disintegration of the body into the atomic state. People thought that His body had been stolen away by His disciples.

The slander of the old world is of no consequence. Each true achievement is needed for Cosmos. The creativity of *podvig* is the same in every process of creation. In augmenting the profundity of the form we create an ageless crystal. The sense of perfection uplifts the spirit of creative manifestations. Christ, being a realist, desired that the phenomenon of transformation should be preceded by a *podvig* in complete consciousness.

One can point out two kinds of *podvig*, the supermundane and the earthly. As an instance of supermundane striving, one can mark a serene passing, such as that of the Great Pilgrim. Let us not attempt to judge acts of *podvig*, for the understanding of evolution is individual and voluntary.

9. Anyone who is able to observe human auras may witness a vivid play of the emanations of light. Plans of rational action can be based on observation of this cosmic flux. Each sign of atrophy is connected with the products of darkness. But where there are waves of Light, where the vital sparks interplay, there is Our Ray.

My Teaching can reveal the waves of the observed *Akasha*. Welcome the joy of the sparks. This is not a diversion but a deepening of the task. Only by manifesting Our Will can you approach. My wish is to preserve the beauty of spirit.

Each motion can be transformed into an achievement of the spirit. Commitment to the evolution of consciousness, and the onrushing whirlwind of events, will lead to a new turn of the cosmic spiral.

10. When alone, spurning possessions, standing firm and unperturbed, not bewailing his fate—only then does the daring one exult.

Thus shall We begin the translation of Our ancient Book of Daring.

When a child plays with a newborn kitten, his mother rejoices at his courage, loathe to note that the kitten is still blind. When a youth toys with the soul of his comrade, the spectators marvel at his daring, not seeing the shackles binding the wretched soul. When a man denounces an assembly of judges, the witnesses admire his courage, not knowing that the daring of his threat has been bought with the jingle of gold. When an aged man comforts himself by deriding death, his friends delight, unmindful that fear has fashioned his mask of derision.

True daring is often unnoticed by people, because in its essence it is unusual. But the heart will tremble in response to the unusual.

Where art thou who vanquished? Where art thou who transformed the tremor into a leap toward the light? Hear, thou who darest! In the deep of night I shall draw near to bless thy sandals. I shall strew thy pillow with sparks of light, for the sleep of the daring one is as the melting away of a lute, when the seven strings are bathed in mystery. The sleep of the daring one is as the calm before the whirlwind, when even the slenderest blades of grass are unstirred.

Does the roar of the lion set the worlds atremble? No—daring is awakened and the royal lotus of spirit unfolds. Brothers, let us gather in the hall of joy! The flower has unfolded; raised is the great wheel. Our Joy descends to the nether worlds and rises to the Brothers in the Supermundane.

We sing to daring Our best song.

11. The chirping of birds has disturbed the moment of rest. Why in the early hours are the birds so tense in their striving? They dare—overhearing the praise to daring. But no one informed them that their usual song would not increase their daring. The darkness shrieks, deafening in its banality. Darkness cannot withstand the daring of light.

When the scales of the Lord have been prepared, we shall awaken early in order to weigh our use of the day just passed. We shall select that which was most daring, in order that these kernels of good may weigh more in the balance. We shall add the sorrows of the old world, for their burden is of use to us. And add the derision of the ignorant. Each of these adds its weight to the cup holding truth. Should we find threats and assaults, let us not forget to add those to the cup also. Why the trembling of the scale? With what wretched, murky tatters have we filled the cup of our wrongdoing? Like last winter's withered leaves are heaped the curses of the ordinary, the dross of yesterday.

Victory to you, daring deeds! For the mighty-winged deeds outweigh all wrongdoing.

Lord, grant me to cast into the flames the deceptive rags of the ordinary. I shall not err in realizing that winged daring has Thy blessing. In the sacred furnace will I forge the *Wings of Alaya*. I know nothing of complaints, cruelty, or aught that could weigh down my new wings. New will be my song!

12. Broadly has spread the praise of daring. The least of the disciples have turned to the path of searching and have approached Us, asking that We judge their striving. Each brought his dreams: "I will destroy all earthly temples, because Truth needs no walls. I will water all deserts. I will open all prisons. I will demolish all swords. I will blaze all trails. I will wipe away all tears. I will travel through all lands. I will inscribe the book of humanity."

But the least one of them turned to the shining stars and said, "Hail to you, brothers!" And in this salutation of daring his ego vanished.

Let the path of the Universe be acknowledged in this daring greeting!

13. The book of Thomas à Kempis, *The Imitation of Christ*, has long been appreciated in the East not only by virtue of its content but because of the meaning of its title. In the midst of medieval idolatry of Christ, the voice of Thomas à Kempis resounded in protest. From behind the walls of a Catholic monastery rang out a voice to clarify the Image of the Great Teacher. The very word *imitation* comprises a vital action. The formula—Imitation of Christ—is an achievement of daring innate in the conscious spirit that accepts all responsibility of creation. Truly, the conscious pupil dares to approach the Teacher in imitation. Such an example brought light into the musty darkness and behind the monastic walls provided the impetus to strive toward creative daring.

In accordance with the groveling medieval consciousness, it would have been fitting to say, "The Worship of Christ." But the ascendant spirit dared to pronounce a call to imitation.

Each step of blessed daring must be cherished as a milestone in the progress of humanity. We do not give attention to monastic utterances. Thomas had no need to climb to the stake—his task was to proclaim not the forbidden but the inspiring formula.

There are two forms of truth. One must be nurtured by the flame of the stake. The other demands spreading without restraint. It is difficult to state which method is the more painful to pursue. Sometimes it is easier to suffer the pain of the stake than to witness the distortion of the disseminated teaching. In either event, blessed be the daring that penetrates the darkness!

14. The world has lost its happiness, because happiness is in the spirit. Those who have turned away from the spirit must endure unhappiness, because why else would they return to the spirit? Therein lies the meaning of great events.

To seek happiness through lies and through murder! One may rejoice that degeneracy is hastening evolution. Crimes are fanning the fire of an extinct world.

15. Imperil, which attracts danger, is the poison resulting from irritability. This poison, a quite substantial one, is deposited against the walls of the nerve channels and then spreads through the entire organism.

If modern science would try to examine objectively the nerve channels, giving heed to the astral currents, it would encounter a strange decomposition of the astral substance during the passage of that substance through the nerve channels—this is a reaction to imperil. Only rest can help the nervous system to overcome the dangerous enemy that can call forth the most diverse irritations and painful contractions of the organism.

He who is afflicted with imperil must repeat, "How beautiful everything is!" And he will be right; because the flow of evolution follows immutable law, it is beautiful. The more refined the nervous system, the more painful is the deposit of imperil. This same poison, by the addition of one ingredient, may contribute to the decomposition of matter.

16. Of no great merit are those who cannot distinguish the swallow from the vulture. But of what merit are those who believe that by plucking the eagle's wing they can turn it into a helpless duck? Beware of hypocrites, especially those immersed in greed—those cunning ones who stir their "spiritual" stew. The manifestation of the inviolability of the world's laws flashes like a sword. There is no spot for the hypocrite to lay his head. The teacher who has not assimilated the Indications of the Teaching is like an ass under a too-heavy load of grain. Likewise, the fisherman who has prepared his baskets for fish he cannot catch is like a fox outside a well-locked chicken coop.

17. Great is the turmoil in the world! A blow against the Teaching acts as a boomerang, smiting the inflicter. The air is alive with arrows.

Dry away the sweat caused by the enemy's attack. At the time of assault I shall speak of matters eternal. Let us rejoice, because opportunities are multiplied. I know that in each hostile heart sprouts a useful seed.

18. Astrochemistry makes it possible to determine the best combinations of astrochemical rays for each organism. Astrology is nothing but formulas of astro-chemistry. He who enters a house permeated with nicotine will carry away with him poisonous particles. Similarly, once someone has experienced directly the action of certain astrochemical rays, he will always respond to this particular combination. Knowing this, it becomes easy to ascertain when to approach a person who is needed.

The much-discussed sunspots intensify chemical influences. People keep repeating about unrest in the world during periods of sunspots, and even those with little knowledge can draw correct conclusions. But if we call to mind the harmful chemical reactions, it is not difficult to understand the saturation of space by the most active compounds, such as oxides and metalloids. How can one lightmindedly deny the evolutionary power of matter when from the Inexhaustible Reservoir rays of immeasurable intensity pour over our heads?

Those with especially sensitive organisms can testify that during the culminating period of the sunspots the rays of the luminary, because of their qualities, become unbearable for them. Also, during the passing of the great meteors, one may feel a quivering of the nervous system. Until now, people have been unable to recognize their place in this gigantic laboratory. That single recognition alone would arm the human organism, and, in place of worried observation of the tremors of the seismograph, would direct the search into the Limitless Heights—as material as tomorrow's repast, as majestic as the numberless stars.

19. Of all creative energies, thought remains supreme. What may be the crystal of this energy? Some believe that precise knowledge is the crown of thought; but it would be more correct to say that legend is the crown of thought. In legend is expressed the essence of creative energy. In a legend's short formula are defined both hope and achievement. It is a mistake to believe that legends are fantasies of antiquity. The impartial mind will discern the legend spun through all the days of the Universe. Each great achievement of a nation, each great leader, each important discovery, each cataclysm, each *podvig* is veiled in winged legend. Therefore, let us not disdain the legends of truth; let us discern keenly and cherish the words of reality. In legend is expressed the will of the people, and we cannot cite one legend that was false. The spiritual striving of the powerful collective spirit imprints an image of true meaning. And the outer form of a symbol is a sign for the world, a part of a world language, which is inevitable in evolution.

Right are the seekers of a universal tongue. Right are the creators of the world's legends. Thrice right are the bearers of *podvig*!

20. The new must be seen as urgent and useful. Inapplicable abstractions have no place. We are weary of air castles. Even the far-off worlds must be mastered in their physical reality. Such mastery as, for example, over a piece of ice or over the chemical heat of the sun, must enter the consciousness, as must also mastery of the minutest products of matter. The retardation of spiritual realization is caused by a lack of attention to the manifestations of nature. Losing the power of observation, man loses the ability to synthesize.

The abolishment of the use of money will free humanity from the blinders that impair its vision. There are moments of evolution when the walls we erect to contain conventional knowledge become obstacles. The time has come for the emancipation of knowledge, and the assumption of personal responsibility for its use.

A free mind has the privilege of searching out new designs based upon unusual combinations. These hitherto undetected threads will lead it to more exalted layers of matter. Beholding play that is timid and limited, the free mind is right to point out new and better combinations.

Rejoice in the Great Play of the Mother of the World!

21. Your discussions about the examples of slander recorded in history are correct. Slander is like fuel to the flame of *podvig*. Slander, when it occurs, is disturbing in ordinary life, but from the point of view of history the flame of slander is multihued; without slander grateful humanity would probably have buried its brightest manifestations.

Tactica Adversa ensures that the clanging bells of humanity are not stilled. The music of the spheres needs accompaniment, but those slanderers maddened by envy imagine that their howls densify the atmosphere so that the symphonies of Eternity cannot penetrate through to Earth. However a good householder finds a use for any and all dross. So, let the torches of slander light the path of unswerving achievement.

By calling Our messengers charlatans, people are acknowledging their unusualness. Coarse are the caresses of the lower animals. And the coarseness of the remainder of the departing race has surpassed even that of the dark ages. It is not baseness so much as coarseness of receptivity that makes the mass of humanity unfit material. It is precisely coarseness that gives rise to light-mindedness and to its consequence—treason.

Therefore, let us define slander as the torch of the savage. But during the night-crossings each fire can be used!

22. There is no judging more erroneous than that based on apparent actions. Looking at only the evident, people lose the thread of reality. Usually, any teaching that leads to a source of reality is called dreams by people.

Most people see life as being without any sign of new beginnings, and see only the evident decay. Thus, one can be completely immersed in the idea of decomposition and easily overlook the valuable new beginnings. New beginnings are wisely hidden; otherwise natural catastrophes would destroy the seeds of new possibility. Inertia is an essential quality of these elements, and in order to imbue them with evolutionary energy that stroke of spirit is needed which can embrace thought. Thus, thought is the communicating link with the elements.

When We speak of the need for fortifying the apparatus of thought, We are warning against the unbridled assault of the elemental forces. Certain periods of planetary existence are subject to assaults of the elements. The one resistance to them is a consistent striving of people toward a renewal of life. This saturation of thought will permit concentration on the Teaching and, like a smiting sword, will cleave the clouds of unapprehended chaos. Thought can protect against the elemental forces, otherwise the balance would be so greatly disturbed that cosmic catastrophes would ensue. Would a year of famine, of drought, of disease not be the result of mass degeneration of thought? One man's thoughts are not enough to resist the elements. A new trend in consciousness cannot yet give the needed form to conscious thought. Only complete realization and responsibility will make it possible to inject power into thought. Otherwise there will be tension without realization, like sails taut in the fury of the whirlwind.

We observe great tension in the magnetic waves as well as in the chemical rays. Human thought has become bent like an untempered blade. Chaos seethes in the depths of consciousness.

Can one endure? The idea of Our Beacon is beginning to penetrate the minds, because gradually it is becoming clear that nothing else remains in the whirls of chaos. How painful to the sensitive spirit! How We watch the waves of unprecedented darkness! The heart can contain only a limited quantity of this elemental poison.

23. What has forced the poisons toward the earthly spheres? The disturbances of the elements give rise to a powerful poisonous gas. Usually this gas is easily assimilated in space, but the rays of the sun are driving the gaseous waves into the layers closest to the planet. Although a dangerous reaction results, those forewarned can overcome the poison. Irritation and its offspring, imperil, combine easily with the poison of space, which is called aeroperil. The laws are alike in all things.

The Teacher sometimes wears a mask against the gas. Of course the action of the poison is not always the same. But sensitive apparatuses are responsive. Cold considerably minimizes the action of the gases.

24. It is possible that some will not agree to accept prophecy, and will say, "I can accept all things but prophecies." Answer, "Then let us set aside this word. More significant for you will be the decrees of the Invisible Government. Your modern heart prefers modern expressions. We do not insist on terms. For Us it is more essential that you should experience the effects of these decrees, that your brain should remember that the Invisible, International Government exists. To you the word *prophecy* jars too unscientifically in your dictionaries; but servile habit will come to your aid in classifying the precise significance of the word *decree*; and your tendency to see conspiracy everywhere will help you to accept the existence of the Invisible Government. In addition, the correlation of fact and effect will prompt your respect.

"We do not quibble about terminology but bring to conclusion a useful action. It is time to replace biblical terminology with more precise expressions. An amulet in a pocket is of no great value to the Invisible Government. What is needed is devotion, tested by conscious action. You thought to vanquish Us upon the field of terminology; but you called forth a decree, the results of which We ask you to contemplate. Guard your words and thoughts. We value the valor of daring; but the cunning of mediocrity is disdained by Our Government."

25. In every chemical experiment there comes a favorable moment when the breaking down and transformation of the original substance begins—this is the moment of creative success. Hence, out of the downfall of Rome one should not deduce the ill fortune of Numa Pompilius. It is simply that the substance has been depleted of its electrons. And it will always be so with all evolutionary actions. People usually do not understand this moment of success. They think that structures should rise continuously, beyond all the laws of construction.

It is incorrect to think that the past experiment of My Friend was unsuccessful. One should not pay attention to those few fools who are encountered on the way. The steps of new consciousness are laid firmly. Thus also the path observed by Us now is laid out successfully. In the same way, H.P.B. was grateful to the deriding drumbeaters, for she knew the true meaning of those, who, like her, were the drums on which the crowds beat. When the crowds perceive only charlatans, approach with attention. Remember that even Buddha and Christ were honored with this title.

26. You often ask how one can reconcile the indicated joy with one's joyless contacts with people. Truly, each Teacher rejoices at the limitless beauty of the far-off worlds and suffers over the stunted stupidity of so many people. How can they be given the key to those far-off worlds? Even after divesting themselves of their leaden burden of stupidity they must still pass through the venomous slime of doubt, and then the terrible state of self-conceit. Then, a great log will fall on the napes of their necks, and, tumbling down the stairs, these snails will dream of clinging at least to the lowest step. From this rocking human spirit one could fashion instructive children's toys. Truly, the snails cling more firmly to their own spots. At least snails do not engage in senseless wars.

27. Having no home is a necessary attribute of the Teacher. The Teacher has a place to stay, but not a home. The Teacher participates in life, but is not touched by the ordinary. The Teacher beautifies a discussion, but does not prolong it. He pities, but does not bewail. The Teacher defends, but does not gesticulate. The Teacher affirms, and is never uncertain. He forewarns, and delays not. If absolutely necessary, He can smite, but will never wound. He is grateful, and does not forget. He evaluates motives, and shows no weakness. Carefully He guards, but does not impose. He fears not, yet is not reckless. And so, cherish the

Teacher, who is revealed for the growth of your spirit. Consciously must the spirit be nurtured.

28. Hatha Yoga cannot be regarded as an independent form. The growth of the spirit changes it into Raja Yoga. It is impossible to name anybody who attained through Hatha Yoga alone. Besides, in a world of darkness and prejudice, accomplishments through Hatha Yoga can even bring harm, by its strengthening of the astral body. The fakirs may adapt themselves to this world of darkness and unwittingly weaken the ascent of thought. Even a person sitting quietly and contemplating can attain further, because thought is the Raja of all that exists. Beauty is born through the lightning of thought. Truly, a flaming Bhakti can kindle new worlds with a thought. And the step of a Jnani will be but the smile of a Raja-Bhakti. Therefore Hatha and Jnana are not original and are insufficient. What sage of wisdom would not be the lord of love?

29. Affirm Our Teaching as your own abode, as your own construction. Let the breath of renewal fill your entire being. The significance of Community is expressed in united thought about the development of the world. The distribution of basic material benefits will result from an understanding of the highest truth. Unimportant are thoughts concerning the lowest material benefits. One should reject thoughts about quantity and strive only for quality. Of the benefit of quality, and of the harm of doubt, one must speak untiringly.

30. After one of Our co-workers had completed a lengthy chemical experiment weighted with responsibility, a child exclaimed, "How prettily he plays with the glasses!" When we see a man climbing a mountain, would we think that he hastens to the Teacher? When we watch a carpenter, do we know what step of the

house he will reinforce? When we meet a woman bearing water, do we know whose thirst she will quench? When we see a closed door, can we know who will emerge first? When we hear sudden thunder, do we know where sped the dart of lightning?

But people almost always assume that he who bends over is picking up a stone for murder. They are sure that he who races astride his horse hastens with slander. They "know" that he who calls out pronounces a lie. They "know" that he who offers his hand is afire with treachery. They interpret every move of others according to their own way of thinking.

Poor ones! Who has bestowed on you the curse of self? Wherefrom comes the prejudice of your decisions? At what crossroad did you hear the criers of slander? Every simple greeting seems to you a condemnation. You expect that the mountains will withstand the threats of the slanderers and the oceans will not dry up from treason.

For you, the Uraeus of knowledge is not yet wrought!

31. It is necessary to distinguish between indignation of spirit and irritation. The fire of irritation must be divided into two kinds. When irritation has an impersonal cosmic character, its poison may be washed away by a current of *prana*. But if harmful feelings, such as conceit or self-pity, intensify the irritation, the sediment of poison will be precipitated upon the centers. Then there is no means to remove it; one can only wear it away by developing cosmic perception.

Quality of thinking must be realized as healing. Gratitude is likewise the finest purifier of the organism. He who has found the seed and realized the care of the Sender can project gratitude into space. Great is the healing power of the emission of gratitude. One must transform everything abstract into reality.

32. The International Government never has denied its existence. It has proclaimed itself, not in manifestos but in actions that were recorded even in official history. One can cite cases from the French and Russian Revolutions, as well as from the history of Anglo-Russian and Anglo-Indian relations, when an independent outside Hand altered the course of events. The Government did not hide the existence of its envoys in various countries. Naturally, in accordance with the dignity of the International Government, they never hid themselves. On the contrary, they showed themselves openly, visited various governments and were known to many. Literature preserves their names and adorns them with the fancies of their contemporaries. It is not secret organizations—of which governments are in such fear—but actual persons that are sent out by decree of the Invisible International Government.

Inimical to international tasks is each perpetration of fraud. But the unity of peoples, the appreciation of creative labor, the growth of the consciousness, are affirmed by the International Government as undeferrable measures. And if one traces the measures of this Government, it will be found that it cannot be accused of inactivity.

The existence of this Government has entered the awareness of humanity repeatedly, under various names. Each nation is warned but once. Envoys are dispatched but once in a century—this is the law of the Arhats. The acts of the Invisible Government conform with the process of world evolution, hence the results are based on natural law. No personal desire is here, only the immutable laws of matter. I do not desire—I know! And therefore decisions, even amidst the turbulent currents, are firm.

One may climb a mountain from the north or from the south—the result is still the same.

33. The phenomena in which you have taken part have demanded calmness. In addition to calmness, one might have noticed the need of a certain tensity. This condition created an accumulation of energy that could be likened to that operating in a hydrant. Therefore, it would be more correct to say that for the manifestation of phenomena a saturated calmness is needed.

34. Striving, during the growth of consciousness, is focused in the center of the solar plexus. Should striving go beyond its proper limits, then the so-called fiery death is unpreventable. An uncultivated consciousness can bear the fiery emotion of striving, but further ascent demands that the treasure be placed temporarily within a guarded casket.

Each thought deposits its sediments upon the walls of the channels of the nervous system. The more perfect the striving the more phosphorescent the sediments. The only place sufficiently protected for that fuel is the solar plexus, which gradually imbibes the sediments from the auxiliary channels. Sometimes such an absorption can be so vigorous as to cause star-shaped painful sensations. Then the Teacher must apply a cooling ray, which aids in drawing the sediments from the extremities to the center. All this is a process of the expansion of consciousness. By triennial steps one can trace the sharpening of receptivity. Each stage requires preservation of the casket for the next praiseworthy expenditure.

Let us guard the law of life that leads up the ladder of beauty and happiness.

35. When one speaks of someone's usefulness it is not meant that he is a pillar of the Teaching. One should take things in their reality, because exaggerating is as wrong as belittling. One must not drag anyone forcibly to heaven. At the destined hour, the blind regain their sight. It is useful to point out the measure of the order of life, avoiding what is unnecessary, so that even the humblest may see the benefit of material progress. But it is wrong to force people to wash their faces. Mark the usefulness of each messenger and do not place the load of a camel upon a donkey.

36. Each movement of consciousness must flow with the current of evolution. Each step of life must be considered as inseparable from self-improvement. A form that has congealed can be duplicated, but in the current, no wave can be duplicated.

Sleep or vigilance, labor or rest, motion or repose, all carry us equally toward the fulfillment of life's plan. "It is like fallen leaves," say the timid. "It is like seeds for the sowing," say the wise. "It is like arrows of light," say the daring.

Whosoever is set affright by the roar of the torrent is not yet born in the spirit. Who soars on the wave may think of the far-off worlds.

37. Answer only when you see that your answer can be understood. Often a questioner is not able to grasp your answer. Then it is necessary to find a consonant chord before sending your thought in a new direction. It is an error to believe that a current that cuts across the thought is less dangerous than a knife severing an artery. You must not intercept the questioner's thought, but must infuse new blood of life by nourishing his nervous system. Each answering word must be given not as a nail in a coffin, but as a physician's ray. A deferred reply may be given in the form of advice.

38. One who desires to join in cooperation must be given an opportunity to show his understanding. Thus, say to the physician, "You can show resourcefulness in applying musk, valerian, and cedar tar." Also, one can demonstrate observation in describing the flow of life. One can show steadfastness in striving to the Teacher, without doubt and without prejudice.

The quality of one's attainments is revealed in life. And we value each mark of attainment. Each hour brings new inalienable possibilities. Clear advantage results from previously manifested achievements— thus, the accomplishments are lawfully gained.

39. It is erroneous to believe that it is easy to lose something on Earth. It is even more difficult to find something. The word *loss* suggests that something was acquired. All that is acquired will drag behind him who acquired. At times it is impossible to be rid of one's possessions, both material and intangible. Therefore We advise acceptance of possessions with full responsibility for them. This permits improvement of the quality of one's possessions and thoughts. To drag along tattered survivals is burdensome.

How to cleanse away the ulcers of thought of cowardice and treason? One cannot heal the aura with cedar tar. One must burn away the ulcers with the flame of shock, and must find courage to endure the pain. But how can courage be found in a state of cowardice? Terror shakes the coward, but for Us terror is entirely inadmissible.

You who acquire possessions—think about their quality!

40. A blind man dreams of material reward. But, if he were to gain sight, he would be astonished to see that he creates his own reward. Ascending in consciousness, a man progresses filled with joy, and the thought of reward would return him into slavery. In fact, there are many slaves, precisely those who try to conceal the servility of their spirit beneath an icy impenetrability and a seeming renunciation of that which they do not even possess. Each one wanting reward is already a slave. Only by a free consciousness, lacking both self-aggrandizement and self-disparagement, can evolution be constructed.

The hammer of spirit is the worthiest weapon of attainment.

41. The bridges crossed between the stages of the expanding consciousness are unaffected by current events. It is a mistake to wait for the stars to be right; the work of the serpent of the solar plexus flows independently. But a special sensitivity to atmospheric conditions accompanies this inner work. The density of the surrounding atmosphere complicates the work of the nervous system. Therefore calmness is needed as a remedial condition.

42. One should distinguish three groups of medicines—life-givers, preservers, and restorers. Let us leave for Our enemies the fourth group—the destroyers. Let us turn our attention to the life-givers, because they act first of all upon the nervous system. The nerve centers and secretions of the glands indicate the future development of medicine. Through these domains humanity will discover the finest energy, which for simplification we still call spirit. The discovery of the emanations of this energy will be the next step in the development of culture.

Metalization in the cultivation of plants will yield useful secretions of the roots. Therefore it is necessary once again to direct attention to the vegetable kingdom. Besides, examine the nourishing properties of vegetables and grains and you will have many surprises. The lack of discrimination in the choice of man's nourishment is astonishing. I speak of the quality.

43. The pupil must not be obsessive, and the Teacher must not be seen as a dictator. Indeed, there is demanded of the student a realization of Hierarchy and harmony of action—the reconciling of the free will with acceptance of the Teacher. The weak mind is usually confused. Of course, the conditions and limitations imposed by the Teaching contradict the meaning of freedom in its vulgar sense. But through culture and the realization of goal-fitness the great concept of the Teacher is formed. The realization of the significance of the idea of the Teacher is a passing through the first gates of evolution. One should not bring to the concept of the Teacher expectations of anything supermundane. The Teacher is the One who gives the best advice for life. This practicality will embrace knowledge, creativity, and Infinity.

44. Do not say, "I do not remember." Say, "I failed to observe." Do not blame the memory, but do look back to note your inability to pay attention. People would sooner fall down stairs than watch the steps.

Do not say, "I do not know." Say, "As yet I have failed to learn." Neither age, nor health, nor conditions of life vindicate the funereal "I do not know." Zeal in life teems with eagerness to learn.

Do not say, "I have decided." Say, "I believe this is fit for the goal." It is easy to increase the goal-fitness, but to change one's decision is unworthy.

Chiefly, do not invite unhappiness persistently, as is usually done.

45. One should firmly tell people that the New World has come into being. People are not prepared to assume their places in the tasks of creation. It is an error to believe that conquest has any connection with the mission of the New World. Whether it is in the conquest of countries or of a special class of people, this belongs with departing ways of thinking. In the process of evolution one can consider only the ascent of consciousness founded upon freedom of opportunities.

In observing the history of humanity's development, entire periods of growth in consciousness can be seen. Let us not conceal that precisely now a book of discoveries and of the light of daring is being opened before humanity. This ripened fruit of the thorny travail of the community is ready to burst with seed. Can one split this fruit with a sword, or crush it through fright or through cringing cowardice, or usurp it through treacherous cunning? No, only unity of consciousness and the gaining of knowledge will bestow on humanity the gift of a new race. The impetus toward this will be afforded not by cosmic phenomena, but by the current of thought.

We shall not miss the ordained date when lightning-bolts of thought will provide the solution for the world. We suggest that humanity not only think about but realize the astrochemical moment of the planet when thought, like a chemical ingredient, will intensify the atmosphere.

In any case, until the significance of the emanations of thought is realized, thought will glide over the foreheads of the skeptics. But the moment does not wait!

46. According to certain symptoms one can distinguish between those nations that are ascending and those declining. The nation that ascends dreams of heroes. But for the worn-out nation the idea of a hero seems wearisome and pointless. Though this nation may be showered with gold, though its conceit still may be impassioned, it will be unfit for *podvig*. The dreams and ardor of real daring have passed out of the walls of the nation that knows only reason.

Everyone remembers the stories of children who left home in quest of happiness; and in the fairy tales of all times happiness is given to these children.

47. People are not averse to dreaming of desired changes in the basic functions of the human organism. The conception of the embryo, the decomposition of matter, the weightlessness of bodies, and deliberately produced materialization, are discussed even in ecclesiastical writings. It would seem that the horizon of possibilities should expand from early childhood and should be strengthened in the laboratories of the exact sciences. But it is precisely there that the imperfection of the race raises an obstacle. The bold seeker devoted to exact science quickly reverts to a common state and begins to imitate the customs of his grandfather.

We saw how the red flame of revolt turned into nothing more than smoke in the hearth. We saw the many banners of light resewn to cover layers of prejudice. We became aware of how lofty edifices were used for bazaars. Timid ignorance has woven its nets and feared, above all, to push away from the mossy shores covered with decayed bones.

The Teaching of evolution shows that human timidity increases before the change of race. But the date approaches, and those who have not learned to swim must swallow their fill of the brine.

Let us watch the leaps of the daring ones.

48. There is an urgent need to prepare the pilgrims to understand the Teaching. The simplest act of improving life will help them to follow this unusual path. Usefulness will lead them to a search for beauty. Life itself will reveal the requirements of goal-fitness. A simple explanation of a task can lend confidence to its fulfillment. Thus will they find the easier, speedier, more useful ways of approach.

The daring of the unshackled man is not an abstraction. The courage of the bird that flies across the sea provides an example for humanity, although no one thinks to consider the swallow a hero.

Nevertheless, air your storerooms and your walls.

49. They will ask, "Who gave you the right to dare?" Say, "We dare by the right of evolution. The right of evolution is inscribed in flame in our hearts. We cannot be deprived of the truth of the immutability of ascent. Both amidst the crowds and in solitude we know our inalienable right. We can affirm that only the blind are unable to perceive the direction of evolution. But when the door of knowledge is distinctly outlined, it is not difficult to strive out of the darkness."

Daring! Should one understand it as an unheard-of achievement? Shall not daring be one's daily repast, and the garment of one's every thought? Will not the prison walls become transparent? And will not the seal of the secret scroll melt away for the one who dares?

In recommending daring, We offer the simplest way. The heart knows the truth of this way. At present one cannot point out any other.

Display daring! There is much conflagration in the world, but it is only in flame that the foundation of the new world is forged. Blacksmith, hold firm thy hammer!

50. When will people understand the significance of thought and word? People still lend greater importance to the spilling of a sack of ordinary seeds than to the spilling of destructive words. Any rodent can pick up the seeds, but even an Arhat may not be able to clear away the consequences of thought and word. When people depart for a sea voyage they take with them only carefully chosen things; but in their speech they are unwilling to pay attention to its meaning, and to the consequences of their words. We do not threaten, but We do point out the first signs of smoke curling from under your shirt.

51. It is right to remember that work with Us has but a single direction—that of co-measurement and goal-fitness. The one who betrays his path is simply bereft of these qualities, and his fate is like that of a kitten at sea.

52. The word *repentance* does not exist in the Senzar vocabulary. What does exist is an expression familiar to you—wise cooperation. Consider the essential hypocrisy in the notion of repentance. It is simplest to demonstrate this to people through an example in medicine. By distortion of thought a man wounds his brother; but no words or thoughts of repentance can heal the wound, whose torn tissues can be mended only by persistent effort. For the restoration of goal-fitness it is necessary to demonstrate wise cooperation. The consequence of action can be cured only by action. No verbal avowals, no oaths, are of importance.

He who has realized his folly must correct it with sound reasoning. Only by wise cooperation can one drain away the folly.

To absolve a repentant sinner for a fee—is it not the most heinous crime? Is not this attempted bribery of Divinity worse than the most primitive kind of fetishism? Light must be shed from all sides upon this terrifying problem, otherwise the human undergarments will never lose their grime.

53. We must also turn our attention again to the serpentine venom of doubt. Doubt is of two kinds: one coils in its lair, in darkness, immobile and barbed. The other is ever crawling, sliding, and whirling. Usually the first is characteristic of youth; the second, of old age. The basis is not so much fear as deceitfulness in the nature of people. People distort their current judgments by these traits, influenced by their own past deceits. Though man is not inclined to self-examination, he is always ready to judge others, using himself as a standard.

Try to catch hold of the tip of doubt. Do not hinder your steps with such soiled fetters. Truly, it is easier to carry a real snake in your bosom than to be strangled by the boa constrictor of doubt.

54. Hasten to reveal the consciousness of the New World. Leave your memories behind. Can the charioteer, driving forward, continuously look back?

55. Truly, do not divide the world into north and south, or east and west. But everywhere distinguish between the old world and the New. The old world finds shelter in all parts of Earth. The New World also is born everywhere, but beyond boundaries and conditions.

The old world and the New World are distinguished through consciousness, not by outer evidence. Age and circumstance bear no importance. New banners are often raised by the hands of the old world, still filled with prejudices. But often in solitude beats a heart filled with the radiance of the New World. Thus, unwaveringly, before our eyes, the world divides itself. The new consciousness grows, unskilled, but full of daring. Despite its experience the old thinking loses strength. There is no power that could hold back the tide of the New World. We regret the useless waste of energy of the expiring consciousness. We welcome with a smile the daring of those who realize their right to expand new achievements. Each mistake, if committed for the cause of the New World, becomes a flower of valor. No matter how skillful the effort to embalm the old world, it remains a skeleton of horror.

The old world rejected the Mother of the World, but the New World begins to perceive Her lustrous veil.

56. It is fitting to realize the danger of the waves imposed on the lower layers of our atmosphere. A one-sided consciousness can cause an unprecedented catastrophe. The collision of waves of sound and light can set up grave brain disturbances.

Whither may one direct one's consciousness? Truly, to the reality of Infinity. This means that it is time to pass from the coarse layers of matter to research into the subtler energies.

57. Let us recall the Legend of the Grail. Titurel, devoted to the Teaching, received the power of Light. His successor, immersed in darkness, bled ceaselessly from an unhealing wound. In memory of worthier days, the remains of Titurel were exposed to view, and the words of the great dead one were repeated. Nevertheless the flame in the Chalice of Truth had already been extinguished. The arrival of a new hero was needed in order to retrieve from Titurel's unworthy successor the Chalice of Truth. Only then could the fire of the world be rekindled. This legend is very well known in the West, but it was originally conceived in the East. Does it not parallel a certain contemporary case?

58. One can pay tribute to heroes, but each hour brings its own judgment. The natural erosion of a section of rock reveals new veins of gold.

Do not tear down the temple of another if you cannot immediately erect a new temple upon the same site. The site of the temple must never be left vacant.

To express the qualities of God, humanity has invented many terms. Each new concept lengthens the thread of knowledge. There are no gates in the East upon which the Name of the Highest Concept is not inscribed. Truly, one cannot enter the regions of the East without knowledge. Let us not forget that upon the very stones the East has carved out its precepts.

59. The lengthiness of the Teaching is in inverse ratio to the measure of consciousness. The broader the consciousness, the shorter the formula. For those who are near, a word, or even a letter, is sufficient. The first command is like rolling thunder—the last is in silence!

60. How great is the play of the Mother of the World! She beckons to Her children from Her distant fields: "Hasten, children! I wish to teach you. I have keen eyes and alert ears ready for you. Sit ye down upon My garment. Let us learn to soar!"

61. You think correctly about the manifold effects of human emanations upon their surroundings. A convincing example is to be found in the effect of a human being upon animals and plants. Give someone an animal or plant, and by noting the change in its condition you can identify the man who is a destroyer of life energy. Like a vampire, the rider can exhaust his horse; or the hunter his dog; or the gardener his plants. Seek the cause of this in the emanations of the man.

Observe and record the history of the sickness of the spirit. The roots of what is physically evident are concealed in past accumulations. I advise that you treat coldly those people with unhealthy emanations. Treatment with coldness will improve them more quickly. Do not regard this as cruelty. We only remind you to open the door sensitively to all who knock.

62. Learn that you bring into the astral plane only what you have acquired on Earth. Ignorance remains there as it is here. One can receive there only what one has learned to desire here. It is almost impossible to acquire there a new broadening of consciousness. Therefore, accumulate a store of consciousness here, that you not enter in a worn-out garment.

63. If you notice repetitions in the Teaching, it means that new details can still be found, or that a command not yet fully applied in life must be stressed again.

One should remember that the benefits of the application of *prana* can be extended over an entire community. One can store *prana* not only for one's own use but, by means of psychic energy, can transmit a part of one's store to others.

In remote times a sick body was surrounded by healthy ones in order to nurture its strength. But this is a kind of vampirism that should not even be suggested. It is quite a different matter when there is a conscious transmission, voluntary and benevolent. This can be not only to one person, but even to several at once if one understands how to apportion the transmissions judiciously. It is an important reality that material benefit can be transmitted by means of psychic energy. Weighty substance is transmitted by weightless energy. This is not just suggestion but a real phenomenon.

64. Our Brothers may sometimes be seen by you with Their faces not clearly visible. If the face is somewhat misty, you may be assured that that Person is immersed in a lengthy experiment that requires a fixation of the gaze in one direction. If a woman's figure is seen with a veiled face, this manifestation relates to the Mother of the World.

65. If a very simple man should ask you the purpose of the Teaching, say, "That you may live happily." He should not be overwhelmed by too complicated considerations. Let his entire being be filled with the realization that the whole Teaching is concerned with improving his life. The understanding of responsibility will come later. First—proclaim the joy and betterment of life.

66. Can one reveal to people the truth of the evolution of worlds when they cannot even be certain of having their daily bread? One must avoid even a hint of offering abstractions.

67. How to awaken devotion? By goal-fitness. How to improve quality? By reverence for mastery. How to awaken creativity? By the desire for beauty.

68. Let children describe their ideas of the New Country. In this way we can observe how the unseen is made manifest. Inspire in the children the impulse to realize their dreams. This is the best task that we can offer them. Afterwards, let them describe a common piece of granite. That will be a test of their resourcefulness. Perhaps the stone will give them an idea of the strongholds of the far-off worlds. Out of the ordinary one can evoke the sparks of beauty.

69. Many times will you hear the common formula: "I left, and then returned." To this, be able to say, "How many possibilities were lost to you during your comings and goings!" Beyond calculation is the extent of humanity's losses because of such truancy. Man departs and returns, each time for selfish reasons. This "great inner work" reminds one of the sputtering of a wick. The skill in hiding the true cause of this moving backward and forward might better be used to polish the floor. But blisters on the soles may require painful lancing.

Ask each one who departs: "Wherein lay the offense?"

70. One should distinguish a narrow consciousness from narrowly-focused energy. Sometimes the Teacher applies a pointed energy in order to stimulate action of the spirit in a particular direction. One must not draw from this the conclusion that the consciousness of the Teacher is also narrow.

Do not show off the consciousness whenever it is necessary to dispatch a fleet arrow. Only the ignorant try to display the dry twigs of their pompousness on their window sills. He whose house is filled with knowledge does not fear to carve a slice of thought.

A sowing of one kind of grain can bring a full harvest, but even more fruitful are combinations of beneficial grains. They will yield explosions of spirit.

71. Urusvati, by suffering the pain caused by the magnetic arrow, experienced the waves of the currents from a distant planet. It is correct to consider the magnetic currents as channels between the planets. The study of communication between the worlds should include research in magnetic waves, but of course the spiritual consciousness must not be forgotten.

72. Have you finally learned to rejoice at obstacles? Can We be assured that what seems like an obstacle will multiply your resourcefulness tenfold? Can We accept you as conquering warriors? Can We send you the arrow of help, assured that you will catch it in flight? Can We pronounce the word of the New World in unison with you? Can We believe that for the sake of the beauty of creation you have burned your outworn garments? Can the Mother of the World entrust to your vigilance the texture of Light? Can the Lion hasten to your aid? Can the Light illumine your path? And finally, do you understand how to apply to yourself the given Teaching? Can We entrust to you the wearing of the given signs? Can We dispatch the ray of perfectment? Can We vouch for your vigilance? Can We construct a stronghold from your understanding of self? Can We rejoice at the steadfastness of your path? Can the Mother of the World call you just? Can the Lion become the protector of your dwelling? Can the Light bathe the new steps? Unbolt your doors! Victory is at the threshold!

73. You know that at an altitude of eleven thousand feet the astral body acquires a special quality. Each altitude has its specific effect on each body. You may have observed that at an altitude of seven thousand feet man can decrease his intake of food. The need for food gradually decreases as one ascends until at an altitude of sixteen thousand feet the decrease is substantial. Above an altitude of nine thousand feet I do not advise the use of wine, coffee, pepper or other spices. Above seventeen thousand feet even strong tea is inadvisable. With the decreasing need for food there is a parallel decrease in the need for sleep; one can consider sleeping for no more than six hours, and at twenty thousand feet four is quite enough. Thus one can understand that at great altitudes one can remain almost without sleep, or food.

At the high altitudes, one should not take valerian—which has been recommended to you—with spices, and it is harmful to consume food in the same quantities as at lower levels. The mountains are important, since they lead one out of the lower earthly conditions. On the heights one feels that one has been freed from ordinary earthly demands. Certainly, if an altitude of eleven thousand feet has a significant effect upon the astral body, then each added thousand feet has an even greater effect upon the physical body. It would be an irreparable error to try to artificially reduce the conditions on mountains to fit our lower earthly habits. Remember and apply.

74. Each outer form distorts reality. One can strain to be alert, so as to diminish the degree of false perception, but everything seen, every reflection, every thought, projects its illusory color.

75. People are ready for every kind of spiritual incest. People are only too willing to unite elements that are incompatible. They try to unite the father element, fire, with the daughter element, water; and the earth-mother with the air-son. If their progeny is burned to ashes they will not blame themselves, and will lay the responsibility on the Heavenly Father.

It is impossible to become accustomed to the light-mindedness of human deeds. Only the spiritual consciousness can discern which are incompatible elements. People are distinguished not only by their emanations but also by the essence of elements, which always remains intact. Precisely in relation to elements are the best combinations found.

76. Hasten, hasten to understand the Teacher! Let us encircle Him with a protective wall of devotion and thereby enclose ourselves within the stronghold. After you have wandered enough you will come to understand that with the Teacher, there is always success. Where defeat occurs, there has been betrayal of the Teacher. Where defeat is, it is we ourselves who have bent and rent and razed the goal-fitting plan. In defeat, we have turned away from the tested arrow of help. Can we assert that in the hour of danger we will proclaim the Name of the Teacher? Can we bear witness to the Teacher's Name? Can we discover the exultation of gratitude to the Teacher? Or, on the other hand, do we sometimes wonder why the Teaching does not accommodate our habits, and why our inactivity is disturbed by the Teaching? Why we are awakened from our self-justifying sleep?

Gratitude and devotion flourish joyously in Our Community. If Our conduit brings word to Us that a co-worker thinks he has sacrificed something in the name of the Teaching, this would compel Us to reject his cooperation. Our co-workers know both how to receive and to give. When you spread Our Teaching do not shout in the square, but simply offer a smile to the approaching ones. Those who come voluntarily will accept the Teacher. But he who is ensnared will gnaw at his chains. We expect joy, and accept only the wondrous flower of devotion. Let us hasten to understand the Teacher!

Affirm success; affirm joy; affirm understanding of progress. Cast away the thoughts that belong to the old world. I shall not tire of repeating this.

77. You know that the members and co-workers of the International Government have always had to obey its Decrees. For the last time let us turn to M., to the historical event of Our Warning. This age-old tradition of forewarning humanity, with each recurring century, is effected in full benevolence; in this lies its basic nature. Otherwise the role of the envoy would not be sincere and persuasive. St. Germain spoke to L. with good intent. Similarly, M.∴ addressed V., and A.L.M. properly conveyed Our Decree. I praise all those who have aided Our envoys with their supportive thoughts.

If Our warrior is told that a mountain is Ours, he accepts the decree. If it were not this way, the significance of the Government would be lost.

St. Germain fell ill after fulfilling his mission because of the undisciplined thought of one of his co-workers. Guard against the harm of undisciplined thought. Think only in new ways. Consider as lost that day during which you did not contemplate the New World. Set yourself problems demanding concrete solutions to life's questions. Do not waste your breath with questions of cosmogony while attempting to scale the heights of Earth.

78. It was impossible for you to divert your attention from the breaking down of the granite cell. When it reached the stage in which it could be compared to the cell of an invertebrate, you saw that the pulsation was almost identical.

79. Whom shall we call the most courageous? Perhaps the tiniest butterfly exposed to the same atmospheric conditions as the lion. Observe the effects of the Teaching upon the humble. Often they bear the hurricane of enlightenment better than those who are considered great.

80. If one can confirm the presence of thought even in a stone, then what a clear rainbow of thought fills space! One must become used to the fact that thought permeates all that exists. Certainly this reality, ponderable and not abstract, remains defined as energy but preserves the potentiality of conscious evolution.

Until recently the sensitivity of plants was considered to be just instinct, but after investigation one now can attribute this "instinct" to the domain of thought. Hence, one must observe upward and downward. The human creature shows a characteristic error in presuming to himself the exclusive ability to think. By the most simple examples, one can demonstrate how human thought is affected by age, circumstances, and nationality. It is striking to see how weak is the rudimentary thinking of the average man; yet anonymously-sent spatial thoughts will uplift his spirit. You know that a radio, with slight alteration, can receive thoughts from space. And thoughts, as living matter, can both nourish and be nourished.

Reflect on the manifestation of thought. Realize its omnipresence and rejoice at the laboratory of thought that, from the mineral cell up to the Infinite, links all kingdoms. The magnetic wave, the electric spark, and thought—these three voyagers greet those who strive into the Infinite.

81. Can thought thunder? The phenomenon of the echo is an example. Thought, like sound, expands in magnetic waves. And the expression "the thunder of thought" is not an exaggeration. Precisely, the nature of thought must be investigated. For instance, is it possible that thoughts of a certain quality and intensity can influence plant life? How do animals react to certain thoughts? And finally, how do thoughts affect "sir man"? How does thought act as an element in chemical compounds? Would it not be advisable to test thought with litmus paper? Could thought not rival virulent poison or music in its power? In general, thought must be investigated as a living factor of existence. Thus it will be possible to build a bridge between the psychic and the material from psychotechnics to dynamics, and even to astrochemistry. Thus should be understood the working of space.

82. Can one trust a blind helmsman? Is it possible to think that the rags of antiquated thought can be worn in the New World? One must understand that the gift of the New World will be brought to those gates that have been opened to it. Truly, the New World wishes to bestow a beautiful garment. But humanity must approach to receive the fabric woven by the labor of the Mother of the World!

83. Spread the grains of the Teaching little by little. Let it imperceptibly flood the being. The time for preaching has passed, and life remains. Inspire the consciousness of your brother with an imperceptible touch, brought to him as his daily bread. Expose and understand his wrath and quench it with goal-fitness. Affirm him in the joy of realized containment. Beware of manifesting miracles to him, but reveal to him the co-measurement of that which passes into the Infinite. Abolish special holidays, and make of life a perpetual holiday.

"My holiday will be yours. My path will be your achievement. My generosity will be your inheritance. You will not notice the generosity, but you will be astonished at your own transformation. I have no need of thanks, but your gratitude will be fuel to you, because supreme above the flames of other offerings is the fire of gratitude."

"Teacher, I see and remember indelibly."

The manifested succession of Teachers glows as a string of interplanetary pearls. Add also your own pearl!

84. I believe everyone can read Our books. I do not see any among those who approach Us who are afraid. Test people's fear. Show them frightening masks, then smile with understanding when their hearts tremble. Where is their trust in the Teacher? Where is their understanding of where power lies? One can distinguish Our people at the first call. Like deer will Our own hasten. I know no fearful mask that can turn them away.

We need not always take examples from giants or heroes. I recall a Hindu boy who had found his Teacher. We asked him, "Is it possible that the sun would seem dark to you if you saw it without the Teacher?"

The boy smiled. "The sun would remain as the sun, but in the presence of the Teacher twelve suns would shine to me."

The sun of the wisdom of India will shine, because on the shore of a river there sits a boy who knows his Teacher.

Just as there are conductors of electricity, so also are there conductors and accumulators of knowledge. If a barbarian makes an attempt against the Teacher, tell him what humanity calls those who destroy repositories of knowledge.

85. Can Our people have their dear ones near them? Of course they can. These near ones will deepen the feeling of responsibility, solicitude, and resourcefulness.

86. One should know that having one's centers open enables one to reduce the imperfection in one's surroundings. It brings not only the development of sensitivity but also the offering of one's own forces for the improvement of one's surroundings. One can observe that the forces emitted for this are in some way absorbed by space, and this degree of openness of the centers is called "Lamp of the Desert." After this follows the degree of "Lion of the Desert."

87. One must distinguish between absolute devotion and conditional devotion. Most often people display absolute devotion when they receive, but each act of giving in return is difficult because of self-imposed conditions. Some accept what they have been given, but then raise obstacles in their own consciousness, and begin to think that the given treasure is but a piece of mold! One should remember that the measure of one's devotion determines the measure of receiving. Faith must be equal in degree to knowledge. Each limiting condition set upon one's faith sets an equally limiting condition on its fruits. Yet no one would wish to be called a conditional disciple. Such a title would provoke offense. The law acts identically under all conditions. But the law does not take offense—it co-measures. Be assured of the co-measurement of devotion.

88. Cosmogony should evoke thoughts that exalt. While the god of an unawakened people is conceived as sitting atop an insignificant ball, the superior spirit peers into the Infinite, adorned in the joy of unbounded knowledge. Do not demean the Infinite!

89. Harmony of auras does not require sameness of color. Thus, a violet aura can be in harmony with one that is green, and a pink aura can make a blue one more visible. In such combinations can be found currents of special intensity. It is even desirable to combine colors, as a guarantee of the future rainbow. So multihued are the vibrations of luminous colors, that it is impossible for the limited range of earthly colors to represent them, just as it is impossible for the range of earthly sounds to encompass the symphony of the spheres. Your earthly lilac and violet have nothing in common with Our heavenly purple.

90. A simple affirmation of respect for knowledge will make possible the resolving of all contradictions. True thinking is impossible without reverence for knowledge. The Teacher advises that knowledge be set as the basis for developing the consciousness. Point out that knowledge builds the path to the One Teaching. Is it possible that humanity cannot comprehend that knowledge emanates from the One Source? Therefore, the dividing line between knowledge and ignorance is the dividing line between light and darkness. We are easily able to bring together the Torah with the hymns of the Vedas, or the precepts of Buddha with the words of Christ, for We do not discern differences between Teachings emanating from the One Source.

91. Reconciling the idea of the finiteness of the universe with that of the principle of infinite space is one of those problems that the pupil alone must resolve. This is called *Summa Summarum*. To help the realization of these concepts of space, We set milestones, but the realization itself must be achieved independently. This corresponds to the degree of "Lion of the Desert." It demonstrates the freeing of oneself from Earth and earthly possessions. This achievement is required for an understanding of the spheres as separate.

Clinging to the idea of the Infinite alone will not bring concrete results. Similarly, attachment to the finite alone will be demeaning. Only the reconciling of these opposite principles will bring a correct understanding of cosmogonical matters. Thus one can make calculations of the finite without demeaning the grandeur of Cosmos.

Urusvati has arrived at a proper understanding that makes possible a further comprehension of the formation of the worlds. Vividly glows the manifestation of cosmic functioning!

92. Note the times of great events. Already the Vedas are coming together with the Tripitaka and the Kabbala. The teachings of Buddha and the words of Christ and of the Teachers are dispelling ignorance. Carefully observe the growth of knowledge in diverse

parts of the world. Both the affirming and the denying ones walk in one direction. The time is unrepeatable, like a gate into the preordained. Dead are those who see the determined hour as an ordinary one.

93. Do not listen to the teacher who demands a fee for his teaching. The Teaching cannot be bought or obtained by coercion. Truly, each one gains access to the Teaching only by proving his devotion by deeds. It is actions, not words, that lead to the Community of Knowledge. If a child strives to that Community, will there not be work for him there? Likewise, will anyone who accepts with full consciousness the statutes of the Community find the doors barred? Can one cite an example when the quest of a pure consciousness was not answered?

Precisely outlined are the statutes of the Community of Knowledge. No cunning can obscure them. Traveler, pay your debt, and walk tirelessly.

94. Some may be unable to reconcile the idea of equality with that of Hierarchy. Equality lies in the potentiality of spirit that all possess. Hierarchy is based on the uniqueness of one's accumulated experience. Therefore it is just to say that a complex of knowledge will be the gate of Hierarchy. Mark the expression "complex," because narrow specialization cannot define the breadth of a Hierarch.

Striving for knowledge, gain the realization of the Teacher. Truly, reverence for the Teacher is the panacea, even for physical ailments.

There is greater difficulty when one's centers are open, for each breath of the old world brings illness and only the breeze of true evolution can restore health. Therefore do not wrap yourself in the old world; attract the young ones to the joy of the New World. In all there is joyous, yet stern goal-fitness.

95. To Him of the great Illumination there came a pupil who sought a miracle, saying, "After the miracle I shall have faith."

The Teacher smiled sadly, then produced for him a great miracle.

"Now," exclaimed the pupil, "I am ready to ascend the steps of the Teaching under your guidance."

But the Teacher, pointing to the door, said, "Go. I don't need you!"

96. I am astonished at the old world; the appearance of sunspots intensifies the discord. The wings of the old world flutter their last, while the open centers revolt. For each advance of the centers a kind of epidermis is needed which grows painfully. Pure air cannot coexist with the lifeless azote of the old world.

97. It must be indicated that all opiates are undesirable on the way to the Teaching. Clearminded vigilance will bring one nearer to Us.

98. Express your prayers by devotional action. Know how to affirm the Teaching each day. Lose not one day, nor one hour. Know how to think of yourself as the creator of a whole world of action. Know how to apply all your forces to every action. Know how to bring the Teaching into every thought. Know how to array your forces as on a battlefield. Know how to feel gratitude as the union of joy and beauty.

End with honor, because the end expresses the fire of one's accumulated achievement.

It is a most heinous treason to know the Teaching and not apply it. Abuse of the Teaching is worse than death of the spirit, because by this act one exiles himself from cooperation and dooms himself to Saturn.

99. I shall point out how to sharpen your power on the edge of My sword. The manifestation of the Teacher can enlighten people, but only if the way is paved with knowledge. The dragon is mighty, and barbed are his coils.

100. The destiny that leads to Us must be forged every hour. The debasement of the idea of co-measurement is a kind of self-strangulation. The postponing of achievement is like drowning oneself.

101. I am witnessing an experiment involving the transmission of human force over a distance. By this one can move any object; for example, one can move the bolt of a door by applying the energy of one's thought to the corresponding energy of the object. This experiment has been known since the distant past. But one should remember that with the establishment of general cooperation among all that exists, the energy of thought unites all spheres of being. Not by using a hammer, but by penetrating objects with our thought, shall we unite them.

"Wisdom in all," recalls the Hindu. "Cooperation in all" will be added to this in the Age of Maitreya. Not only by command, not just by harmony, but by the lightning-bolt of directed thought are the co-workers united.

Cooperation of the layers of matter is characteristic of the New World. Each era has its own call. The power of thought will be the evocative principle of the New World.

Try to observe the life of so-called inanimate objects. Observe your effect upon them. The one who converses with objects is not always a subject of ridicule. Enwrapping them in thought creates a special atmosphere. Likewise, a pillar of swarming thoughts can penetrate to the regions of the far-off worlds. Regard thought as a real force in life, then gain firm control over the flow of thought.

102. Contemplate each approach to Us. Become irreplaceable. By night cover yourself with Our Name. By day gird yourself in the armor of devotion.

103. In the relation between Teacher and disciple, the Teacher can instruct only within the boundaries of what is permitted. He uplifts the disciple, cleansing him of outworn habits. He warns him against all kinds of treason, superstition, and hypocrisy. He tests the disciple, openly and in secret. The Teacher unbars the gates to the next step with the words, "Rejoice, brother." He may also bar them with the words, "Farewell, passer-by."

The disciple chooses his own Teacher. He reveres Him as one of the Highest Beings. He trusts Him and brings Him his best thoughts. He cherishes the Name of the Teacher and inscribes It upon the sword of his word. He shows diligence in labor and flexibility in achievement. He welcomes trials as he welcomes the dawn, his hope directed to the unlocking of the next gate.

Friends, if you wish to approach Us, choose a Teacher on Earth and place your guidance in His care. He will tell you in time when the key may be turned in the gate. Each one should have a Teacher on Earth.

104. Be fortified in the thought of My desire to show you the best path. Consider how imperative it is for you to help Me in this desire. Let nothing of the outworn obstruct your striving. Remember that one stumbling horse can impede an entire caravan. Therefore say, "Walk with certainty, otherwise your fate will be to fall upon a spear."

Your approach to Us quivers on the balance; do not try to hide it.

Let us pronounce the prayer to Shambhala:

"Thou Who didst call me to the path of labor, accept my fitness and my desire.

"Accept my labor, O Lord, because by day and by night Thou beholdest me.

"Manifest Thy hand, O Lord, because great is the darkness. I follow Thee!"

Walk as though ascending the mountain of joy. Great is the scope of the battle for the regeneration of humanity's consciousness. The Teacher rejoices at your decisiveness.

105. Disciples are of four types. Some follow the Indications of the Teacher and ascend in proper order. Others, behind the Teacher's back, follow the Indications to excess and thereby often harm themselves. Others, in the Teacher's absence, take occasion to prattle and thereby destroy their path. Others, behind His back, criticize the Teacher and betray Him. Dreadful is the destiny of these last two kinds!

Let understanding of the concept of the Teacher be affirmed.

106. Right is the one who rejects coarse, indecent, or ambiguous expressions, for their origin lies in ignorance. Speech must be beautiful, clear, and deeply meaningful.

107. The steps of acquiring Knowledge are: alarmed, inquiring, knocking, harkening, remembering, transforming, sword-carrying, puissant, lamp of the desert, lion of the desert, co-worker of the Creative Principles, creator.

Each degree is subdivided thrice. The order must be passed gradually. The one who strives can attain swiftly, but the deserter casts himself down.

108. Who is the traitor? The slanderer, the one who fails to speak, the one who misappropriates, the hypocrite, the denier, and the one desiring the downfall of the Teaching.

Dark clouds are easily dispersed by the whirlwind; the invisible whirlwind of consciousness acts in the same way.

109. The heart knows its friends! Therefore, carefully examine your friends lest you admit into your heart a casual passer-by. The Teacher is your closest friend. Do not add to His burden.

110. The degree of "Lion of the Desert" especially permits the fulfillment of one's thought. Therefore one must be particularly cautious. The degree of "Lion of the Desert" knows no offense. Who could offend? The great heart can contain all.

Joy is easily attained if at each moment you feel devotion to Us. Satisfaction is within reach of those disciples who value the clouds, realizing that without clouds the sun would scorch. The Teacher can act where His hand is not tied.

111. The Teacher loves battles and knows how they fill Cosmos with energy. The Teacher stands with you. How, then, can you fear the precipice? How, then, can you fear great beasts? To search for fleas in one's bedclothes is petty. But to hold in your hands the sword of Solomon and the command of Maitreya bestows on one the morning light. The realization of the unprecedented battle rings out as a jubilant trumpet.

We must not differ in understanding. Otherwise, Our reasoning will see achievement where yours sees only downfall. Restrain the fool from trivial decisions. In flaccid, outworn judgments is hidden a deadly poison.

112. I realize how difficult it is for the hungry one to wait for his soup to boil, but it is necessary for the dangerous microbes to perish. While preparing ourselves for space, let us gaze into the far-off worlds. Let us feel ourselves as participants with them. The link with them makes the densification of the astral, or subtle, body more achievable, and the sounds of the far-off worlds may soon be discerned. Connections of the far-off worlds with the physical body will be possible in the approaching future.

113. Indeed, human desire forms each one's own tablet of commandments. What the slumbering spirit desires, the awakened one receives. But the tide will carry away the scum of unstable thoughts. Participation in planetary tasks is the best tempering of one's sword.

He who succumbs to counter-currents will not again find his stream. Thus can one accept the battle of the world. He who will not wash his face in the flow of the current will lie as a stone on the path.

One can impart to few the sacred Mystery. Their number is small, but space itself harkens to them, for, like a human furnace, they fuse and temper the thoughts of the world. Let people guard thought!

114. The karma of one's actions cannot be compensated for by inaction. He who built a pyre to incinerate Truth will have to bend and remove each cinder. The command of justice neither burns nor smolders. It flares up, unexpected, and consumes the strongholds of obstruction.

The success of the cosmic structures differs from human expectations. The human mind is like a beginner at a lesson, trying to avoid answering, sugaring his tongue. But how then can one proceed? Only by the realization of the nearness of the cosmic structures. Who are the judges and who the judged?

Does the music of the spheres signify the victory of human presumptions? Or does it hail the purification of forgotten Truth? There is a prophecy that reminds us of the condemnation and then the purification of a sacred city.

115. Often We are asked why We do not hasten to destroy a harmful entity. This must be explained clearly, especially since you yourself have a weapon for such destruction. I shall take the example of a physician. Often the physician is ready to cut away a knot of diseased nerves, but possible damage to a sympathetic center stays his scalpel. No being is isolated. Numberless are the layers of the karmic web that binds even the most disparate beings. In the flow of the karmic stream one can trace currents linking the most unworthy to the most worthy. Therefore the one who cuts must first anesthetize the channels that unite the streams of karma. Otherwise the individual destruction, even if justified, can cause harm to the whole. Thus the means for destruction must be resorted to with the utmost caution.

116. The least insincerity in devotion and in one's acceptance of the foundations of renewal can affect the state of one's health. Such insincerity can nest deeply in the crevices of the consciousness. Insincerity is exceedingly contagious, affecting the emanations of others.

If people could realize the harm they bring to themselves and others by halfway decisions! They may cleave the consciousness and bring on its death. As often happens, illness begins unnoticed and a fatally dangerous operation then becomes inevitable. Thus does human downfall result from the bite of the tiniest adder of insincerity. One must warn, but one cannot change others. A steed jumping the precipice cannot be halted.

The planet can easily be exploded into innumerable stony meteorites, thus increasing the number of dead satellites in the universe. Yet, cosmic justice must be fulfilled. Some time will be needed to determine whether Community will be voluntarily accepted.

By that time, relations between the worlds will have developed sufficiently for the reality of the astral world to be recognized, and then the very existence of Earth will come into question. Either it will become a beautiful garden of achievements or it will fall into the abyss of decay, when our most worthy spirits will then be sent to populate other planets.

117. Why can flame flare out from under one's feet? True striving is like fire, unstoppable as the whirlwind. The ardent comprehension of Our Decrees wings one with fire. Such fiery self-encompassment is like a wall; from behind it, you observe the battle unharmed, but are vigilantly ready to dispatch your arrow.

The New Dawn will come, relieving Me of the exhausting night watch. Humanity's burdensome thoughts are hammer-blows on the foundation of life. But it is possible to find reinforcement in the moment of decision. Therefore I can say, "Nevertheless, rejoice!" The issuing of flame from the soles of the feet can be an indication of the beginning of a new stage of great achievement. You have been told so much that by now you should not belittle yourselves by undue attention to insignificant dates.

By the sound of the trumpets, the warriors recognize the moment for advancing into the field of battle. Manifested warriors, what an untamed current, never repeatable and obscured to the eyes of the world, rages about your camp! What has impelled you to keep your swords sharpened and your shields at the ready? You will say "We know the marked dates of Earth and nothing can dim our sight. The Keeper of the dates has confided to us the combination of forces, and the decisions. Patience has turned to immutability. Yesterday we trembled with expectancy, but today we rejoice in the ardor of battle, knowing that the destined battle will lead to victory."

"Lord of the Seven Gates, lead us sunwards who have passed through the midnight. Thine are our arrows, O Lord. Without Thy Command we shall not enter the city of rest. Neither an hour, nor a day, nor a year will arrest our way. Because Thou, the most speedy, holdest the reins of our horses. Because Thou also didst pass this way and give Thy patience as guarantee. Tell us, Keeper, whence flows the stream of patience?"

"Out of the mine of trust."

Who knows where the messenger changes his steed?

118. Often we hear self-satisfied exclamations, "I am already transformed! I have already attained!" Wavering "I," have you truly examined yourself? If you have attained—good be unto you! But is it not really that the surroundings have changed? And are you not appropriating another's attainment? Where is your vigilance? Are you not inviting an illness of the spirit?

It is wrong to think that Our Communications are without effect. On the contrary, each Decree bears with it, as a whirlwind, Our protection or criticism. Can it be otherwise when each manifestation of smugness carries its own harmful contagion, when each act of narrow-mindedness is at another's expense? Each Command inattentively heard is like an arrow in the heart, each sneaking away like a chain that strangles. You know that all is suspended in space. Who would be willing to drive in the nail of his own condemnation? We hasten to help you to complete your karmas in order to rid the speeding ship of unnecessary loads. At the destined date strain your ear to grasp every word of the Teacher.

119. Each act of reverence for the Teacher shows an understanding of the Teaching. Each sign of reverence for the site of the Teacher's labor will show deep understanding and devotion. But these signs of attention cannot be prompted. These signs must by themselves flower in the consciousness. The Teacher will not demand, "Pay your respect to Me!"

120. Can the so-called miracle be expected? The most important characteristic of a "miraculous" phenomenon is, of course, its unexpectedness. The very substance of human consciousness makes such phenomena elusive. The ordinary consciousness creates obstacles by presuming conflicting conditions. The Adept of knowledge can only ask, "Dear humans, do not distract yourselves with cries of expectation when the vessel of universal essence is already producing a blessed combination. Can one expect the turning of the ship toward the right, when Our Hand directs the rudder to the left?" Only one with a clear and infallible understanding of what is immutable can be a co-worker in the world process. If a room seems empty to the eye, can we affirm that it is truly empty?

Let the phantoms of ignorance not limit the horizon.

121. I affirm, and you should understand, that what seems impossible today may be feasible tomorrow. The Teacher uses His power to safeguard your achievements in all their beauty. The misfortune of people lies in their lack of understanding of the process of incarnation and the complexity of the circumstances surrounding achievement. For example, solitude is the best friend of achievement, but sometimes witnesses are needed, and the karmic conditions then become more complex.

The Teacher can point out the most necessary channel of action. The Teacher can protect to a certain degree, but the shadow-dance of the past will continue its round. One should concentrate one's thought on finding the right attitude toward these demons. When you see a doorkeeper you do not concern yourself greatly about his mentality. Also, when you meet a condemned criminal you do not discuss cosmogony with him. While on Earth, one must often polish one's treasures, and on this path many demons are encountered. We can recall many encounters with frightful entities during Our past lives. The elements are closely involved in one's earthly attainment. The elements stand guard on both sides. The battle of fire with earth will have its resultant phenomena, and untimely manifestations should be expected. Earth is the guardian of old ways of thinking, but fire is the rebellious outburst of evolution.

What an unprecedented battle We are conducting in the lightning bolts of the elements! The indestructibility of the primary substance provides firmness in the battle, and the knowledge of the continuity of existence provides wings of attainment.

Say, "Sisters and brothers, labor unceasingly, and your wings will grow in the rapid flow of day and night."

And to the incredulous say, "You will feel warmth, and your life will be sweet—you can find these by turning to the Teacher. But do not cast stones of disbelief on the path."

In the battle of the elements each worn-out consciousness is as a wall against light. Say, "Do not entangle the web of life."

Each thunderclap releases many discharges of positive and negative energies. Consider the battle for the fulfillment of Our Plan as unprecedented. Consider all the mirror-images as true. But do not confuse their dates. Each given year has its own significance.

122. That a situation is without solution is only imagined by those who would rely on other people rather than upon the power of their own thought. Grief experienced by others flows like the ripples of a stream; but the images of Truth, which you call ideas, rule the karma of the world. It is astonishing to see how images of Truth participate in the spatial battle. While the multitudes disintegrate in a blind fury of ignorance and betrayal, the thoughts of Truth weave their heavenly nests, which for real evolution are far more vital than any worship by entire nations.

You understand both the work of reality and the work of Maya. Spatial thought is reality, while what people generally pay attention to is Maya. Bear in mind that each of Us could grieve over the low level of those on Earth; but this would have no effect on the evolutionary plan because it is thought that creates. Images of Truth provide to each body, whether it be evolving or disintegrating, new possibilities for flight to higher spheres. Each Teacher of life bases His power only upon images of Truth, and creates the future by His thought, not by the consciousness of the crowd.

The ashes of past fires may dim the vision, but the fires of new images of Truth glow in the Infinite. When we have transcended the narrow boundaries of ethnicity and nationality, is it not all the same to us which planet is nurtured by spatial thought? The only important thing is that the thought be filled with a realization of the Common Good. Then the crosscurrents of nations will not distract the eye that is directed toward the inevitable evolution.

Reverence for the dwelling place of the Teacher should not be reverence for the soil, or for temple rituals, but for the igniting of justice in space.

We often exhausted Ourselves in improving the condition of humanity, but do not regret having sent even one evolutionary thought. These thoughts take root and flourish like an enchanted garden; and as magically invisible are the workers in this garden. Know how to direct your thought to the Common Good and We will always be with you.

Let us end with a legend: "Let us look at the stars. We were told that the vessel of Wisdom poured its contents from out of *Tushita*, and the drops of the miraculous draft became aglow in space. But the Teacher said, 'Thus glow the tips of the arrows of thought, because thought pierces the radiant substance and creates worlds.' "

Creative thought, do not cease to adorn space with thy flowers of light!

123. Said Solomon, "I shall set thee at the crossroad and make thee silent and motionless. Before thee will pass the signs of events. Thou shalt restrain thy human curiosity, and thus shalt thou peer into the predestined flow of the current. For beyond human thought is borne universal thought."

Thus, observe the flow of events as though you were counting sheep from the top of a tower.

124. When the Teacher severs His ties with a disciple, the ring received from the Teacher must be returned by the disciple. This should not be seen as a rare occurrence. The karma of obsession or weakness of spirit can easily set a barrier between the disciple and his Teacher. Self-correction by the one expelled can bring him back to the point at which the path was interrupted. The disciple must understand the need for haste and apply himself to this task.

It is difficult to see as a qualified disciple one who has no questions to put to his Teacher. Of course, questions and answers will come in due time, and the living tissue of trust will saturate space.

125. Thus does the disciple approach the Teacher: open, ready to shed the old-world tatters, striving toward the new consciousness, eager for knowledge, fearless, truthful, devoted, keenly vigilant, industrious, knowing goal-fitness, and sensitive. He will find the path of trust. Maya will no longer tempt him. Mara will not terrify him. On the bosom of Earth will he find the Stone from the far-off worlds. For him, life will be adorned, ability strengthened, and superfluous words erased.

"Teacher, I have succeeded in withstanding the stabs of heat and the horror of cold. My bodily strength has left me, but my ear remains open. And my body of light is ready to tremble at Your call. And my arms are ready to carry the heaviest stones for the Temple. Three Names are known to me. Known to me is the Name of the One Who Veiled Her Face. My power grows."

Thus shall the disciple address the Teacher.

126. The misfortunes of humanity result from an inability to distinguish between the signs of good and the signs of evil. People first apply the signs to their own future, because thinking primarily through themselves, they see no world beyond themselves. With a measure such as this, how can one have true perceptions? The chief and most heinous consequence of such limitation is that much of what is good and useful is not separated from the harmful. Numberless are the instances when an indication given for the future is applied to the immediate moment and thus loses its intended usefulness.

Sometimes the destiny of entire nations can be expressed in a simple formula. But people want to appropriate for themselves what is meant for the larger group. And the given formula is then crumbled like a piece of sculpture under a crude hand. This crudeness of individual limitation is a most harmful contributor to the dissolution of valuable opportunities.

The very rare threads of light from the far-off worlds are generally applied to routine, instead of being used for the solution of world problems. Therefore, with trembling heart, embracing all, approach world tasks. Through the crevices of catastrophe sense the tremors of Earth, and by the rocks of upheaval ascend the sphere of world understanding.

Woe to him who has scattered the seeds of the world only in his own garden. But joy to him who has contributed every seed of his understanding to the Common Good. Such is Our instruction to those who approach world tasks.

127. Energy and will are the true rulers of karma. He who renounces self, who strives for the Common Good, who is devoted in battle and joyous in labor, acquires, at least for a moment, an Arhat's enlightenment, which makes him lord of his own karma. The realization of enlightenment may be defined as straight-knowledge. True, this straight-knowledge may be lost, or may never be realized. These meteors of spirit race by in space, bearing away the happy opportunities of unconscious humanity.

The consciousness of an Arhat bestows advantages, but exacts full responsibility. But how many can sense the joy of responsibility? At the time when one must assume responsibility, one must also have the courage to see oneself as an Arhat who leads the battle unaided, able to withstand the assault of the elements with his wisdom and his will.

For the ignorant, an encounter with the elements is a fantasy. But you already know how often the elements are involved in the actual life of people. The Teaching has often pointed out the effect of physical manifestations upon the human organism. Energy creates a correlation between the elements and the tension of the human organism. Will is born from experience and an attention to the phenomena of existence. Thus, "insurmountable" karma can be subject to human influence.

128. It is not enough to establish facts; their inner meaning must be understood. We have discussions about the future during which it is permitted to offer the broadest range of ideas, but We must support them with facts and analogies. Such games of forecasting are the best relaxation. They awaken dormant centers and give birth to new thoughts. Our Teaching results from experience and prognosis. Therefore, advise your friends to ponder upon the future. It is futile to consider whether the current moment is successful or unsuccessful. Only by projecting fact into the future do we ascertain its value. Thus is molded the reality of the future.

We are opposed to baseless fantasies, but We welcome each goal-fitting prognosis. If the best building-blocks for construction can be found, and if the will can join them, then one can be certain that one's plan is valid and will be accepted. The cause of unfitness or frailty of any structure lies within ourselves. The horror of destruction is caused by discord between consciousness and reason. The narrowness of human logic and reason can undermine the foundations, when the consciousness is already celebrating victory. If the logic of evidence finds its true role in the understanding of reality, then one's decisions are made firm. Think thus about the future, and in the midst of the desert erect walls of knowledge. You know that every stone put into these walls must be vital and needed. Their strength will resist all assaults of the enemies of knowledge. Treasure each hour devoted to constructing the future. The major forces of humanity are made possible by man's foresight. Whence comes courage? Whence striving? Whence the ability to overcome? From foresight.

129. Treason must be foreseen. Every sign of treason must be uncovered. If fear is multicolored, then how much more so is treason. Let us be vigilant.

130. You will say to him, "It behooves us, even in the midst of great turmoil and revolt, to preserve our calmness of spirit."

He will reply, "Your truth is not new. But why should I strain for calmness of spirit when my body trembles with tension?"

Answer him, "This is the law of self-perfectment."

He will reply, "This too is not new. Where are the advantages of self-perfectment?"

You will answer, "The exercise of calmness leads to mastery of moving through the various bodily states."

At the change of body, the spirit that has not sought to advance enters a condition of torpor and wanders about depressed by its vague memories. Indeed, memories of the low physical state plunge it into complete darkness.

It is essential to avoid indifference while changing the body. Refinement of striving will provide calmness during the transition from one state of existence to another. Thus is achieved the quality of an Arhat, who never interrupts the flow of consciousness and constantly strives toward the future.

Tell your listener that one can prepare the eternal *Amrita* of spiritual perfection only through vigilant experience. Could one who is conducting an important experiment fall asleep? So also, We, ever alert in consciousness, will unite Our lives into an unbreakable necklace. To some, this advice will seem like an abstraction; but We know all the practical realities of the process of perfectment.

Also, one must understand another ability of the Arhat. One must know how to pass through certain periods of life unnoticeable to the eyes of others. Arrows of excessive attention destroy the purple protecting net. This phenomenon may soon become visible. We do not hesitate to offer the concept of the Arhat, until recently unknown to science, as something that can be proved by experiment. Thus can a bridge to the far-off worlds be built, and life will be discovered where only death had been anticipated.

131. The addition of other subtle energies to the physical and chemical manifestations of life will increase their influence upon humanity. If the chemical properties of rays from the more distant planets can affect the human organism, then certainly the very close emanations of Earth, influenced by those innumerable cosmic formations, provide a lever for the strivings of humanity. Patterns of change in human activity cannot be perceived by subjecting apparent fragments of evidence to human logic.

How, then, without a study of all the surrounding processes, can one unravel the knots of the apparatus of thought? Somewhere pink rays flashed out, and a prepared uprising of an entire nation died down. Somewhere the currents of the oceans changed, and altered the patterns of world trade. These are crude, obvious examples, but how many more subtle causes and effects fill space and furrow the strata of humanity!

You, who determine the destinies of nations! Enter the laboratories, climb into the observatories, and, though you may not at once discover an analogy with social problems, your searching intellect will grasp the complexity of the structure of reality. You will realize the inseparability of the fate of human evolution from the cosmic processes. Therefore, real unprejudiced knowledge will be the sure guide to the future. He who separates the science of human sociology from the cosmic processes will thereby cut off his own legs and doom himself to a crippled life.

132. Conceit and suspicion are horrible diseases. The first gives rise to stupidity and ignorance. From the second issue lies and treachery. One must keenly discern the true motives of one's co-workers. The shield protects those who, through sincere striving to enlightenment, can make straight the convolutions of darkness.

Not the happy fool of popular tales, but the warrior, vigilant, with foresight—such is the image for the present time.

133. You may ask, "How many fields of knowledge must one conquer to avoid stagnation?" Of course it would not burden one's thinking to master three—the ethics of the fundamentals of existence, the subject of past lives, and observation of the visible aspects of nature. This not too burdensome triad could purify one's consciousness.

134. How does Our Community so easily avoid irritation? Do not overestimate the role of the quality of consciousness, for it is the fullness of labor that is at its foundation. In labor and in the utilization of *prana* lies the mystery of group harmony. Such cooperation is possible, and Our followers must not be confused by the diverse characters of their co-workers. Hard work and the proper use of nature will provide the correct attitude for the laboring community.

135. One may rejoice when the dates of great events flow by. No destruction can impede understanding of the growth of new cosmic opportunities. Such opportunities fill one with joy. If one realizes them, it means one partakes in them. And even a partially conscious participation in the cosmic process is already a great victory of the spirit. Striving toward the far-off worlds is the natural tendency of the human spirit, which remembers its interplanetary experiences. It is essential to direct humanity toward the path to the far-off worlds. This direction can take us through the mockery of ignorance to true reality. The manifestation of the far-off worlds will transform life upon the planet's crust. Predestined realities will drive away the stagnation of petty thinking.

136. Often people entrust themselves to a fiery steed, not realizing that even a mere gnat can throw the animal into a rage. Often people try to navigate in a frail canoe when every stone is a peril. Often people sit beneath the beams of a house which the slightest tremor of earth can cause to collapse. All this is of course known; nevertheless people think they can evade danger as though danger were not a constant companion to existence on Earth. People traverse life, blindly happy, unaware of the adjacent precipice. But if the inner sight is sufficiently developed, the voyager of life will see each cosmic irregularity. He will be painfully tormented by the seeming impenetrability of the path. But how will he gain the courage and strength to

71

cross all chasms of what he now sees as a crumbling stronghold? Certainly, only by realizing the relation of the present transitory hour to an inevitable future.

137. People do not want to understand group work, which multiplies the forces. The dodecahedron is one of the most perfect structures, with a dynamic power that can resist many assaults. A group of twelve, systematically united, truly can master even cosmic events. It must be understood that the enlarging of such a group can weaken it, undermining the dynamic force of its structure. Therefore you notice Our formations of small groups. Of course, various karmic conditions can attract more and diverse karmic elements to the group. One cannot expel them forcibly, but one can quickly live through their effect. The duty of each developed participant of the group is to realize who the uninvited guests are, and to exert all will power to settle the old accounts of life.

Sometimes even decent motives can draw unworthy individuals to a worthy person—a sort of overloading of a ship with unfit cargo. But the helmsman must guard the quality of the cargo and cut away the unfit. Especially avoid empty promises; these promises cling to the ship like barnacles. Recognize the merits of the worthy one, but do not burden him with promises. A united group must avoid mutual promises. A realization of the future structure should be the sole basis for unity. I speak not of magic circles but of the influence of real groups.

138. You rebel justly against any sowing of filth in life. Indeed, animals act more cleanly, because their imagination is unstained. Without fear one must eradicate the base habit of implanting filth in the eyes of youth.

139. The fire of *Brahmavidya* can be perceived only through the eyes. Words cannot express it, writings cannot express it, for its flame is within the thought that is not expressed in the physical shell. Only the lens of the eye can transmit the sparks of highest thought. Certain eyes can discern the sparks of the cosmic rays that the crude sight will think is simply the light of the sun. In order for the naked eye to perceive the cosmic ray as the sparks of *Fohat*, the fire of *Brahmavidya* is needed.

The human word is ineffectual in expressing the nature of *Brahmavidya*. One may partially penetrate it with the spiritual sight by facing the outburst of rays with closed eyes. The growth of the fire of *Brahmavidya* will later permit perception with open eyes of those components of the rays that are imperceptible to any physical apparatus. This possibility is already akin to the domain of communion with the far-off worlds. It flashes up as unexpectedly as each illumination of consciousness. It does not respond to forced development, but comes when sufficient sensitivity of the organism has been developed. The Teacher does not force this possibility, but He rejoices when the sight is carried from darkness to light.

The same is true of perception of the sounds of the far-off worlds. At first they appear undeniably in the depths of the consciousness and then, unexpectedly, they fly into the open, exultant ear. Those who do not understand enlightenment will not understand whereof I speak.

140. Worst of all are those people who cannot trust, and know not the power of trust—they are passing shadows!

141. We do not abandon Our brothers-in-labor on Earth. We measure their true opportunities for success against the earthly evidence. A sower can always change fields without forfeiting his usefulness. So also can Our brothers change their field of labor when they know that Near Ones vigilantly watch their creative work and striving of spirit.

We are often asked about the death of Upâsikâ. Was it really impossible for Us to postpone her departure until the completion of the books? Thus ask the near-sighted ones, who cannot embrace the supermundane conditions. It would have been cruel of Us to bind Upâsikâ by exacting a vow that she remain in her unhappy circumstances. On the contrary, We searched for the right combination of conditions, so as not to impede the progress of that spirit. It should be known that if that best combination had been missed, Upâsikâ would have once again been subject to attacks. Also, the opportunity for the right incarnation for her—in time and in place—would have been lost.

With true cooperation, each brother must know that the best possibilities have been chosen for him. This knowledge will be his sustenance through all difficulties. It is the pledge of the Community.

Can the individual himself know when he has begun or completed something? In the physical body it is impossible to know all about oneself. Many lives forge one chain of consciousness, and one should leave it to the faithful Brothers to pronounce the hour when the Lotus will open. They can decide on the needed goal-fitness, and in this decision and in the depth of trust lies a mastery over karma.

142. Let us take an example from the animal world. When organisms sharing one kind of blood separate, the process always evokes a feeling of being incomplete. The litter of tiny, blind newborn creatures so unconsciously turns to the forces of nature that only compassion takes notice of them. But time passes, and they become a powerful pack. It is true that they fight with each other, but they unite to attack the enemy. A new force has been developed despite an insignificant beginning.

And let us take the example of a structure. For the construction of a new house the old building is demolished. Each stone, each beam removed from the old nest cries out against the injustice of such an act. But the demolition is completed, and a new energy is ignited. Kali the Destroyer has become Mother the Creator. Out of the fragments of the old, a new structure is built. New energy floods the space. With such simple examples one is reminded of the need for the regeneration of energy.

If We are told about a form that will exist unchanged for a millennium, We will first of all regret the unprogressing nature of the spiral of energy around such a structure. Great action will ever be Our joy. We call destruction creation if it contains a striving to the future. Conscious creation of a new current of energy leads to an understanding of cosmic currents. Therefore, ponder the need to manifest motion in thought as well as in action.

All have heard about the coming of the New Era. Can the new arrive in inaction? It is better to welcome a new blind puppy than an aged parrot that repeats old things. Examine the stream of the Teachings of life that have been given to humanity. Each, without affecting the preceding, opens new gates to knowledge. The enduring realities of life are fundamental to each given Teaching. Therefore they should be studied not for learning, but for application to life. Only in this way can you create the current of energy.

143. We know of entire empires that were built successfully because flexibility was maintained in their planning. For example, those who besieged a stronghold retreated temporarily for reinforcement. And afterward their multitudes became an intimidating army, the very sight of which terrified the seemingly unassailable stronghold. By an irrational, single-minded application of energy, their entire army would have been destroyed, but the introduction of a new current of action provided new power.

The creation of the stronghold of knowledge is victory.

144. Vessels brimming with spirit! Thus do We call those people who, on the basis of the experience of past lives and their decision to attain, expand their consciousness and thereby enter into an understanding of the foundations of evolution. If this definition seems unscientific to some, say, "Can't one compare a great toiler in the spiritual realm to a Leyden jar?" Of course, for thus is the outer energy accumulated, and in due time a discharge follows. Hard is the strain when the potential is ready but the time has not yet arrived, because the sensitive apparatus has already absorbed especially dangerous particles related to Primary Matter.

As is known, Primary Matter itself—*Materia Matrix*—does not penetrate to the earthly sphere because of the whirling of the infected lower layers. But the so-called *Fohat*, which is the granulation of Primary Matter, can reach the earthly surface in the form of sparks and can even be discerned by some eyes when a ray of sunlight crosses the planetary ray, coloring the sparks according to the chemical composition of the ray.

In addition to *Fohat*, the earthly surface is reached by the outflow of radiant matter, *Materia Lucida*. To a certain eyesight it will be perceptible as radiant currents and spots of light in space. These manifestations may be taken for a peculiarity of sight, or even for defective sight. But knowledge will reveal the deep significance they have for the organism.

On the one hand, when they are recognized, the sparks of *Fohat* and the streams of *Materia Lucida* have a benevolent effect, for they imbue the spirit with an understanding of the necessity of evolution. On the other hand, being parts of the fiery element, they burn and can cause inflammation of the centers. The manifestations of the fiery element can be compared to the most intense colors of electrical discharges; but the electrical light-scale is limited, whereas the variegations of the light-sparks of *Fohat* are beyond imagination. The light of *Fohat* is comparable to that emanating from precious crystals. Nurturing the psychic energy, *Fohat* paves the way to the far-off worlds, whereas *Materia Lucida* weaves the strengthening of the consciousness. One strengthens, the other leads into the limitless ocean of perfectment. These are the wonderful gifts of Great Aum!

145. At first you were both shown how the basic laws of matter work. You participated in levitation and in experiments with the materialization and teleportation of objects. These were performed not for amusement, but for the purpose of seeking serious knowledge. After that you were shown the astral world, but not for immersion in it. Expanding the consciousness, you received the ability to see auras and images of earlier incarnations. Having finished with the semi-material world, we then approached cosmic clairvoyance and clairaudience. Using the opened centers of Sister

Urusvati, rays of different kinds and the structure of the most subtle substances could be shown. Thus we approached the realization of far-off worlds, which is close to the element of fire and therefore dangerous. That is why a period of treatment with cold was needed. The results were brilliant—because of having achieved the so-called prismatic sight, it became possible to perceive the granulation of *Fohat* without undue shock to the organism.

Why is it important to experience the manifestation of *Fohat*? The granulation of this finest energy is at the basis of cosmic condensations. This means that it is precisely *Fohat* that is the father providing the impetus for the formation of new spatial bodies. He who attains knowledge of the far-off worlds will feel the strength and beauty of the crystals of *Fohat*. This is a difficult experience, and We rejoice for Urusvati, because the physical body is rarely capable of assimilating the finest energies.

146. Every false accusation, suspicion, or statement immediately burdens the sender. It is foolish to hope that the consequences of a lie can be averted or hidden. Precisely these consequences root themselves, just as promises do, in a karma that must inevitably be outlived.

147. One should firmly understand the difference between expectation and striving. In expectation there will always be a time of inactivity, whereas in striving there is always a flight into the future. Such a difference can be understood only by one who is not satisfied with the flow of present life and thinks of the continuous flow of existences on other planets.

148. Let us consider the contrast between the wisdom of Earth and that of the far-off worlds. Certainly, if the spirit has for long been striving toward the perfection of the far-off worlds, life on Earth will be but a gathering of fragments.

All experiments in the fields of subtlest energies best occur in those hours when you are easily separated from Earth, and are filled with an unrestrainable striving to the wisdom of the far-off worlds. Any earthly sensation appears as nought compared with this flight into the Infinite. Yet there are times when we must strengthen the pillars of earthly wisdom. We rejoice at the wisdom of the far-off worlds, but should not forget the earthly wisdom.

149. Today Urusvati heard the music of the spheres, the rhythm that strengthens the realization of evolution. It is not the theme precisely, but the rhythm that is the essence of the music of the spheres. And it is the degree of purity of the sounds that determines the quality of the interplanetary conduit. These sounds are heard on many far-off worlds, but on Earth they can be heard only at high altitudes, and only by those who have a musical ear. However, the ear that listens for the music of the spheres must be protected from the wind.

150. Everyone who even once has regretted his work for Our missions creates an impassable barrier between himself and Us.

151. I vouch for health wherever *prana* is consciously safeguarded. Evolution is inseparably linked with the improvement of the life of the people.

For example, in Asia the question of the use of fuels must be approached in a new way. Mineral fuels must be utilized properly, and nurseries must be established for the planting of trees.

But even on the heights there have always been ample deposits of combustible materials available, and therefore people of Asia have long been afflicted by hydrocyanic acid fumes. This has been a serious threat to the progress of life in Asia, and to life itself. There will always be health where there are conscious efforts to preserve *prana*. The improvement of conditions of life must be an inseparable part of evolution.

The snarling of dogs can lead to the rhythm of a symphony, but the stillness of a cemetery can be more frightful than the whistling of the wind.

152. The more perfect the spirit, the more infallibly it understands the deep suffering of earthly life. And yet I myself speak again and again about joy, the joy that lies in the realization of the far-off worlds. Let us take a simple example. Through the darkness of night your carriage rushes homeward. The pouring rain should depress you, but instead your spirit is jubilant. Why? You know that your home is near and that the darkness and rain do not keep you from discerning those close to your heart.

What does the misery of earthly life amount to when the far-off worlds have become real to us? Make haste to realize the path to the far-off worlds. Only this broadening of the understanding of life will provide your spirit with the foundation of the path of joy. Otherwise, about what can one rejoice? About the inevitability of reincarnation? When one lacks vision of the future, however, incarnations are only fragmentary pages from the book of life. Animal reasoning does not need perception of the future, but man's will to knowledge impels him to understand the change of lives. Only by such thinking does man receive the right to joy, and by striving he can approach cooperation with the far-off worlds. Not by gazing at the sky, but through daily life will man multiply life's riches and discover the meaning and relative value of many daily events.

153. Everyone who has understood the fundamentals of evolution has the responsibility to transmit his knowledge to some others. In this, the one who transmits the knowledge, whether he is great or not, is subject to the same law: he must pass his knowledge on without violating the freedom of others. The fundamentals of evolution can be realized only voluntarily, and can be applied in life only through the striving of the awakening spirit.

One must rebuild one's entire life for the new step in evolution. This is impossible for one who is not ready to offer himself in spirit to earthly service. In fact, this offering is of the greatest importance for the completion of one's earthly path. From the most ancient precepts of Vedanta We know of this principle of liberation. Facing this new step of evolution, it is Our duty to repeat again and again about this propelling force.

154. You have often asked about those spirits who have departed from Earth for the far-off worlds. But, having seen the sallow coloring of our planet, you understand the goal-fitness of crossing over to where the beautiful reality exists. One must fulfill one's obligation to Earth by promoting the foundations of evolution. In this way one achieves the highest cooperation with humanity. But no glass dome can hold back the branches of the growing oak.

Let all ascend who can, striving to the heights!

155. One must give attention to the middle brain, for in its development lies the attainment of yoga in life. This development, as experienced in one's life, proves to what extent the Yoga of everyday life is superior to any artificial ascent achieved in isolation from reality.

156. The rhythm of truth is an invincible stronghold. It is not a pile of words, but a rhythmic sound, that carries decisive significance. Why try to conquer with words when the lightning bolts of rhythm can drive away the most harmful beings? Of what use is it to compose lengthy letters when thought pierces the consciousness instantly? Indeed, the Teaching about thought and the action of will has already been distorted by people. They have endeavored to compensate for their own weakness of will and thought by mechanical means. All the artificial hypnotic devices for lulling one into a trance, including glittering playthings, are ridiculous. And the crossing of the eyes is unnecessary! The one who realizes the true Yoga of Life knows that the lightning of truth can strike down, but can also resurrect.

When We speak of the need for honesty, We do not have in mind unworthy people. We point out the direct path of perfect truth, devoid of any personal element. This opportunity can be perceived through straight-knowledge. The experience accumulated in the center of the Chalice gives invincible knowledge. The center of the Chalice is close to the blood reservoir, for blood is the wherewithal for our passage on Earth.

Thus, the truth is not an abstraction; it is the realization of cosmic laws based upon direct experience. Therefore, though an honest accountant can make an error in his figures without becoming dishonest, an accurate but hypocritical person will not gain the power of spiritual effectiveness.

It is right to consider initiations, meditation, and concentration superfluous practices; these concepts must be expressed in one's actions. All artificial magic must be left behind.

157. The moral darkness of the nations increases. The fiery flower is obscured throughout the entire expanse of the planet.

158. People believe they can attain perfection by many methods. This multiplicity of mirages lulls the mediocre mind. But one really has only two ways to live: either wisely and ardently to seek the realization of Aum, or to lie in a coffin like a log—self-centered and impoverished in spirit—assuming that one's destiny will be taken care of by something or someone else.

It would seem, then, that a true striving toward realization of supreme possibilities should fill the greater part of human life as a most essential and engrossing occupation. But in reality the light of knowledge has been replaced by the conventional dogma of religion; and man, meant to be a thinker, worships his dark corner of idols, hanging amulets upon himself without even understanding the meaning of their symbols. Repeat this to all those who sleep in the darkness of the ordinary.

There exist no half-measures; there is either striving or the paralyzing cold of death. Moreover, striving is replete with the joy of cosmic realization, whereas the stiffening of death is filled with terror.

The governments that try to conceal their poverty of thought behind a mask of conventional success are doing the work of grave-diggers. Thus, it is necessary to point out to the younger generations the approach of the Yoga of Life.

All preceding Yogas, given from the highest Sources, took as their basis a particular aspect of life. Now, at the dawn of the age of Maitreya, there is needed a Yoga comprising the essence of the whole of life, all-embracing, evading nought. One remembers the example of those unignitible youths in the biblical legend who valiantly sacrificed themselves to the fiery furnace and thereby acquired power.

You may call this the Yoga of Life. But the most precise name will be Agni Yoga. It is precisely the element of fire that gives its name to this Yoga of self-sacrifice. While in other Yogas the dangers are diminished through practices, in the Yoga of Fire the perils are increased, because fire, as an all-binding element, manifests itself everywhere. But it also permits mastery of the subtlest energies. Fire will not lead away from life; it will act as a trustworthy guide to the far-off worlds. For what but fire saturates immeasurable space?

Thus, with a smile of joy, greet the fiery life.

159. Why is the Yoga termed Fiery? Its power enhances the vividness of life and extinguishes all that is unworthy. The manifestation of fire brings light into matter. Properly speaking, where there is fire, there is clear evidence of progressive perfectment.

We know instances when the tensed aura attracted the Fire of Space and enveloped itself in greater luminescence. This is how one's physical link with the finest energy is established. And We especially value it when one can sense the highest energies in the lower layers of the atmosphere and discern the unusual possibilities that descend upon mankind.

The pits of darkness require a powerful disinfectant. Only fire can pierce their harmful emanations. And if you are told that the element of fire is dangerous, answer that danger is the crown of achievement.

160. Can we think about battle only in terms of victory? What seems like failure is the root of strength. Success is like multicolored blossoms. But tap the roots, because in them is found the sap of power. I suggest that power be understood as being gained from the accumulations of experience. We are again in the garden of life, where experience assures attainment.

161. Let us see wherein lie the similarities and differences between Agni Yoga and the preceding Yogas. Karma Yoga has many similarities with it as far as earthly realities are concerned. But when Agni Yoga provides ways to the realization of the far-off worlds, the difference becomes apparent. Raja Yoga, Jnana Yoga, and Bhakti Yoga are all separate from the realities of routine life, and because of this they cannot enter into the evolution of the future. Of course, an Agni Yogi should also be a Jnani and a Bhakti, and the development of the forces of his spirit makes him a Raja Yogi. How beautiful is the possibility of being fit for performing the tasks of the future evolution without rejecting the past conquests of spirit! One should not boast of bringing innovation, because only by a synthesis of the old and the new is a renewal of possibilities attainable.

162. Each danger brings its advantages. When tempering a sword in fire, certainly the flame is a danger, but it also heightens the subtlety of receptivity. A similar fiery synthesis results from the development of the center of the larynx. Therefore, Agni Yoga is created upon the manifestation of Fire, the life-giver and the creator of will.

163. He who would swim must dive fearlessly into the water. And he who has determined to master Agni Yoga must transform through it his entire life. Why do people think they can begrudge to the Yoga a portion of some idle hour, while giving the rest of the time to impure thought? Truly, all actions must be infused with purifying one's fiery striving.

Recall how I began with you the attainment of Agni Yoga. Similarly, lead your disciples into the domain of the mastery of the Fiery Yoga. Like sculptors, begin to shape the different surfaces of the raw matter. Suddenly and continually strike sparks of the fire of life from the surface of chaos. As the play of the Great Mother gathers power in the spiral turns of the energy of *Fohat*, thus fearlessly offer to people a complete—more complete than expected—understanding of the whole of life in the realization of the Infinite. Do not be concerned with the rising and falling of the spirit. These are only turns in the spiral of motion. Far worse are a continuous inattentiveness and self-concern.

Let Agni Yoga lead on the path of building the flame, a process equivalent to the unending creation of cosmic formations. This most synthesizing Yoga exacts an obligation to construct one's entire life in accordance with a discipline that is externally imperceptible. If this essential discipline is not seen as chains, but is perceived as the joy of responsibility, we can consider the first Gates open. When cooperation with the far-off worlds is embraced, then will the second Gates be unbarred. And when the foundations of evolution are understood, the bolts will fall from the third Gates. And finally, when the superiority of the densified astral body has been recognized, then will the locks of the fourth Gates fall away. Together with this ascent the fires of the centers of knowledge are ignited, and amidst the lightning bolts of the subtlest energies, straight-knowledge unfolds. Cherish, then, the fire of knowledge and guard the growing power.

164. People talk much about the aid that should flow from Our Abode. But let us examine the ability of people to accept Our help. Each person who yearns for assistance has already decided selfishly the direction and measure of it. Can an elephant find room in a low cellar? But the seeker of help cares about neither its proportion nor its suitability. For him, lilies should flower during wintertime, and in the desert a spring must burst forth; otherwise the Teacher's merit is small.

"But, you who claim to be creator of the desert and lord of the cold, you caused your own thirst and shuddered from the cold of your own heart. My spring of pure water remained unnoticed and you did not turn to regard My flowers. You encumbered your way with selfishness and found time only to protect your precious feet from the thorns that you yourself grew. My help therefore took flight like a startled bird. My messenger returns in haste, and white Lobnor bays mournfully. My help is rejected."

But the traveler continues blindly to call for help, while wending his way to the site of his future destruction. We always advise alertness, flexibility, and open-mindedness, without which one cannot keep in step with reality.

165. The path of the hermit is not Our path. One must offer to life the flowers of experience. Besides, who would choose for himself the easy way of an unperturbed existence? Who would choose for himself the role of spectator at a battle? Henceforth, there should be no spectators or slumberers, because Flame is at the threshold.

166. Everyone has within himself some kind of Yoga, even if only in a rudimentary stage or in a distorted form. People can be classified not only according to the elements, but also according to Yogas. Often in a hypocrite you find a perversion of Bhakti Yoga; in an overbearing athlete, Hatha Yoga; in a zealot, Raja Yoga; and in a bigot, Jnana Yoga. But what can match the heights of the true Yoga, which links the earthly consciousness with the cosmic pulse? Can one

imagine anything that could replace the fundamental striving of the incarnate spirit; something that could imbue one with astral understanding; something that would make clear the purpose of mankind's existence? It is the study of Agni Yoga that brings one closer to the far-off worlds.

You may ask Me what physical exercises are useful in Agni Yoga. I advise a short period of *pranayama* in the morning, no longer than five minutes. One should abstain from meat, except smoked meats. Vegetables, fruit, milk, and cereals are always beneficial. All alcohol is barred, except for curative purposes. Narcotics, such as opium, are inimical to Agni Yoga. Cloudy skies are burdensome for an Agni Yogi. I advise insulating one's footwear with rubber and taking morning walks, avoiding smoky air. With courage must all events of life be faced, for it is impossible to decide where is the good and where the bad. He who brings the true Yoga into life fulfills his greatest mission. Thus, before us is the foundation of Agni Yoga.

167. Some may ask, "Is the path of those who bring Truth an easy one?" Of course the path for the person carrying Truth is hard. The fiery path can never be made easy. It is as if a dome descends upon the head of the bearer of Truth and presses upon the centers of the brain. Only conscious battle can lead the spiritual toiler to the fulfillment of his task. And a cloud of malice will pursue him because he strives to bring the planet out of its isolation.

Can one call him fearless who pronounces himself fearless, or can one call him learned who proclaims himself as having acquired knowledge? Truly, each one worthy of attainment performs his tasks, declaring them to be neither good nor bad, but performing them just as he must. Thus is the path laid for the completion of his incarnation. Will the one who completes his path call it burdensome? The completion of the last step should fill the traveler with joy, because he knows Whom he approaches.

168. Can one ascend and descend in isolation? Truly, no being can act without affecting his surroundings. Not only does he stir up the various layers of the atmosphere with each action but he literally drags his near ones with him. Man must realize his responsibility toward the universe. A person, with each elevation of the spirit, is of substantial aid to others. But a person falling in spirit may thereby even kill someone. Beyond the range of one's conscious thought flows a constant unconscious interaction, embracing wide circles, limited by the law of karma and the affinity of auras.

It is not always easy to decide when one is a murderer and when a benefactor. Only as beacons of Agni Yoga can we with justice illumine the workings of chaotic thought. But for this we must consecrate ourselves in sacrifice to Agni Yoga; and few can love the dangers of self-sacrifice. Therefore, what is said is comprehensible to only a few. But one can cite numerous examples, such as how one who became insane in Asia was the cause of the death of another in Europe, or how one who rose in spirit in America healed another in Egypt. Hence the efflorescence of beneficent thoughts is a flaming flower of spirit.

169. Just as Fire is the all-embracing principle, so does Agni Yoga permeate the whole of life. One can notice how one's consciousness is gradually sharpened, how the real values of one's surroundings become clear, how one's understanding of the immutability of the cooperation of worlds grows. Thus life fills with the signs of highest understanding. Truth as reality enters one's daily life.

Courageous seekers of Agni Yoga face the inevitable pains caused by conflagration of the centers, and also suffer a painful sensitivity to all injustice. But what do these dangers mean compared with the realization of the true liberating path!

Agni Yoga is like the Morning Star, which heralds the approach of Light.

170. During the development of the centers one feels incomprehensible symptoms, which science, in its ignorance, will attribute to quite unrelated ailments. Therefore the time has come to write the book of observations of the fires of life. I advise not to delay, because it is necessary to explain now to the world the manifestations of the reality and unity of existence.

New concepts are entering imperceptibly into life. These signs, visible to few, are at the foundation of life, penetrating all its aspects. Only the blind fail to perceive that life is being filled with new concepts. Scientists should be called to cast light on this new evidence.

Physicians, do not fail us!

171. An Agni Yogi must renounce the conventional in all national cultures, although temporarily he belongs to one of them. The Agni Yogi renounces narrow specialization in his work, although he can possess a superior knowledge of one thing and the mastery of it. The Agni Yogi chooses spiritual relationship over blood relationship. The shield of an Agni Yogi lies in his consecration to world evolution and in the stern banishment of prejudice from his heart.

172. The yogi must keep his organs of respiration pure. For this, hot milk, valerian, and mint are prescribed. The yogi must keep his stomach and his bowels pure; licorice and senna are prescribed for this. The yogi must keep his lungs pure, and for this he is given aloe, and also resins, prudently used. The yogi must keep pure the all-pervading soma, for which he must make use of musk. But purity also requires vitality of the glands.

173. The yogi is not given to hypocrisy; the yogi is not given to gossip against those belonging to the Brotherhood. Such gossip is equal to treason in its consequences. The yogi knows how much he himself is affected by his own thoughts. The yogi welcomes each sign of evolution. The yogi valiantly recognizes the evil of cosmic refuse and quickly destroys the sources of untruth.

174. The Teacher watches the progress of the yogi. Signs of his progress will be the ability to hear the voice of the Teacher and also the development of a keen sense of justice.

175. The confirmation of the yogi in his path will be a full participation in the evolution of the worlds. But one particular quality distinguishes the yogi—he knows not death, for the awakened consciousness experiences no interruption of existence. Thus, not for a moment does the yogi interrupt his service to Truth. Gradually does he who attains Yoga ascend upon the ladder of the worlds. Unceasingly do his mission and his service flow. The retention of consciousness in his varied sheaths makes the yogi's achievement vital to life.

Until now, only very rarely, and under special conditions was Yoga achieved, but the present stage of evolution of the spirit demands that Yoga be brought into life. And the thoughts of the young generation must be directed to this end. Neither zealotry nor weakness of faith are needed by Us, but each wholesome transformation of life will be noted and supported.

176. If we desire to introduce Agni Yoga into life, the goals must be presented to others in familiar terms. Ask the disciple if he wants to receive the support of the Teacher. Does he want to receive spiritual and material help? Certainly he does. Then, let us enter on the path of trial. Useful are sudden tests by cold and hunger; useful are sudden tests by distrust, by treason, by falsehood, and by superstition.

Observe how the frail spirit bows before the wind, how his stomach growls for food, and how his lips violate the most sacred principles. But see how he then can go forward, poor, self-sacrificing, smiling at cold and hunger, trusting in the power of the Cosmic Principles in his ascent; eternally young, ready to undertake the achievement of realization.

When you insist on the application of Yoga in life, then you will be true teachers.

177. Affirm the justice of the entire new structure of life. Strike especially at those who claim for themselves what others have attained.

178. The same unalterable Truth is given to humanity repeatedly, but clothed in various garments. Invariably, it is distorted in less than a century by confused minds. Therefore, it is the duty of a yogi to purify Truth. When the newly cleaned face of Truth smiles upon the devoted searcher, then joy can speed to the far-off worlds. Space proclaims that the purpose of life has been clarified. And the countenances of the Bearers of Truth are smiling ones. Rare is such a smile, but Yoga can evoke it. Therefore, the path of the Yoga of Life illumines life.

179. Even when facing the greatest battle, we must continue to follow our usual daily plan. It would not be correct for a battle to disrupt the current of life. Battle is our destiny, and one must simply include it in the daily plan.

180. A sorcerer veils in unusualness the most commonplace action. But the yogi brings even the most unusual manifestation within the boundaries of the ordinary, for he knows the goal-fitness of nature.

A yogi is neither old nor young. Not old, because he knows the path of steady ascent. Not young, because he knows the cumulation of previous experiences. A yogi can pass unnoticed through life. A yogi smiles at foolish words, and smites ignorance.

"I am the fearsome smiter of the defamation of Truth. I take upon myself the responsibility for the purification of the old world. Unyielding will I be in opposing the onslaught of pettiness. I will assume the courage to oppose the fury of evil!" Thus affirms the yogi. And in the power of this affirmation he tempers his sword of Truth.

Deem it happiness to embark on the path of the Yoga! The past offers its best fruits to him who begins the Yoga, and the future will disclose to him the vast field of action.

181. We taught you to grasp the essence of ideas, without succumbing to their superficial meanings. Just as Buddha taught the development of an entire topic from a single word, so must you broaden the understanding of your disciples by building upon one word or sign. But chiefly, try not to repeat to the unprepared. If the receptacle of spirit is ready, each thought will pierce like an arrow. But if decayed tissue has already clogged the channels of the centers, no Yoga can be achieved at that time.

Certainly the Teaching of Yoga will to some extent be useful for all, even if they cannot attain the higher spiritual manifestations. The practical teachings of Yoga can in any case improve health, strengthen memory, and purify thinking.

But where are the signs of the achievements that exalt the spirit? First the inner fires of the centers will be kindled. Then will be heard the voice of the unseen Teacher. And finally the external flame, which binds the individual consciousness with the consciousness of space, becomes manifest. Then will become possible the contact with the wondrous, perilous, subtlest energies—with all that transforms life and eliminates the concept of death.

The strains of contact with the unusual sometimes necessitate special conditions in one's life. Sleep is decreased. Lying down becomes painful. Muscular tension impedes the work of the spirit. Each poisoning of the aura causes suffering. Naturally, these aggravations can be prevented without leaving the path, and the light of Yoga will be vaulted by the all-embracing light of space.

Is there any other path to Nirvana?

182. More about signs of Yoga—if the consciousness permits, when one begins to breathe freely and deeply on the heights, then the path to the highest layers of the astral world is within reach.

The path to Yoga is open only to the one who recognizes that his knowledge is insignificant; who seldom thinks of the distinctions bestowed upon him by others; who has not taken part in any wrongdoings of religions; who, remembering about reincarnation, does not overvalue his earthly bloodline; who can yearly repeat the planting of his garden, smiling at the storms that undid his past labors; who has lost the ability to slander; who has aimed his striving search toward the Invisible Supreme; who has rejected the companionship of all betrayers of Truth; and who has encircled himself with purity of thinking, which produces an invincible aura.

Truly, I say, the Agni Yogi must receive his merited place on Earth and above, for he has enveloped himself in the subtlest element. And when the coward cringes, the Yogi girds himself in fiery armor, for he is without fear.

Remember the baptism by fire, the fiery cross, and all the flaming Chalices, which I disclosed to you long ago as symbols of the coming Yoga. The symbol of fire has informed all teachings, for application in life. Thus, the manifestation of fire has come closer, and the element of water has been replaced by that of fire.

183. I entrust you to extol the Name of the Teacher so highly that nothing debasing may touch this link uniting the worlds. I entrust you also to offer your help to those who knock untiringly. I entrust you to speak of the purpose of life on Earth. I entrust you to reject all that demeans communion with Us. I entrust you to affirm the fact of Our Existence.

The understanding of Our Teaching will essentially transform the lives of those who accept it. It opens new possibilities; otherwise why assume the burden?

184. Among the achievements on the path of Yoga is included the possibility of communion with the Teachers. In this regard one must distinguish two currents, the single current and the spatial one. The single current evokes the response of one chosen Teacher. The current of space not only brings one into contact with several Teachers but also provides the possibility of receiving knowledge from Cosmos itself. It is necessary to understand the different ways in which one's energy is expended when in contact with these two currents. Just as a lamp responds variously to different currents, so do the centers vibrate to the currents of space. Truly, caution is needed to bring into daily life the combinations of such varied energies.

You have an example of the difference between two currents, and you know that the single current has less effect upon one's health. For future research it is important to know with which of the currents you are dealing. Many scientists will not be able to find appropriate methods to study this. Why is it that one person under observation is less in need of special treatment, while the spirit of another can flutter, like a captured rare bird, so that ordinary remedies are thrown off without effect? On this level of Yoga one is brought in touch with energies that are applied with great difficulty to contemporary life. Sometimes, after contact with an unusual type of energy, one must cease contact for a considerable time; but the overly zealous spirit does not permit this rest to his centers, and then We admonish, "Caution!"

Agni Yoga is only now entering life, and those who have consecrated themselves to the influence of these forces endure particular difficulties, almost as if they were aliens on Earth. Therefore We say to scientists, "Do not err in your deductions."

Many think they are ready to dedicate themselves to evolutionary achievement, but the conditions are most severe, and the one who cannot cast a great net had better not approach this great ocean.

185. Some of the young may ask, "How should one understand Agni Yoga?"

Say, "As the perception and application in life of the all-embracing element of fire, which nourishes the seed of the spirit."

They will ask, "How can I approach that knowledge?"

"Purify your thoughts, and after determining your three worst traits, sacrifice them to be burned away in fiery striving. Then choose a Teacher on Earth and, mastering the Teaching, strengthen your body with the indicated medicines and *pranayama*. You will behold the stars of the spirit; you will see the flames of purification of your centers; you will hear the voice of the Invisible Teacher; and you will acquire those subtlest perceptions that transform life.

"Help is ready for you who have entered, and your mission is given. You have realized that joy is a special wisdom. You will not return to the stream's old banks. You have embraced in your consciousness the battles of space. Misleading evidence no longer has meaning for you. You are an attaining co-worker and brother!"

186. For an Agni Yogi, the repetitive movements of work like carpentry, smithery, and hand laundry are harmful. One must be prepared to withstand the battles of space. One must also understand how much the fire, brought into one's life, refines the organism. I, by the justice of Hierarchy, decree that the achievement of introducing the new Yoga is superior to all other missions!

187. Agni Yoga must be introduced into life, but its bearers must not differ externally from others in life. The Agni Yogi lives unnoticed. He needs no human distinctions. He observes, but will avoid attention from others. For the current of space, the arrows of the crowd's attention are unacceptable, because the work of evolution is not wrought by the crowds. Even the single current at times requires protection from the random arrows of the crowd. This does not mean that there should be even the slightest alienation from life. It is necessary only to evaluate the goal-fitness of one's surroundings.

A yogi ignores seeming misfortune because he discerns the causes and effects of unforeseen events. What people usually see as accidental is the result of influences persisting from the past, even the most remote. And where others will turn away from misfortune with disdain, a yogi perceives the true possibilities. Do not be amazed if the yogi's heart responds to the most pitiful dog in which he sees the seeds of devotion, or if he suddenly calls the humblest child to be a future co-worker.

No sooner do people call a yogi stern and cold, than he will unexpectedly perform an act of true love and compassion. Most probably, the intent of this act will be falsely judged by onlookers. Being called a deceiver is an honor for the yogi, because evolution is an abomination to the ignorant. We speak both for humanity and individuals. The beast of ignorance, however, is alien to those who build.

188. With each century a special kind of Yoga is introduced, appropriate to the world's condition. The earth element is inapplicable when a fiery cure is required. Nor will water or air serve in place of the wings of fire. Like an inevitable cataclysm that sweeps away continents, so undeferrable is the Yoga of the realization of the fiery power. The ability to recognize the right time for right actions is the mark of an enlightened consciousness.

189. The yogi has few possessions, and among them are no unnecessary ones. If an object has importance for all, then, after being used, it must be returned to the common treasury. A yogi's everyday objects may occasionally be given to trusted people, but more often, in order to avoid the mixing of auras, it is better to burn them. Sometimes, however, it is useful to give to another an object that has been permeated with a particular aura.

A yogi recognizes the true nature of objects and will not keep any unworthy objects near him. The question of material possessions wastes too much of people's time. The culture of the spirit demands that surrounding objects be of the highest quality. In the future, people must be free from the need to devote attention to their physical needs. The basis of communal life assumes for each co-worker the provision of reasonable comfort, which will safeguard strength and labor.

Can a yogi without penalty waste his time and energy? It must be remembered that at times the dissipation of strength and time is equivalent to suicide. Similarly, reading the Indications of Truth without applying them to life is regarded by Us as ignorance. The ray of realization of the tasks of evolution will inspire recognition of the best creations. Therefore weigh carefully the true quality of what has been revealed to you.

190. On the way to Us do not forget to take all that you recognize as valuable. It is instructive to develop an understanding of values. Often, even people who know something of the domain of the spirit continue to give their attention to mediocre and ugly things. They forget that ugly things serve the forces of darkness. A yogi must know quite clearly the true quality of everything.

191. It is too early to concern oneself with the downfall of the planet when one has not yet recognized one's own downfall. One should first cure one's own wounds, then walk with those who labor. A new approach to everyday life will provide an understanding of its every detail. A yogi does not fly off to nebulous regions, but does keep the silver cord of contact with the far-off worlds.

192. A yogi is tested continually by his Teacher. In the same way, a yogi tests those who come to him.

Explain the meaning of the tests by cold and hunger, and all other measures. An ignorant person will be puzzled about how to overcome feelings of cold or hunger. The one who understands the essence of things knows that these sensations cannot be made to disappear, but the spirit can be strengthened so that nothing will unsettle it. A hungry one will find means to satisfy his hunger if his spirit has not descended to an animal condition. A cold one can warm himself as long as his spirit understands why he must protect himself. Without this, there will be only an animal-like irritation, confusion of consciousness, and downfall.

It is proper to add that adaptability is the best way to deal with the traps of life. A yogi appraises instantaneously the value of goal-fitness. If in order to expose his yogism he is offered a piece of meat, he would of course prefer to eat the meat than to disclose his secret. The effect of the meat can easily be purged, but the effect of permitting the secret to fall into treacherous hands would be irreparable. Then it sometimes becomes necessary for Us to project a smiting ray, though this is only rarely permissible.

I also wish to remind you of the importance to Agni Yoga of creative work. You were bidden to compare two different interpretations of a musical composition, and your spirit understood the differences in their effect. Thus is consciousness raised by the touch of Truth, and one more abstraction becomes a reality. And how beautiful is the realization of constant testing! Therein lies motion. Can a Yogi of Fire succumb to inactivity?

I do not say this just for your ears, but for application.

193. A skilled archer, even in this age of firearms, is still a skilled marksman. Likewise with Yogas. Except for Hatha Yoga, all Yogas are beautiful in accomplishment. It would be unwise to belittle any of them. One should only speak of which better applies to the present stage of evolution.

194. A yogi should understand atmospheric conditions in order to know how to make use of them. Even an ignorant observer can clearly see that electrical waves can substantially affect normal processes. Also, magnetic whirlwinds and precipitations of humidity will have various effects on the psyche. Magnetic whirlwinds and all electrical manifestations are Our friends, but atmospheric precipitations impede the fiery current. We use an atmosphere charged with electricity to convey, even to those who are unprepared, the usefulness of concepts unknown to them.

The exit of the astral body is also helped by magnetic waves. Therefore a yogi must be sensitive to all the unseen processes of nature. For this the yogi needs, first of all, contact with *prana*. Windows should not be closed, except perhaps when the humidity is overly dense. Long, warm baths without abrupt movements are useful. Generally, abrupt movements disturb the motion of the aura and We avoid them. A speedy rhythm does not disrupt one's link with the atmosphere, but convulsive movements wound the aura, like needles.

Many atmospheric observations can facilitate the building of the future. But unfortunately, one must recognize that even mosquitoes know atmospheric conditions better than men. Yet people think that by claiming the title of king of nature, they have the right to know nothing.

195. Covering the fires of the centers with layers of soma is sometimes necessary, otherwise the sharpness of outer influences would inflame the centers. Again we come to the need for balance, called by Our Teacher the golden mean, which may also be seen as the fullness of understanding.

196. You know about the harmful effects of various fuels. Therefore one should pay attention to the proper construction of fireplaces. In any case it is best not to remain long near a hearth, knowing what manner of guests the emanations of food, especially bloody foods, attract. Therefore it is better to have smoked meat and poultry, when eaten cold.

One must with equal caution guard the purity of the air in one's sleeping room. One should remember that during the departure of the astral body the physical body remains unprotected, and if the air is poisoned, the appearance of undesirable guests is unavoidable. Mint is the best disinfectant. It also aids the astral body, which leaves the physical body more often than we think. It may at times wander aimlessly, staying close to the physical body, or it may enter upon a new course of action and gain much knowledge. The imperative duty of each one is to create the best conditions for one's astral body.

Also, one should take care that no dirty water collect in the house. Indoor fountains and aquariums are usually undesirable nurseries. Besides, why torture and imprison fish and birds?

I also wish you to keep one room, or even a corner of a room, in absolute purity, dedicated to the Teacher. You can keep near the window an armchair, in which no one is permitted to sit. Also, do not admit the curious. For them, you should behave in a most ordinary way, so that their intrusiveness will pass lightly over your aura. All these counsels are salutary for Yoga.

197. One should think about Our actions and testify to their rightness. The least doubting thought will divert the arrow far from its target. Then it would be better not to touch Yoga at all. An obscured consciousness is a remainder from the animal state. Who has need of clouded thoughts? No one would want to receive obscure answers to their questions!

It is necessary to purify the current of one's spirit. But We are not chimney sweeps, to forcibly clean the channels of your spirit! Simply say that people themselves must make it possible for Us to be of help.

198. A yogi has no habits, because habits are nothing more than the decay of life. However, it is natural for a yogi to have his own way of action. It is not difficult for a yogi to cut the bonds of habit, because his state of tense alertness constantly reveals to him new approaches to problems. Inertia is the skeleton on which ignorance grows. How many kingdoms have collapsed because of inertia!

199. Our Teaching is not strong in the hands of those who do not apply it to life. Tell this to the co-workers in all countries, so that they may immediately find the means to fortify life through the counsels of Yoga. There are too many talkers and too few doers. I see no need for general lectures; but individual conversations are needed. Also, do not hide the difficulties or the advantages of the Teaching. Relate Yoga to world events, because a new system of life must be introduced, without which social movements will be nothing more than a masquerade of old ideas. The severe discipline of freedom can rebuild life only when a new understanding of the conscious use of psychic energy enters into everyday life. Repeat that a new understanding is needed for application in life!

200. Revelations are only for the few. The crowds will not know of the turning of the ship; and in the morning they will ask, "Where did the sail disappear to? Why is the shore so empty?"

"Because you did not notice the loading of the precious cargo, and you slept through the east wind at dawn."

One cannot speak openly to the crowd, because at the approach of the morning light it still hears the voices of night. One can strike the hydra of ignorance only with a blow unfamiliar to it. It is the yogi's duty to learn to strike unfailingly.

He who strives unceasingly for the higher knowledge will be unwaveringly vigilant. Whom else can one call a warrior? And whom a plowman? Who is a guide? A yogi should be called by all these honored names. But the time will come to reveal the field he plows. Who can measure its cubits when the field of the yogi is space? Who can point out the yogi's victories when their fires are glowing within him? Who can number those saved by the yogi if he guides them without even asking their names?

201. There exists the false impression that a yogi possesses unfailing health, as it is usually understood. But can a sensitive instrument be made from a sturdy log? Does not the value of the strings of the *vina* lie in their ability to resonate to the finest intervals of tone? Equally resonant is the sensitive apparatus of the yogi. Indeed, to him alone are known the indescribable fleeting pains, which, like the tuning of the strings of the *vina*, transform his being.

One must understand that We will not claim that the path of Yoga is without danger. How can one avoid pain during the transformation of one's centers? The fire of cognition always burns hot.

You know by now that what is said here is not abstract symbolism. All the usual names given to these pains are useless, so long as science does not hasten to understand the significance of psychic energy or spirituality. The farther people are from an understanding of the dangers of Yoga, the farther they are from unity with the Highest Consciousness. Random flights of consciousness are of no value. What is needed is an incessant song of soaring. The *vina* may not always be sounding, but its tuning is kept harmonious.

Those who seek Yoga only for their health should instead partake of a glass of wine and discuss lofty ideas without applying them to life. For the health of a yogi rises and falls like the wings of a soaring eagle. The eye of the yogi sees like the eagle's eye, which you already know. The calm of the yogi is like the tensed power of the ocean.

202. The health of the yogi is comparable to the tuned *vina*. The same may be said of the work of the yogi—at times resounding, at times silent, always wrapped in the garment of goal-fitness. The aim of the yogi is to fill space with beneficent affirmation and to direct energy to wherever Truth has been debased.

Can one criticize a yogi for arriving suddenly, or for departing without warning for long periods of time? Attachment to a particular place must be abandoned. Only thought and action should decide the earthly dwelling. Therefore traveling will always be an inseparable part of Yoga. How else can be born a sensitivity to the need for change? Where is independence tempered, or the solitude of realization? The yogi's work reverberates, and gains its expansion from space. A yogi must be familiar with space and be able to bring the word of space to the people of the world.

203. Those who seek out the yogi for instruction in the Teaching will not be of equal worthiness. A yogi must be able to understand who comes by accident; who may become a pupil; who may in the future become a pupil-teacher, learning to perfect himself by helping those who come to him. It is worse for those who involve themselves in the Yoga and then try to return to their old life. Truly, it is easier for the astral body to return into the clutches of the physical body than for one who has acquired even a grain of knowledge to return to the darkness of ignorance. Warn those who want to know about Yoga. We cannot permit people to keep their delusions.

204. Many dream of acquiring the shield of the yogi, while finding it too troublesome to forge the needed sword. But the ability to strike cannot come through watching another wield his sword.

205. "Awaken, slumberer!" People love to repeat this call. It is especially amazing when this is repeated by those who are themselves slumberers, and who continue to sleep. Some sleep for years; some sleep through an entire life; some occasionally fall into sudden slumber and drowsily repeat thoughtless words uttered by others. Let us not speak of the occasional passers-by; even those who are already on the path are subject to spells of animal sleep. Then it is the task of the Teacher to awaken them, even, if necessary, by a stroke of lightning. Indeed, sleep can easily lead to possession.

Blessed India! You alone have guarded the concept of Teacher and disciple. The Guru can pilot the ship of his disciple's spirit. The Guru can dispel the attack of sleep. The Guru can raise the drooping spirit. Woe to him who has dared to lay false claim to someone as his Teacher and who then pronounces light-mindedly the word Teacher while actually honoring only himself! Truly flowers the spirit that has understood the path of ascent, and he fails who droops in uncertainty of thought.

One can ask a Hindu boy if he would want to have a Guru. No word is needed in reply, because the boy's eyes will shine with desire, striving, and devotion. The fire of *Aryavarta* will burn in his eyes. The stream of the *Rig-Veda* will flow on the slopes of the mountains.

Who can describe in words the entire succession of Teachers? There can be a realization of it as a serpent of knowledge; otherwise lacking this, there is only darkness, sleep, and obsession. There is no need to terrify, but one should tell all who have approached the Yoga, "Your support is the Teacher. Your shield is devotion to the Teacher. Your downfall is indifference and duplicity of thought."

He who smiles alike on the friends and the foes of the Teacher is unworthy. He who betrays the Teacher, even if only by reticence when speech is needed, may not place his foot on the threshold.

206. You have received the signs of Yoga on the heights. You saw for yourself that neither the cold nor the altitude injured your health. How then can one who has not conquered the cold endure the supreme tremor? How can one contemplate the far-off worlds when fearing even the heights on Earth? How can one think himself a freed spirit if any passing sensation of hunger is not conquered? An over-full stomach is a sign of the cessation of ascent, though a right measure of involvement in earthly life must be maintained.

Yoga provides many advantages related to cosmic consciousness. Yoga provides a spatial current and Our aid in all useful actions. An understanding of cooperation gives the only true approach. It is most important to understand the Yoga in its practical application, in order to give Us the possibility of responding in a practical way.

207. *Amrita* consists of the accumulations of the finest energies. What else should we call the saturation of the yogi's striving with all those properties that we have already spoken about? Each striving of the yogi is imbued with a priceless combination of energies. Let us call this combination the discus of striving. The strivings of the yogi rise precisely as does the luminous disk of the sun. No actions of the yogi are without purpose; otherwise he could be compared to a man who without purpose has climbed to the summit of a mountain and gazes about in amazement. But the yogi acts, and the action itself is transformed into beauty.

The disciples of a yogi learn to act in the same way, from the first moment of understanding. It is especially important for the pupil to control himself in the Teacher's absence. Often, just at such times, because the concept of the Teacher is still unrealized, the disciple's imprudence permits excessive freedom, and thus the way to *Amrita* is closed.

208. The laws of energy awakened while one follows the path of Agni Yoga act inevitably and with precision. No one who has stepped onto the path of Yoga can deny that his life was fundamentally changed by it. His life was either expanded broadly or was diminished, depending upon the qualities of his spirit.

We say to all, "Accept the full Chalice of *Amrita*." But freedom of choice rests with each one.

209. Be cautious with a tuned instrument. It is like a torch in the dark. Disturb it, and you harm yourself. For its path between the worlds is inviolable. And the yogi's striving shines like the sun. His path is not easy.

210. It is said that a yogi has no desires; actually, he is filled with striving. A desire is not active, because it creates expectation, and expectation is the mother of passivity. Striving, on the other hand, is a generator of motion, leading to ascent of the spirit. It is said that the yogi knows no love; but in truth, he is full of compassion. People think of love only as constricting bonds. But compassion is boundless, a co-worker of Truth. It is said that a yogi is endowed with inexhaustible powers; however, like a diligent gardener, he must tend his own plants in the garden of opportunities.

211. The Druid Mother safeguarded against distortion the teaching entrusted to her. So shall the Mother of Agni Yoga safeguard the Teaching from malicious misrepresentation. However difficult the fiery path of Truth, service in vigilance permits no treason. The sun-sword does not falter in the hand nor does the knee bend to untruth. Thus must be understood the Teaching that brings with it the forging of a new life. It says: "You have heard; you must understand that from this moment you have accepted responsibility for any distortion!"

212. Rejoice! rejoice! rejoice! For the yogi must know the wisdom of joy. The teaching of the Blessed One is to safeguard the joy of spirit. He who feels the presence of the spirit already rejoices in recognition of his boundlessness.

213. It is especially difficult for the spirit who has developed new possibilities but who, because of external circumstances, is unable to express himself. The closest example is that of a covered cauldron, boiling in the Fire of Space. Applications of cooling currents are then needed. The Fire of Space, which makes even stones red-hot, has an unbreakable bond with the channels of the centers. Therefore the Teacher says to even the most self-sacrificing yogi, "Caution!"

214. The crystal of *Materia Lucida* can be seen only rarely in such a size as was made visible to you. For this, there is needed a special converging of magnetic currents. The crystal seems in some way to be attracted by the Stone. It sharpens the center of the third eye, and also serves as the substance for astral construction on the highest plane. The crystal relates to the finest energies and also to the energy promised to humanity—if humanity is willing to accept it. The light of *Materia Lucida* can be intensified infinitely, and will provide illumination, which, without requiring the consumption of any material, can assume any form. This is a challenge that can be met, but the desire of humanity is first needed. Without it, access to the currents of finest energies cannot be given. The power of these energies is linked with psychic energy; hence each abuse is destructive.

It should be remembered that not only for illumination but also for healing is *Materia Lucida* irreplaceable. It will be the best remedy for calming the nerves, for it is a bridge between the psychic energy of humanity and cosmic energy, the reservoir of which is inexhaustible.

215. An angry person is like a bull. But the one who strikes a blow for justice is like a luminous spirit. When will people comprehend the wondrousness of becoming like the Highest Beings? As yet, they are abashed at this thought.

216. This is why it is important, especially at the present moment, to direct attention to Agni Yoga. In each century there is a powerful awakening of psychic energy in humanity, but usually this beneficent indication is not understood by people.

Let us take an example. At the beginning of the nineteenth century there rose a tide of romanticism without, however, an understanding of its essence, or, properly speaking, without heroism. In the middle of the same century the world became enveloped in a negative materialism, failing even to study the true properties of matter. The close of the century was given over completely to decline, even though a reassessment of values had been indicated. The beginning of the present century was marked by war and national upheavals, although the recognition of psychic energy pointed toward the conquest of other worlds. Thus by free will were the destined values perverted. In the middle of our century there will flash forth signs of new, as yet unmastered energies, and again people will scurry about in false directions. Therefore it is time to give the signs of the true path to those who can see. Let them have enough time to familiarize themselves with it, remembering how little time is left.

217. Do not be too hasty in choosing disciples. Apply three tests to the approaching ones, so that they may reveal themselves unsuspectingly. Let the first test be the affirmation of the General Good; let the second be the defense of the Name of the Teacher; let the third be the demonstration of independence of action. If one, during a task, begins to threaten—reject him. If one whispers around the corner—reject him. If one thinks that he is overburdened—reject him. I do not speak about traitors. By the ways in which their tasks are performed, you will know the tested ones. Freedom of will abides in all, and the planet itself is in the power of the human spirit.

218. When we speak about the subtlest energies, we should know the signs of their manifestations. The word *subtlest* indicates that the quality of their effect will differ from that of ordinary manifestations. The highest energy is the least perceptible. It is the consciousness that controls the power of the universal energy. The consciousness of space permeates the brain substance. This process cannot be demonstrated; it cannot be measured. Thus the spokes of a wheel rotating at a certain speed appear motionless, and it is only the movement of the surrounding atmosphere that indicates the degree of tension. Likewise, in processes involving the finest energies, the effects are visible only from afar. Just as colorless cyanic acid is undetectable to the eye, yet shows powerful effects, so does the energy of consciousness invisibly begin its striking action and reveal its effects in the surrounding waves of space. Likewise, the finest vibrations of radiant matter are hardly perceptible, yet are blinding in their gross manifestations.

The same law is evident in other processes. Let us take as an example the way in which people are influenced. A speech is made and the crowd is quickly convinced, but the later effects are much less evident. Nevertheless, one cannot affirm that the first effect was the strongest. It is quite possible that the people's consciousness was changed and thunder was replaced by silence. And the power of silence has already been spoken of. Thus new, quite understandable circumstances are invisibly formed. Ordinary people notice them only in their finality, but a yogi can perceive the entire process of formation in all its subtlety. For a yogi, the saying "nothing is accidental" means that a rainbow of influences exists. The formations are stratified in many colors, and it is valuable to remember this. As in chemical, so also in psychic achievements do we take care to avoid unchanging methods. Monotonous uniformity cuts off a multitude of possibilities. Each seeming unexpectedness produces a new pattern in reaction to the subtlest energies. What benefit can we bring to evolution if we do not understand the multiformity of influences?

219. What can one call an Agni Yogi? Certainly, a supporter of Truth. The perceiving of Truth is as natural to the Yogi as light is to fire. The growth of sensitivity in a yogi cannot be described; it sharpens the five known senses, and also the seven senses related to the astral body, which can only rarely reverberate within the earthly shell, like a resonator. Thus, one should pay great attention to the feelings of an Agni Yogi. From them comes Truth, like light from a flame.

220. Agni Yoga is not just the progressive development of human ability; it leads one to a balanced contact with the fiery cosmic energies that reach our planet at the prescribed time. This fact must be clearly understood, otherwise a succession of sicknesses will spread, and their treatment by external measures can only lead to disastrous results.

How can one be cured of these fiery illnesses? The inner fires must be utilized as a useful, psychically active force. How can one cure the pains in the spine that are caused by the awakening of *Kundalini*? He who knows will welcome the pains and relieve them by rubbing in mint. How can we stop the burning of the third eye when it begins to function? Is it not wiser to help its development by shielding it from the sun? Long ago people knotted their hair on the crowns of their heads in order to protect this channel. Can one stop the movement of the solar plexus when it begins to rotate? Any forcing of the solar serpent can result in injury to the brain. Equally dangerous is any interruption of the functioning of the center of the Chalice. Of course, any poisoning by narcotics, such as opium, will stop the movement of the centers; but then, decapitation would be even simpler!

One can imagine what confusion would be caused by these inexplicable movements of the centers if we did not think of them in terms of psychic energy. Strange as it may seem, a study of the physical traces of imperil can lead to an understanding of the accumulations of psychic energy. One can observe the traces of imperil in any nerve channel. But it also can be noticed that, around the granulations of this poisonous viper, is gathered another substance that absorbs it—accumulations of psychic energy are found there too, because each energy has its physical crystal.

Whoever has seen the crystals of *Fohat* and *Materia Lucida* knows how visible are the crystals of even the most subtle energies. The true direction of research will be towards the study of both the physical plane of energies and the invisible energies saturating space. The way of the metaphysician has not brought meaningful results, and the alchemist is resting in his coffin. But chemistry will uncover tangible reality when it reaches a true understanding of psychic energy and all-binding fire.

I consider it necessary for Us simply to provide opportunities, for freedom of the will must not be violated. Whoever wishes to will understand! Explicit formulas should never be given. There must be room for free will.

221. The accumulation of imperil has been shown to you. It is precisely that poison which causes much trouble to people. Do not forget that meeting with even the grossest ignorance is not worth provoking one drop of imperil. Indeed, imperil does not remain only within; it evaporates and permeates space, for the purity of which we are all responsible.

222. Free will is a subject that is interpreted in many ways. One sees it as willfulness; another as irresponsibility; a third as the madness of the ego. Only the one who has gone through the discipline of spirit can realize how strict the reality of freedom can be. The abuse of freedom is a festival of ignorance. People cannot reconcile themselves to the Hierarchy of Knowledge, nor can they respect discipline of the will. But is any Yoga possible where there is no responsibility for one's will? Each yogi wields his sword directly over his own heart; to that degree is he responsible for every action of his will. The consequences resulting from the will of a yogi may be indescribably severe, but he has chosen them consciously. Thus, one can see the yogi as a tireless warrior, always on guard.

Whoever is sure in his will—let him enter!

223. Claws do not frighten you; roaring does not terrify you; animals wag their tails and stand ready to serve you. Thus precisely, the path of Yoga transforms dangers into fiery blossoms. When I advise you to preserve your earthly cumulations, I mean only the armor of your spiritual strength. We condemn waste. Each accumulation is a step toward freedom. But where shall we set the limits of permitted accumulations? By straight-knowledge and experience, the Teacher will confirm what is permissible. A yogi is able to do everything, but not all is permitted to him. Where then are the borders of limitation? A yogi's responsibility is to his spiritual accumulations, for they are his only treasure. The rest is nothing more than the arms of the warrior, returned to his commander after the battle. About this there can be no doubt.

"Lord, take my weapons, my shield and my smiting sword. How weighty seems my helmet, which in the battle was lighter than a feather! My anklets fetter my steps and my gauntlets are like shackles on my wrists."

His Commander will reply, "Each weapon is meant for certain battles. Lay aside thy now-useless arms. They shall be given to one who succeeds you in this stage of thy spirit. Each battle has its appropriate arms. Thy sword is now too short for thee; therefore I give thee a spear of light and far-flying arrows."

Whoever has seen his enemy at sword's length will know how to shoot the arrow of victory. But many warriors do not know which weapons are appropriate, and therefore fall before the enemy's stroke. He who has succumbed to the enemy's stroke through incaution merits no honors. This rule of battle applies to every yogi.

224. The subtle body of the yogi, when liberated, visits different planes of existence. Flights into space and descents into the depths of the planet are equally possible. A study of planetary cataclysms will provide an understanding of the stratifications of life. It can be observed how animals became fossilized when caught in a mineral flow. When moving through the subterranean channels, the yogi can see to what extent the foundations of our planet have become worn out. Thus the spirit of the yogi becomes familiar with the conditions of ancient formations, and afterward nothing can appear to him as stable or complete. Such a realization is needed for the progress of the spirit. A striving toward perfection will come through an understanding of imperfection.

225. It is a mistake to think that the ascent of consciousness can be accomplished by attainment of supernatural exaltation. As below, so above: labor and

experience everywhere. Consciousness nurtures the growth of the subtle body. Even the slightest sensation contributes to the texture of the subtle body. It is precisely this that is usually overlooked by people. They think that one great action can compensate for a succession of small, petty deeds. But who can say what is great and what is small? All actions of a yogi take into account the most detailed considerations. One can see keen observation and precision in every act of a yogi. In his actions, no prejudice, no useless habit is permitted. He walks like a lion. He strikes unhesitatingly, but does not crush what is unworthy of notice, or too weak to threaten. Thus, one must evaluate the true meaning of one's every action.

One must not delay until tomorrow the planting of a new garden; only immediately and without delay can one strengthen the nursery of consciousness. The gardener studies each new root found in his garden. And for the yogi, each thread of consciousness will be a thread to the far-off worlds.

226. A yogi in his labors is like a stonecutter, or a goldsmith fashioning the most delicate work. A yogi is indeed like a goldsmith, who can fashion with the finest touch an intricate design. Likewise, a yogi can pierce the signs of human intent that are invisible to others. He strives toward that which is usually invisible, and learns to discern the real causes of events. Experience gained through alertness is the yogi's.

Can a yogi resign from life completely? He is so close to spiritual perfection that he cannot long endure even the usual interplanetary form of existence. Yogi U., known to you, for this reason created a special form of interplanetary existence for himself. It then was recognized as being of use to humanity and was included in Our research into the densification of the subtle body. I cite this example as indication that everywhere personal conscious labor is needed.

The manifestation of corruption in the Subtle World impedes humanity from proceeding steadily toward perfection. But the Subtle World is corrupted by the earthly world; thus, the healing must begin from the earthly world. Therefore, the study of Yoga leads not only to self-perfectment but also to the improvement of the Subtle World. The yogi, by consciously changing the state of his body, achieves a greater tension in the work of the spirit. He shortens the periods of rest between incarnations, but even during his rest continuously directs his thoughts toward useful action. Thus, through incessant labor, he unites the separate worlds and affirms the realization of all that exists.

227. Each cosmic achievement carries with it the possibility of danger caused by carelessness. People can master new energies, but if they are weak in spirit the danger of possession is increased.

The problem of possession should be approached scientifically. Two aspects of existence should be remembered. First—the continuity of life through different states. Second—the influence of the will of one upon another. Thus, beings existing in subtle bodies of different levels can direct thoughts to those on Earth. This unrealized energy can aid in the unifying of the worlds. However, uniting with the highest also opens the path to the lowest. You already know how much the lower spirits try to attach themselves to earthly emanations. Therefore, people should be warned about the need for steadfastness of the will, because possession is the most inadmissible condition. Only the intervention of a third will, firm and pure, can terminate this violation of the law, which affects people without regard for age or position.

It is the physician's duty to watch the sick for symptoms of possession by an alien will. If the physician is himself sufficiently pure and unafraid of calling the unwelcome guest to himself, he may apply his own will. But then, even the departure of the possessor from the patient is insufficient for a complete cure; because for a thousand days the danger of relapse still exists, and the ailing one must watch his thoughts closely. Physicians should be warned about this.

Countless are those who want to impose upon people their most degraded thoughts. But in order to save the endangered one it is sufficient to have power of will and to find the right rhythm of command. It is the duty of the yogi to eliminate harmful influences.

228. Open centers provide a channel for cosmic evolution, but mediums are like rudderless boats. All humanity must pass through evolutionary channels toward perfection. Closed centers keep people far behind. Open centers are symptoms of right development, but with them comes the danger of mediumism. A medium is but an inn for disembodied liars.

229. By making use of the magnetism of the heights and the opened centers of Sister Urusvati, We were able to study in her the crystals of *Fohat* and *Materia Lucida*, the accumulations of imperil, and the emanations of psychic energy. Consider that if the emanations of psychic energy are visible to her naked eye, then they have real substance. And whatever is tangible can be concentrated to make possible the collecting of a new vital force. Thus it is precisely through the experimental methods of the laboratory that the mastery of new energies will be approached.

Using their own natural emanations, people can create a store of new vitality. The energy scattered throughout space can be directly apprehended. This is why it is necessary to pay attention to the development of psychic energy. This is why the City of Knowledge, high in the mountains, is so needed.

230. It is necessary to study attentively the cases of so-called split personality. At its worst, it is a form of possession. At its best, it is a reliving of a former incarnation. Sometimes the spirit is so close to a former incarnation that he relives it. It is necessary to observe carefully a person with this condition, which has nothing to do with the consciousness of the present incarnation. One should not trouble him with questioning. But here, also, the yogi can be useful. He can give the command not to touch the past. You notice that We do not touch upon past incarnations except when absolutely necessary, so as not to evoke emanations of the past from *Akasha*.

231. One must not, like a carnival barker, entice people into one's courtyard. Yet, even the Great Teachers sometimes overused the Chalice of conversion, fearing that the Teaching would remain untransmitted. But each Teaching is given out in its proper time. It pervades space and emits emanations that have their effect in unexpected ways. We see that much that is broadly proclaimed is quickly swept away in the first wave of confusion. But, in contrast, it is remarkable to observe the growth that follows a quietly invisible sowing.

Often a ridiculed book is thrown away but later finds its merited attention. Also, the burning of books increases their influence. It is not persecution that one should fear, but popularity. This must be repeated again and again, for people attend too much to the voice of the crowd, and do not understand the point-lessness of groups gathering without purpose.

The yogi knows how to transmit the words of the Teaching sparingly but wisely. To broadcast everything to everyone is to inflict calamity upon space itself. Let few but vigorous trees constitute the future forest. Weedy thickets choke one another and also harbor harmful beings.

In each manifestation of nature one can study the ways of growth of the higher organisms. The conception and development of thought are characteristic of the higher organisms. Fragmentary thoughts are of no importance, but ceaseless and precise thought can, like a tree, be a pillar of the Teaching.

232. Who will accept useful Guidance? The one who has left behind all thought of life's comforts. To whom can be given arms for battle? To the one who will not desert the battlefield.

233. One should not seek afar that which is near. What irreparable harm to humanity results from the extensive searches into magic! Instead of working to improve their consciousness, seekers limit themselves to repeating formulas of others, without any knowl-edge of their meaning and rhythm.

What is so inimical to evolution as the petrified for-mulas of magic? The astral world has been separated from the physical world most of all by the ways of magic. Of course, possession is often the result of mag-ical invocations. Mediumism is the bedfellow of magic.

The magic formulas that have been given out to the public are intentional distortions. In them some things are missing that were reserved for oral transmission. Certainly a yogi is the very opposite of a magician. A magician stands on petrified formulas. A yogi constantly inhales the fresh new breath of Cosmos. The one is old at birth; the other is always young, throughout all changes in his life. The one attempts to strike with words not of his own making; the other smites with his free thought. The one defends himself with pitiful pinpricks; the other is shielded just by the armor of his glance. Yoga has nothing in common with magic.

234. You have seen how a stream becomes a powerful torrent after it gathers to itself other streams and passes through waterfalls and rapids, merging them all into its own current. Thus also for the yogi, there is no categorizing of streams of knowledge into good and evil. He assimilates all kinds of knowledge, finding proper use for each.

One should accustom oneself to the assimilation of all kinds of knowledge. Is there any kind of knowledge that we can regard as beneath us? How can we trust ourselves if we reject information that may be needed?

235. It is correctly observed that certain pains are called sacred. Through them the spirit ascends, and there is no other way. We do not know even one instance when the consciousness was able to ascend without bodily pains. Understand how attentive one must be to every manifestation, for with each hour we can expect a transmittal of the highest energies.

236. It should be understood how, in every sense, trust increases one's possibilities. But what kind of trust is the best? And what doubt is the worst? The inner trust that needs no words of affirmation is the best. The fleeting doubt is the worst. It is not the gnawing serpent of doubt that is most to be feared, because with just one achievement the serpent can be destroyed. But the swarm of small worms of doubt requires a lengthy cure. The strongest trust can be upset neither by thought nor word. It would be better to swallow a deadly poison than to remain in the illness of doubt. He who is shielded with trust needs no other armor.

237. To reach the Teacher there is but one way—to walk without glancing back. Any thought of failure is already a defeat. The one who knows the direction of his flight is like an eagle soaring across an abyss. You know about the magnetizing of circumstances.

238. It is karma, the fatiguing aftereffect of previous incarnations, that can bring not very savory fellow-travelers to us. But when each encounter is over, there comes relief, as when property belonging to others has been returned. No less than half of all earthly encounters take place because of past incarnations, in the way that cork figures are drawn together by application of electrical energy.

The broad influence of karma brings about many complicated levels and degrees of relationship. To resolve them, it is better to pay than to receive; for each payment terminates a debt from the past, whereas receiving binds one again.

239. One must become accustomed to the thought that nothing useful is ever lost. One must become accustomed to knowing how many dangers surround one. One must become accustomed to the realization of the burden of knowledge. Buddha taught his son to maintain joy, because this is a most difficult challenge on Earth. It is better to suffer the burden of knowledge than to remain isolated from reality.

240. One should examine all ideas about death. Setting aside those who think of suicide, if a life is dedicated to labor, is there any advantage to having a lengthy life in one body? No, it is more useful to divide the time into several experiences. Economy of energy is a fundamental principle of the universe. To enter a new house filled with fresh air is to open the opportunity for new accumulations of experience.

One duty of a yogi is to dispel excessive awe of death. One can retreat to such a state of limitation that just moving to a neighboring town becomes a major event. Worse, one could fear to move from one room to another, and even a change of garment would present difficulties. People who fear change fear death most of all. They fear to think of it, and think of the present moment as an ultimate condition. Even the skin on our body is constantly renewed, yet we do not summon grave-diggers to bury the shed epidermis. Then why not draw a parallel from the microcosm to the Macrocosm, recalling all that is said in the *Bhagavad-Gita* about the indestructibility of the spirit?

241. Can a yogi feel fatigue? Of course he can; he can even become ill. But he will know that a new store of energy must then be gathered. He will know where energy was overspent and will, without losing equanimity, make use of valerian and musk.

It is a joy to know that our bodily apparatus can obtain the needed restorative energy. Fatigue from the past is happiness for the future. A new reinforcement of energy is always an advance over the past. This means that fatigue is our friend. It is because of it that the wise serpent sheds his skin. The serpent knows that the success of this regeneration depends on rest, and does not strike during the new growth. Therefore, the person who knows what in him is fatigued will wisely prescribe rest for himself, summoning other of his centers for his work.

242. It is painful to think that only a few people are filled with the desire to give all, to give to space, to give to the invisible worlds, to contribute truly to the knowledge of those whom they do not even know. For these few, such a broadening of concerns from ordinary life leads to new thinking.

Existence in space is not easy. For the blind soul it is an impenetrable wall. When the way leads away from city streets, the heart will be able to endure the impact of poisonous substances. Otherwise, it is incalculably difficult to accommodate both the earthly and the eternal.

243. All reality is built according to the laws of space. Thus, the moments of inception of sickness and convalescence are imperceptible. Often the beginning moment of any phenomenon can be grasped only through continuous observation, because each lawful act is parent to many others, the laws of which lie in the realm of the subtlest energies.

244. "To those in the grave I give life." This is the clearest affirmation of reincarnation and the continuity of existence.

245. Why is Earth so sick? Because the rays of the heavenly bodies cannot penetrate its polluted aura. To what will man be reduced if he ceases his communion with the supreme consciousness and sinks into base ignorance? From the greatest of the worlds to the microcosm, the law is one. Losing their realization of the great worlds, people have wandered from the understanding of perfection. The great worlds have become for them a foolish fantasy; and for them, self-perfectment is an unnecessary or even dangerous pastime. Slaving for their daily wage, they yearn only for the end of their path as they see it.

Religions have frightened humanity with their dogma of final judgment, and have thereby deprived it of daring. Whoever submits blindly to a state religion is like a donkey staggering under a burden imposed upon it. Can one accept a religion enforced by police order? Can one accept on faith the decisions of strangers who take fees for communing with heaven?

Therefore, in the presence of a state religion, the responsibility of the yogi is great. Fearless, testing, indefatigable, the yogi must help humanity to remember the Law of Unity. Like a flashing sword, the thought of the yogi is a lightning-bolt through space. Ready to alter the ways of communion, ready for achievement, ready to accept the condemnations of the ignorant, the yogi exhorts humanity to contemplate the causes of their incarnate lives. By doing this, the quality of their labor and learning will be changed. Knowing the possibilities inherent in people, who would not wish to dare valiantly? Does not the victor's crown belong to the one who teaches courage to humanity? Without this the heads of people, like those of swine, will remain glued to the refuse of Earth.

246. The present race has been distorted in many ways. The people of this day want to see and decide everything for themselves. This is quite admirable, but it can lead, in an unanticipated way, to nothing, for after having seen for themselves, people return, unaffected, to their previous ways. Even the most striking experience leaves no trace upon their daily life. It is amazing to see people who, thinking of themselves as scientists, overlook the most useful phenomena. For them, any discovery made in the most recent one hundred years is still a questionable hypothesis.

Whence comes this inflexibility of thinking in our race? This kind of moribund process has attended the end of each race. This is old age, this is a dying out, this is a rejection of evolution. Therefore I constantly advise dealing with the few, regardless of their social position.

Equally distorted is the question of help and of the quality of labor. People desire only the help that meets the needs of their own egotism, and, like those who are departing from a place, do not think of quality of labor at all. Let at least a few assume some responsibility. Thus, through responsibility shall we reach flexibility of thought.

247. Changes in language are welcome to Us. Through such changes, inflexibility of expression and, more important, of meaning, is avoided. The ages pile up habits and lead to petrifaction of thinking. But cataclysms and disruptions of governments bring unexpected ideas and new words. Old expressions lose their relevance and fall away, taking with them the antiquated customs.

It is not the letter of an expression, but the way it is understood, that can be especially dangerous. For example, if I say, "Circumstances are developing for success," people follow their own way of understanding and hear it to mean that circumstances are favorable. But an understanding of success must be much broader than just good or bad. The success of a design depends not on its uniformity of colors but on a full range of contrasts.

It is equally difficult for people to understand the relativity of good and evil. The one or the other is revealed only in the light of its opposite.

A realization of the dynamic motion of spatial bodies, unrestrainable and eternally new, would help people recognize the impelling principle of life. Thus each moment of life would achieve mobility and would demonstrate its link with the past and with the inevitable future.

The spirit striving to the future will not burden itself with the tatters of the past. It seeks ways of expressing newly-encountered concepts, and tears down the barrier of words. One would sooner forgive a failed effort than accept the encrusted, habit-formed greeting of a wizened grandfather. It is through motion that we extend the horizon of ideas to which we were attached by the circumstance of birth. Physical lineage is of a different order entirely from the heritage of spirit. Hence, willingness to change outer forms will aid the striving of the spirit.

All Teachers pointed out the transitory quality of objects in order to teach the importance of motion. Not asceticism, but a wise use of things was indicated.

248. The ability to penetrate to the real meaning of words lies in the receptivity of the inner center, not in analyzing the structure of speech. Submit the simplest idea to a thousand people for discussion, and you might receive only one correct interpretation. One should train oneself to a true understanding of speech. Yoga will aid in approaching the true understanding of thought. The understanding of different languages originates from the receptivity of one center—the larynx.

It is useful to read to children in the schools some texts in unfamiliar languages, observing how an unknown tongue is grasped. The hand easily adapts itself to familiar objects. The consciousness will easily grasp sounds familiar from the past. How many useful observations could be readily made! Yoga constantly teaches this joyous alertness.

249. Material objects may be valued, but there is danger in overproducing them. The most harmful thinking can originate when one is surrounded by unneeded objects. Stretching out like snares are the threadbare ideas about the use for and distribution of objects. The old ways of a bygone age bring prolonged suffering. Whereas new ways of production can generate unexpected currents of thought.

If we deal with objects, then we should not treat them with indifference. The quality and meaning of everyday objects in evolution are important subjects to consider. Truly, a new house needs suitable new objects, but to find them is almost impossible. Thus, human thought must be directed in quest of new solutions. However, for the building of new surroundings one must realize the true direction of one's life. But how can people think about a transformation of life when they continue to pass through life like animals, with no idea of past or future?

Put a question about the purpose of life and you will receive only senseless answers. While space itself cries out for energy and decisiveness, the crowd continues to remodel its old caftans. For example, treaties have brought humanity to its present disasters; and still new treaties are being written on the basis of these worthless texts. New garments continue to be fashioned out of useless remnants.

It is shocking to see how the dwellers of Earth have obstructed their own way. It is not prayer but stern labor that is needed. This must be repeated, again and again. The dates have brought imminent possibilities. Is it possible that the "traders" do not perceive it?

The yogi appears at the right time and points out the happiness that lies within reach. The yogi can be a builder of life because he knows the true values and knows co-measurement. Life itself brings to the surface the urgent need for the Yoga of Life. Otherwise, how and by what signs would people determine the right direction for their striving?

250. If the event of the appointed date is inevitable, then all circumstances are useful: fire illumines the way; thunder awakens at the hour for vigil; the shower washes the mud from the path. There are no counter-manifestations. Our Rays indicate the turns of the way and cover it over with the dome of safety. If We warn about the narrowness of the subterranean passage, We do it just for your knowledge. Only when a change of path is needed do We halt you and send a new Indication. Sometimes it is preferable to circle a mountain than to suffer fatigue climbing the steep crags.

We deny nothing, for that which exists is undeniable. But it must be applied. Then there can be neither grief nor despair—only support.

We know all the grasses that grow in Our meadow; We value their every property, and therefore We do not call any of them weeds. Each is harmful when used at the wrong time; each is beneficial at the right moment.

251. Of what do We speak? Of the quality of devotion and also of alertness—the ability to see clearly. Devotion—irrepressible, all-conquering, creative, adorning the path. Alertness—all-penetrating vision, all-comprehending, indefatigable, strengthening aspiration. Are there many who can cultivate within themselves both devotion and alertness? Where will the devoted but unseeing ones arrive? Should one safeguard the eyes of those who can see but are traitors? To those who are devoted, all plants can be entrusted. To those who can see, all flowers can be shown.

The concept of devotion is vastly demeaned. People are quick to show discontent. Not lengthy is Our list of those devoted to Us. Cherish each evidence of devotion. But the true measure of devotion is revealed only at times of difficulty. And the ability to see is tested only through the cover of mist. Our Shield is simply the understanding of devotion. People usually understand devotion as love, readiness, or solicitude. But these fragments of devotion are only a smile of sympathy, whereas true devotion is radiant, like a warrior ready for battle. Speak often of devotion, and praise alertness. People need affirmation.

252. Every illusion can be made real, for it carries a seed of reality that can be enhanced and revealed. Illusions should be regarded as fireflies. Who would want to extinguish something that brings light?

Know how to smite the darkness of hypocrisy, but let each petal of sincerity live.

253. Adornment of the future with the blossoms of inspiration is as the light of dawn. But each adornment of the past is a wreath laid on a grave. He who affirms the power of the future is Our warrior. His own power is multiplied by the treasure of the future. Just as the hour of striving is like a whirlwind, so is looking back akin to decay. All the past must be burned away for the Yoga of Fire.

254. The striving of most people has little to do with psychic energy. Certain properties of this energy have been completely lost to their consciousness. It is most difficult for humanity to realize the infiniteness of energy and its ability to act independently. People easily sense energy in relation to physical actions, but they little realize something much more remarkable— that psychic energy can act independently at great distances. Like a cannon ball that speeds from the cannon producing its individual effect, so our energy can create results completely independent and long-lasting. Of course the durability of the results depends on the reserve of energy. One can project energy consciously, but one can also project it subconsciously if it is directed frequently in the same way. When the cannonball of energy has been propelled afar, then one may feel a temporary exhaustion of energy. But he who knows this can happen will not be concerned. On the contrary, he will reinforce the act of transmission with his own consciousness.

You have heard the legend about a whirling cloud above a site of special significance. This is based on the same idea of projection of energy. The projected energy may be so powerful that it can cause physical manifestations, for the fusion of energy with the elements produces most unusual phenomena. But during periods of great activity, this energy becomes separated from its source, and one must expect a certain fatigue, accepting it as the natural consequence of the depletion of the treasury.

Under circumstances that admit of no delay, the separated energy acts. Of course, any new structure attracts the consciousnesses most akin to it. The dispatches are sped as help, bringing courage, alertness, and resourcefulness. And often neither the one who receives nor the one who has sent suspects what has occurred. The divisibility of the spirit makes possible the dispatch of energy. The energy acts through the accomplished transmission, and the one who has sent it becomes inactive, as though fatigued and resting. How many such sendings are speeding through space! Will not some of them lay the foundations of new worlds?

255. You place a torch and at once, out of the darkness, a multitude of insects swarms around it. You manifest psychic energy and immediately new, diverse conditions appear, small and great, far and near. Psychic energy is a true magnet. Many would be surprised to learn that a metal magnet and a psychic magnet are governed by the same energy. This basic energy of consciousness is disseminated by the all-pervading element of fire. Sometimes it is indiscernible, but often it can act either on a truly cosmic scale, or within those who have a developed consciousness, in which case the ascertaining of evident results requires no deep observation. Thus one can link the most dissimilar domains of nature to the one origin.

How can one fail to understand that of the vast range of universal energies some affect the centers in unexpected ways, thus uniting the various kingdoms of nature? Thus, a stone is linked to human consciousness.

Of course, modern science cannot fully explain the essence of a magnet. Waves of consciousness, like the tides of the ocean, inscribe in space the images of creation. Little observed are the magnetic currents in individual beings of all kinds. But the mass thought of humanity is already familiar.

Like contagion from an unseen source, similar thoughts spread. Some force gathers them, directs them, intensifies them. Those who used to place a magnet over the crown of their heads in order to deepen the consciousness knew fragments of the Great Teaching. Collecting the magnetic waves out of various realms, they reinforced their store of psychic energy. One can really unite several currents and effect a renewal of consciousness. For this, one must primarily learn open-mindedness. This is the first condition for the development of consciousness.

256. The Keeper of the Seven Gates grieved: "I give people an endless stream of miracles, but they do not perceive them. I provide new stars, but their light does not alter human thought. I plunge whole countries into the depths of the seas, but human consciousness remains silent. I erect mountains and the Teachings of Truth, but people do not even turn their heads to the call. I send wars and pestilence, but even terror does not impel people to think. I offer the joy of knowledge, but people make a gruel out of the sacred feast. I have no further signs to turn humanity away from destruction."

To the Keeper spoke the Most Exalted: "When a builder lays the foundations of a building, does he tell all to everyone who labors on the structure? Some of them will know the given dimensions, but only to few is disclosed the purpose of the building. Those who dig among the stones of past foundations can hardly comprehend a new one. A builder should not be grieved if there is no understanding among his workers of the real meaning of his plan. He can only assign the tasks appropriately."

Thus, as regards the consciousness of people, we shall know that those who cannot understand or harken will be fit to undertake only the menial work. Let the one who has understood be firm as a hundred thousand sages. And the signs, like inscriptions, will unfold before him.

257. How should one understand the benefits of obstacles when one is told that psychic energy, acting as a magnet, attracts all possible advantages? Truly, when a large ship increases its speed the resistance of the waves increases too. Similarly, many obstacles are brought about by our own striving. It is this process that attracts to us unexpected actions by an opposing will. If they are very strong, our own counterstroke will develop accordingly. Most important, the currents opposing us should be strong, because then our flame is ignited.

Consider this inflaming useful; a conflagration would be dangerous. By inflaming I mean when the crystal form of the flame of the center is retained; conflagration is when the center flares up in a blaze.

When someone is said to be depressed by circumstances, be assured that he lives unignited, and that any encounter with an obstacle confuses his consciousness. Sometimes it is difficult to discern the moment of confusion, yet it poisons all subsequent actions. But when the step is firm, the counterforces are beneficial. They generate lightning, and the thunder shakes distant mountains. Pettiness begets pettiness, however. Therefore, when bidding people Godspeed on a journey, bid them also to shun pettiness.

The future is constructed by lightning-bolts of realization. The power of these great sparks depends upon the strength of the counterforce. Clearly then, success will not come from embarking on a voyage in a tub across a stagnant pool.

When We say, "Set sail," We mean that you must try the ocean; the grandeur of its waves will give you joy. Does not the testing of one's strength lead to a growth of power? It may seem impossible to cross an abyss, but you have already crossed many an abyss and smiled. You see, I do not speak of fantasies, but of that which has already been tested and for which there are witnesses.

Courage comes from knowing one's path. Otherwise, each one who tries a closed door would already be seen as a hero. What awaits behind the threshold? The Agni Yogi smiles at this.

258. We will affirm the concept of "by human hands." Why do We insist on the need for action by human hands? It would seem easier to expand humanity's possibilities by providing access to some new subtle energies. But, once again, the heart of the matter lies in the consciousness. As long as the finer energies are not realized they will not be beneficial to people. In fact, it must be understood that energy not consciously realized can even be destructive. An unrealized energy, like an unbridled elemental force, can demolish all surroundings. Realization is almost mastery, and it is already co-measurement. Until humanity begins to realize the true meaning of energy, it is essential to insist upon the principle "by human hands."

We do not withdraw possibilities. We do provide an egress from present conditions. It is time to begin to realize the existence of all that is beyond your present grasp, the chain of indescribable energies so near to us. If salt is on the table, that does not mean that we have already ingested it.

259. Many concepts should be considered in the light of yoga. Can one live without desire when even the spirit is incarnated by desire? Desires are like sparks igniting motion. Then what does it mean to say that a yogi is free of desire? Let us take the precise meaning of the words: a yogi is free, not from desires as such but from their burden. He knows himself to be free because he is not a slave to desire. On the path of goal-fitness, a yogi, applying co-measurement, relinquishes desires in the name of the most essential. This ability to change easily is at the core of the yogi's liberation. Nothing hinders his progress.

It is precisely the inert, stillborn desires that become the chains of bondage for humanity. It is people who chain themselves with such bonds. Either incaution or the karma of others brings on the infection of desire, and a person, instead of progressing, loses all ability to change.

Pay attention to those who stand and wail. What arrested their way? What forces diverted them from the contemplation and understanding of the world? The most minute, almost indistinguishable, desire burdened them and obscured their vision. How monotonous has their world become! Their desires, like parasites, depleted their energy. Desire can be worms and chains, or sparks and wings. The liberated one soars in realization. The one enslaved wails in despair.

260. Many indestructible concepts have been distorted, and they must be restored to their true meaning. This is so for the understanding of solitude. Nowhere is it said that a yogi must be physically alone, but for him solitude of spirit is inevitable. Consecrating himself, the yogi grows the crystal of his individuality. And the more generously he gives, the more he remains untouched.

Also, one should reconsider the true correlations of sound and color. There is a stage in the development of psychic energy called luminous, when the essence of a being begins to emit light. This "resounding" of light is evidence of a degree of proximity to the realization of the far-off worlds. Thus the color green in the aura signifies the ability to perceive the essence of things. And other powers are unexpectedly gathered from space. And the manifestation of light, radiating and "resounding," is a bridge to the Fire of Space.

He who gives is indestructible as flame! He who fills himself with light is striving toward light!

261. He who fears for his life cannot be a hero. And he who pointlessly wastes his life will not be a hero. The hero carries the vessel with care, ever ready to offer it for building the future world—as in everything, the weighing of opposites. A yogi will understand this.

He will understand the value of restraint, yet will never be satisfied. The hero is truly insatiable for achievement and hungers for action, yet is ready at any time to restrain himself. He acts for spirit, but does not detach himself from Earth. Unstoppable, never retreating, he will not abandon what he has begun, and will not initiate any action that is less than selfless.

Let us manifest the consciousness that is able to distinguish between self-concern and concern for the General Good. Fine is the borderline between self-gratification and labor for the evolution of the world.

Only a great consciousness can discern inner motives. Only a great consciousness can ignore the intrusiveness of external opinions.

Logic has poisoned many a statement. Decisions are too often reached by an exchange of words, rather than from their meaning. The Teaching can open one's eyes only when it is accepted in the fullness of its meaning. One may pass through the Teaching as over the tiles of an ornamented floor. Its design is unseen in the darkness; light is needed to discern it. In the darkness, the design seems unimportant, fit only for a lighthearted dance. The most sacred symbols can be trampled by the feet of ignorance.

It is not the eye but the consciousness that prompts caution. Would one in any way want to impede the work of the Teacher? The joy of renunciation in the name of the Teacher is like a luminous rainbow.

"Lord, accept my possessions if they are of use to Thee!"

262. Although much is spoken about obstacles, little use is made of them. Understanding how to make use of obstacles infuses joy into one's work. But as soon as an obstacle appears, people usually begin to think of their own feelings, forgetting the advantage that has been offered to them. People prefer that everything be done in a usual way, by conventional means. But We prefer unexpected actions and equally unexpected results. People are happy when the occurrences in their lives are the most ordinary, but We wish them greater success than this. Teach them to weigh the real harm and the usefulness of what occurs. It is difficult to send currents of unusual success to people when they prefer to avoid unusual ways. We all know people who live in self-satisfied comfort. If they could only know what they lose because of their ease! People want to preserve all their petty habits, forgetting that the habits of the spirit follow from the habits of the body. The spirit weakens, and begins to fear courageous action. Thus, people become commonplace, with the same conventional joys and sorrows.

Let us learn to rejoice at obstacles, knowing that the welcomed obstacle can be used to speed success. And this success will be like a fishnet overfilled with an abundant catch. Therefore, let us direct our eye to our surroundings and understand from what perils we are being protected just by our devotion to the Teacher. But often we trust the Teacher in great works and are less certain in small ones. Often we see the great obstacles, while overlooking the multitude of small ones that lie within sight. After all, a small, unnoticed scorpion strikes just as poisonously as a large one. An eagle eye is needed, not so much to discern the mountain as to see the smallest grain of sand.

263. It is a joy that you already understand the meaning of the battle. Multitudes are drawn into this battle, without recognizing times for rest, or times of danger, or times for joy or for fear. Before sunset gnats swarm, but they cannot know their purpose.

The world battle draws in all beings, but few understand the true meaning of what is happening. "Let us await the morrow," so people think. But for them the morrow comes only after the next midday, and they miss the dawn.

264. To the Blessed One is attributed the following:

Once the Blessed One visited the ruler of Rajagriha. The ruler called His attention to the immaculateness of his reception room. But the Blessed One said, "Show rather the cleanliness of your sleeping chamber, your bath, and your hearth. The reception room is contaminated by many unworthy ones, but in the place where your consciousness is created, let everything be spotless."

And likewise said the Blessed One, "Distinguish between those who understand and those who agree. He who understands the Teaching will not delay in applying it in life. He who agrees will simply nod and extol the Teaching as remarkable wisdom, but will not apply this wisdom in life. There are many who have agreed, but like a withered forest they are fruitless and without shade. Only decay awaits them. Those who understand are few, but like a sponge they absorb the priceless knowledge and are ready to clean away the evils of the world with this precious liquid. He who understands cannot help but apply the Teaching, for, realizing goal-fitness, he accepts it as a solution to the problems of life. Do not spend much time with the agreeing ones. Let them first demonstrate application of the first call."

Thus is attributed to the Blessed One the goal-fitting attitude toward newcomers.

It is not fitting to keep dipping a vessel into an empty well. The sower does not spread his seeds onto naked rock! The ones who just agree will readily accept the benefits, but will be horrified by the first obstacle. Therefore, test through obstacles.

265. The touch of the fine energies is like that of the most delicate veil. But only the one who knows their true value may wear them. So discern the spirit that is ready and flaming. He who does not accept the gift of spirit withers. Through ignorance, which is still with us, the dark ones destroy themselves.

266. Solitude of the spirit leads to a clear perception of the forms of the future. The Spirit of Darkness, pondering how to still more firmly lash humanity to Earth, thought: "Let them keep their old customs and habits. Nothing binds humanity so much as habitual forms. But this is fit only for the multitudes. Far more dangerous to us is solitude, in which the consciousness is illumined and new forms are created. Therefore, time in solitude must be severely limited. People must not be allowed to remain alone. I shall provide them with a reflection so that they may become accustomed to being with their own image." Thus did the servants of Darkness bring a mirror to the people!

267. Each one who approaches Us already has an idea about the process of passing into another state of being. One can compare him to a person who has learned to travel, whereas an inexperienced traveler fears even to step on the gangplank of the ship.

268. Life rushes by like a waterfall, but not many perceive its motion. Those who yearn for rest regard life as if it were a tomb. What is rest? This concept is an invention of the dark ones. What manifest timidity people reveal when they speak of rest! For them, rest is idleness. This kind of rest is always an earth-bound joy, a joy of doing nothing that is not Ours. Is nature ever idle? We, as parts of nature, are subject to its laws.

One does not always have to be running. Nor need one choose for himself a life of seclusion. Even a plant, for example, though rooted, exists in a state of constant activity.

269. You correctly remarked that We often repeat discussion of subjects already covered. But if one follows Our discourses, one will see an ascending spiral of thought. It could not be otherwise. If even once an inferior thought were admitted it would cause a breach in the spiral. The same would result if, in one's thought, one were to leap over a great distance. Again a breach would occur. But no lines of life can be wilfully severed. This is evident in every manifestation in life. The question is only whether the consciousness can steadily ascend. Yes, of course, but only if we agree to understand rest as a time for the purification of thought. Thus shall we avoid the chief enemy.

270. Everyone has his enemy. The importance of one's enemy indicates one's own importance, just as the size of a shadow is determined by the size of the object. One should not concern oneself too much about one's enemies, nor should one regard them with disdain. No one exists without a shadow.

Akbar, called Great, regarded his enemies with attention. His favorite counselor kept a list of his enemies. Akbar often inquired, "Has not some worthy name appeared on the list? When I see a worthy name, I will send my greeting to the friend in disguise."

Further spoke Akbar, "I rejoice that I have been able to apply in life the sacred Teaching, that I gave people contentment, and that I was made more prominent in the light by the shadow of my great enemies." Thus spoke Akbar, knowing the value of enemies.

Friends do not reveal the greatness of a Teaching as much as do its enemies. If an enemy is a shadow, then slander is a trumpet call.

271. The consciousness understands the idea of motion best when it is presented in familiar forms and symbols. One should understand the true value of symbols to the consciousness. For example, the symbol of a small boat is far better than that of any modern ship; a boat, because of its vulnerability, responds more directly to the danger of the elements. Even in its seed, the spirit is subject to the action of the elements. Therefore it is good to be a friend to the elements, especially the all-binding fire.

272. The Teacher never belittles. Only when something has taken place can it then be described.

273. The meaning of the various kinds of relationship that exist between the Teacher and His pupil should be clarified. Indeed, the steps of approach to the Teaching will differ. There is so much attraction on the first steps, and much responsibility on the later ones.

It can be noticed in the astral world that those with a half-developed consciousness do not strive upward. An ordinary level of consciousness is sufficient to spare them from suffering, but not enough to inspire acceptance of their duty for self-sacrificing work. The same can be observed in the growth of the spirit. The first calls are pleasant and benevolent, and, like a child, the cared-for beginner has no responsibilities. But consciousness grows and the spirit becomes worthy of special tasks. These tasks contradict the outworn ways of mundane thinking, and therefore involve new difficulties and dangers.

Truly, only a few learn to rejoice at the need to face and conquer obstacles. Many more yearn to return to the bygone half-developed consciousness.

On this new level, Our instructions become less frequent and more brief, and one's work depends more on one's ability for independent action. Friends will be few, obstacles will pile up like seemingly unscalable mountains, and achievements will seem insignificant. The influences of the subtlest energies will not be so evident. The intermittent, so-called sacred, pains will torture one. The divisibility and transmissions of the spirit will still be beyond explanation. But above all this will arise the striving to fulfil the desire for the General Good. Spiritual cooperation will grow, unlimited by space. Emulation of the far-off worlds will change one's perception of one's surroundings, and spatial work will cease to be an empty idea. One's assigned tasks will become a joy, as if they were one's own chosen labor. It cannot be otherwise. Of course, this joy is not expressed in goat-like frolics. A true understanding of one's surroundings may provoke a stern face, but one's life is nevertheless transformed, and one can observe the coils of the Earthly Dragon from a higher vantage point. Fearlessness, already sent in the first call, brings one closer to the new waves of light.

274. Akbar's court historian once said to the ruler, "Among potentates I observe an insoluble problem. Certain rulers kept themselves unapproachable, aloof from the people. These were deposed because they were considered to be unneeded. Others entered too much into daily life. People became used to them, then deposed them for being commonplace."

Akbar smiled, "That means that a ruler must remain unseen, but still must enter into and direct all events in his country."

Thus spoke the wise ruler, pointing out the way for the future.

Invisibly visible!

275. Vedanta correctly states that the spirit remains inviolable. The fiery seed of the spirit maintains its elementary wholeness, because the essence of the elements is immutable. But the emanations of the seed change with the growth of consciousness. One should understand that the seed of the spirit is a fragment of the element of fire, and the energy accumulated around it is consciousness. This means that Vedanta concerned itself mainly with the seed, whereas Buddhism spoke of the perfectment of its enveloping bodies. Thus do the changeable and the unchanging coexist.

It is quite understandable that Buddha, Who directed humanity toward evolution, taught the nature of that which changes, whereas Vedanta expounded the unchanging foundation. You can add any chemical ingredient to a flame and thereby change its color and size, but the essential nature of the fire will remain unchanged. I do not see any contradiction between the basic principles of Vedanta and Buddhism.

276. It is true that in India there exists an awareness that the subtle energies will enter into life. One should be prepared for a future scientific understanding of this. Although darkness greatly lowers the quality of the energies, the open consciousness can assimilate some part of the energies, as when dark clouds block the rays of the sun, but a portion of light and heat can still reach Earth. All great teachings are without inner contradiction, but there is no way to prove this with the customary scientific methods.

277. It is correctly said that the invisible forces are stronger than the visible ones. Also correct is the realization that the closeness of the Teacher is inalienable.

145

Indisputably true is the idea that the currents of space influence the whole of life. Is it possible that people have not noticed the intensification of the currents since the year of the Earthly Dragon? The tail of the Dragon is a magnet, but the Dragon's hopes are in vain. It cannot receive the salutary energy while crawling on the ground. It is precisely to this year that the sign of the Dragon is sent. One should beware of the hands of the earthbound. During the next ten years one can expect to see many cunning betrayals.

The New Era begins amidst thunder and lightning. What is it that will evoke the storm? Of course, the extreme dullness in people. How tediously will this ten-year span drag itself out, even though the advent of the new energies is already at hand!

278. Often the Teacher finds himself in a very difficult situation with a pupil. The pupil promises to follow all the instructions of the Teacher, but no sooner is one received than reasons are immediately found to alter it. The Teacher experiences a similar difficulty when He is accused of being inactive. Imagine the situation of an archer when he is tensed for his shot and behind him someone cries, "Why does he not shoot?"

Small children, even without knowing the reason, tend to obey the guiding hand. But adults often alter the instructions given to them to fit their own moods. They are like people who, when their house catches fire, abandon irreplaceable manuscripts, but save their beloved bedding.

Whence comes this disrespect for the Instruction? Indeed, from lack of trust. It is amazing how readily gifts from the Teacher are accepted, but how easily forgotten is His best advice. How many carefully planned transmissions are rejected, how many useful actions disrupted, because of people's light-mindedness!

Reverence is rendered with one hand, while the other tosses the given pearls over the cliff, forgetting that discarding into space one's personal instructions is a pollution of space.

Pupils often forget that their chosen Teacher, out of experience, will never belittle them. How much, then, must cooperation be valued, firm in trust!

When you yourselves become teachers, insist on the immediate fulfilling of your instructions. Do not give orders too often, for then they become commonplace. But if the work requires it, make the instruction concise. Let it be known that your instruction is irrevocable. Put more simply, the student should follow, reconciling his free initiative with cooperation. A distorted instruction is like a derailed train. It is better not to accept the gift than to disrupt the transmitted wave.

279. You have heard the legend about the increasing heat of the throne of Indra. At its source lies a psychophysical process. The special tension of the surrounding psychic atmosphere causes purely physical reactions. These in turn increase vividly the tension of the fiery energy, and it becomes necessary to reestablish balance.

280. Amidst his enemies' assaults, Akbar was asked why there were so many attacks. Akbar replied, "Let the enemies have something to do."

281. What is meant by "mad in God"? Why were the prophets of antiquity called madmen? Precisely because of the fire of straight-knowledge, which isolated them from all else, a valuable quality that severed them from the ordinary, everyday ways of thinking.

282. People can take protective measures against the crude manifestations of the elements. But by the time of the advent of the new, subtler energies it will be essential to have found new ways of dealing with these energies. Until recently, people hid themselves from lightning beneath a tree or they ran away terrified. But now they have found practical methods of self-protection. Of course the same thing will also occur with the subtle energies. If this is realized in time, much harm can be avoided.

How can attention be directed to the new energies? By keenness of sight, enhanced by straight-knowledge. Soon people will be divided according to the quality of their straight-knowledge. Those with an open consciousness must be known and paid attention to. Not education, not experience, not talent, but precisely the fire of straight-knowledge opens the direct path to Shambhala. It is precisely the fire of straight-knowledge that enables one to perceive the unique qualities of the new signs in the midst of daily life. In the future, all organizations will guard with special care these sensitive co-workers. Such consciousnesses are like milestones upon a straight road. The new scientific research will be inspired by the fire of straight-knowledge.

Not ascetics, not fanatics, not the superstitious, but those who know the Yoga of Fire are the ones who will choose not to abandon the rudders of life. Truly, their sacrifices will be great. They will constantly be confronting new explosions although they could have chosen a calm existence. But rest is not a property of fire, for fire must constantly destroy in order to create. Such fiery strivings test one's feelings, as in a crucible.

At present it is not yet entirely understood why We care so much about the advent of new possibilities. But soon people will search for ways to apply new revelations that have not yet been explained in life. Then someone will remember the Signs of Agni Yoga.

283. When you are called dreamers, say, "We know only action."

When you are asked where to find confirmation of the Teaching, answer, "Only in life."

When you are asked why you do not defend the Teaching, say, "It is impossible to respond to ignorance."

When someone slanders the Teacher, say, "This very night you will regret your irreparable error."

284. The meaning is important, not the form. Independence of action is most important. Conciseness too, is a mark of progress. When we live on the border of the two worlds, we see an image as if in relief. Thus, when the messenger transmits a message, he knows more than he imparts.

285. Truly, much time is needed by those who seek the right path. But those who have found the path can then apply their forces for achievement. We wish them to go forward exultantly. Each of their steps is a joy to Us. We are ready to send them strength, so that they do not fall.

One must live through difficult currents; even the ship in its voyage must face the obstacles of the elements.

286. Success in life can be found both by those who with particular clarity understand the essential nature of things and also by those who have accepted their own very distorted perception of things. The difference lies only in the consequences. Those who have realized the nature of things are not attached to them, but the distorters are slaves to them. If someone finds no success, it means that he has remained at the fulcrum of the balance rather than placing himself in either cup.

What is the measure of whether things are understood or distorted? Whether or not the conditions of one's life have changed. If nothing has changed, it is because there has been no action of thought. Those who are slow to understand cannot succeed. The majority of people are dragged down by their own weakness and inertia. Life is like chains to them, whereas life should be a conquest. The guarantee of success lies in action.

287. *Mahayana* is to *Hinayana* as Buddhism is to Vedanta. *Mahayana* knows and reveals the nature of the world of the elements. *Hinayana* emphasizes karmic causes and effects without concerning itself with the immediate consequences of causes. The Teaching strikes sparks from the chaos of the elements. One may study these images, but it is equally correct to concentrate on cause and effect. If we call Buddha the Cause, then Maitreya is the Effect.

288. Naturally, a mirage does not disclose reality, but is a reality in itself. Therefore it is correct to recognize the reality of Maya, even while knowing all its treacherous distortion.

You who know the path, find the fire to attain the Goal!

289. The Blessed One spoke of three spiritual teachers. One received divine gifts, then abandoned his earthly labor. Another received these gifts, then dropped the thread of understanding of life. The third one, having received the gifts, and knowing how to tie the thread of understanding, continued to bear his labors on Earth. His usefulness exceeds that of the others.

The cross is the symbol of life. When the Great Plato was departing from Us, his last advice was, "Create heroes!"

290. Did the heroes of ancient times resemble today's heroes? Did the heroes of antiquity need an inexhaustible store of enthusiasm? Their achievements were brief, and one explosion of fire was enough to feed their energy. Now, the extended duration of achievement, with the complete depletion of forces in the earthly atmosphere, puts an unbearable strain on the energy. The most powerful stroke, the sternest call, can flash out from but a single explosion; but continuous and repeated action requires a whole sequence of currents of energy.

The present-day hero is sustained by the realization that from no earthly quarter can he expect cooperation. When he says, "I will not abandon the field of battle," he already finds new strength. We are ready to provide the strengthening current in accordance with the firmness of his decision not to abandon the battle. We do know, however, how difficult it is to carry light in the darkness, because this light is seen by others, but not by the one who carries it. Besides, those who sleep cannot stand the light.

In general, take note of those who do not need darkness for their sleep. The fire of their spirit dispels the darkness. We recognize the fighters by certain habits. When their eye wanders in the darkness and they shudder at the gloom, We comfort them with the words, "Space harkens to you."

The sower does not count the scattered seeds, for he is the sower and not the reaper. Who goes most joyously to his labor? The upright sower—not the bent reaper. With his right hand the sower broadly scatters his seeds. The wind carries away many seeds, but the sower sings, because he knows that the field is no longer empty. He will depart when the field is full. It does not matter to him who will reap the harvest or who will collect the new seeds. The task of sowing is given to the most trusted toiler. Large is the field, but the skilled hand does not tire.

We are told once again, "Create heroes."

291. It is quite correct to say that if one were to measure the time spent in malice, humanity would shudder.

Fame, as commonly understood by people, is an absurdity. It is permissible only as shoes for comfortable walking.

292. External phenomena seen today are on the lowest level. You know that levitation is possible; but if all humanity were to rise for no reason into the air, what madness would follow! You know that the weight of objects can be decreased or increased, but in humanity's present state this ability is still premature. The striving toward realization of the spirit must first be made firm. The clue to many such manifestations will then be found in the power of the will.

293. Especially harmful are crossed currents. Even in the physical life, people prefer arrows coming from one direction to those coming from many directions. One can easily understand the depression of mood caused by arrows flying above one's head from unknown directions. When such a saturation of space cannot be avoided, it is especially important to guard one's health. The blood pressure increases, and the tension of the centers causes depression. A single known enemy, however strong, is better than these unrecognizable taps. The Teacher is especially attentive at such times, especially if the fires of the centers are already strained. But these life explosions are unavoidable. Every affirming conscious activity will evoke a vortex of thought, and if one's spiritual development is already great, then the counteraction of unbridled spatial waves is also great, and burdensome. Naturally, people with undeveloped centers do not even notice the shower of arrows, but this does not mean that they should be envied. We speak of constant joy, but this joy is a special wisdom.

294. People love mystery, and the realm of spiritual study would bring them to many a closed door. Why then do people avoid what is unknown to them? Because in school they were always instructed to act like everyone else.

Direct the spirit into the unknown! Such striving will bring about new ways of thinking.

295. The Teaching requires not only an open consciousness but also a desire to commit oneself to its step-by-step application. A mind obscured by conventional ways cannot accept the Teaching. Those not close to the spirit of the Teaching ignore the usefulness of its books. Such people are not needed, even if they are curious.

How can such scattered seeds be dealt with? They do not even believe that there may be another outlook besides their own. Standard calculations are made everywhere in one uniform way, but the thinking process varies, depending on the surrounding conditions of life. Compare the ways of thinking in the village, in the city, in travel, and in flight. In each case the bases and methods will be quite different.

One can understand and apply the Teaching of Agni Yoga only after having been in touch with other Teachings of Life and then feeling the need to find beauty and new meaning in one's existence. Clouds of doubt do not oppress the person who seeks by any means to find a way out of the labyrinth! The command of necessity infuses one with resourcefulness, and helps one's ability to consider concepts not yet understood. When one's attention is taken by the inexplicable pains, then even the narrow consciousness will remember Agni Yoga.

Generally, there is no need to meet in person others who have accepted the Teaching. The ways of necessity are unpredictable. And do not present the Teaching as too accessible, for this breeds contempt. One can tolerate ignorance, but to demean is not permissible. Searching for the Teaching causes no harm.

296. A desire for knowledge is prompted by forgotten knowledge from the past, just as imagination is based upon former experiences.

297. Which time can teach people to discriminate between the great and the small? The time of contentment alters and distorts reality. The time of wrath bends the sword blade of life. The time of sorrow humiliates. The time of enslaving labor dulls. It is difficult for the unliberated consciousness to discern anything in the darkness. Can one anticipate a time when people will comprehend the power of psychic energy? Like madmen they play, even in the face of imminent explosion, and in their error they regard their planet as a most solid body.

It must be recognized that people want to forget grievous events. The destruction of entire continents is carefully removed from the old writings. Equally well-concealed are many indications regarding events that were fateful for the world. "We do not like to torture ourselves," say the earthly authorities. They are ready to hide from themselves their bankruptcy and their defeat. Earthly rulers say, "All is calm in our kingdom." Their self-satisfied repose and inactivity guarantee them their thrones. Usually they admire the sunset but sleep through the sunrise. But the Invisible Government says, "It is absurd to hide what exists."

This is because we must carefully learn from past events.

Seek the energy that, if consciously evoked, will transform your existence. Do you not wish to be armed in time? Even the last hour can teach humanity. We are not prophets in sheepskins. As ordinary physicians We warn, "It is time to perform a vaccination." But there are reckless braggarts who feast even during a pestilence. The cemeteries never lose their new tenants.

We speak for the sake of those who can live.

298. When beginning a work, know how to rejoice at its inception. Usually people are eager to see the flowers and fruit. But true researchers rejoice at the first seedling, because this is the awakening of life.

299. If a teacher says, "I have ten thousand pupils," ask, "Is it possible that everyone is given entrance?" Quantity precludes success. The size of an army was never the sole guarantee of victory.

300. I affirm that Agni Yoga is a light on the path. It is of no consequence how travelers make use of this blessing. The way is indicated to them. Those who discern the signs of fire will come.

Thus do I wish to strengthen those who have realized the urgency of the Teaching of Agni Yoga. One should not delay until the time when the torrent drives the crowd in search of salvation. This would only be knowledge gained under threat and terror, and such knowledge is of no value. It is necessary to know those who are guided by a free consciousness. Only those who know the purpose of a battle can participate in it. Slaves driven by force are not needed. I consider it right to protect sincere striving rather than to search for the fragments of a broken vessel.

301. If in the circle of activity there appears a child who is apparently drawn to it with special reason, smile upon him and develop in him the awareness that these activities are a home to him. Children sometimes come to this activity in response to a special call. Give them what has been prepared for them by their own past. Heavy with juice is the fruit when the roots are strong.

302. One should observe certain precautions in Agni Yoga. Beyond a certain level one may notice pains in one's back. One should then take care not to bend down, because the pillar of energy is rising like quicksilver in a thermometer. Therefore an upright position of the spine is advised. Similarly undesirable is work that requires a tension to one side, such as tree cutting. The flame is vertical in its structure, and thus does each fire act. The taking of slight precautions will not separate people from life. One can quite unnoticeably introduce into life ways of action that are not harmful.

Only a sense of beauty can lead to synthesis. Power comes not from the muscles, but from the consciousness. Even in everyday life, the nerves rule the muscles.

303. The hands of the enemy are ever ready to destroy the works decided upon by Us. The ears of the enemy are cocked to hear slander that can be used against Us. It is not enough to say, "Rejoice at the enemy." One must learn to understand his ways. The enemy is like the unknown quantity in a mathematical problem. But this unknown can be determined using already-known facts. Hence, it is possible to take the measure of each detected enemy.

Consider carefully the circumstances in which your actions are taken. Learn to remember the conditions under which certain feelings came to you. We will return to them again.

An enemy is something unknown, one which must be recognized, conquered, and transformed into the familiar—properly speaking, the cognized. During this process one should also observe oneself. Approaching his quarry, the hunter must calculate each of his actions.

You will be told repeatedly about the awesome occult mysteries, but you will approach simply, confident in yourself. We regard knowledge of one's own situation as the first condition for battle. The unknown becomes familiar when it is approached. It is of no use to speak of it beforehand, when even its boundaries are unknown.

Essaying investigation into everything, we must agree on the methods of research. We will know the direction of our action, but will not put obstacles in our way by making premature decisions about enemies. Let us combine insight with real action. When any aspect of the unknown becomes familiar, that will be a conquest—without astonishment, without a shudder, and even without excessive enthusiasm. For each hour, even the most inactive, may bring us closer to the unknown. The Great Unknown may be thought of as a friend, but for the researcher it is more useful to think of it as an enemy. All features of the unknown correspond more closely to those of an enemy. We speak always of fearlessness, but this is not needed against a friend. The achievement of victory also presumes the existence of an enemy.

If I bid you be victors, that means I foresee a battle. The Great Unknown, like an enemy, lures one to victory.

304. The Teaching of Wisdom is not a textbook with numbered pages. The Teaching is one of indications for life as applied to each necessity. Just as

157

lightning flashes wherever a sufficient electrical charge has accumulated, so does the Indication speed to wherever possibilities have increased.

While affirming the common unity, the Teaching of Life must address itself to each person. The Teaching offers solutions to one's daily problems. Sometimes it seems that the Teaching repeats already discussed themes. But compare these directives, and you will see that they touch upon entirely different problems in life. The outer signs have no significance. People can grow pale, or blush, for different reasons.

Let us examine and apply ourselves fully to resolving the most important problems in life, and leave details to the flow of karma. One can often affect the direction of the main stream, but the details always carry the marks of predetermined karma. Though these details may have no great significance, they are what people usually remember and use as a basis for judgment. Also in the performance of one's tasks and experiments, one should not expect the details of their application and flow to be identical. What is evident means little.

Our Indications foresee all possibilities, and in their manifestation they are quite varied. The danger lies elsewhere. Often a person, having mastered a possibility, then becomes careless about it. The festival flower is brought down into ordinary life, as something ordinary. Of course flowers are always pleasing, but it is better to transform everyday life into a festival of the spirit than to dirty the flowers with everyday dust.

Again we come to the idea of life as a chalice of wondrous remedy. To drink the poison of the world and be reborn with full power! This ritual comes from ancient legends. We see it in Egypt and in Greece. Shiva himself performs it, and a whole chain of

Redeemers drinks the chalice of poison, transforming it into *Amrita*.

When We say, "Be different, and do not deprive yourself of the Chalice of Achievement," We thereby indicate to you not to darken your life and not to spill the Chalice. I confirm how much is given to you. Every particle understood and applied will give new life. Thus, witness the rain of possibilities and rejoice at the rainbow.

305. A staircase has been revealed, with ornamented steps. But why is the lower step so decorated, while higher up the ornamentation grows simpler, until on the last step one sees no decoration at all? The design on the lower step is so intricate that its entire surface is covered. Perhaps no design is needed on the upper step. Truly, I see no ornamentation at all at the top. Thus, think simply.

306. The Breath of the Mother of the World, the Giants bearing the burden, and the Redeemers who have accepted the Chalice—these three images were born close to the one law. The accumulation of spatial psychic energy causes shocks in parts of the planet. Those organisms that are attuned to the Breath of the Great Mother resound in response to the explosions of spatial bodies. Can such shocks be regarded as an advantage? It is precisely as when, for the performance of a superb musical creation, one chooses perfectly tuned instruments. Of course, when such instruments are few, the pressure of the currents will fall upon just those few. It is not necessary to prove that it is better to accept the burden of the world than to be detached from the activities of life.

When I speak about being careful, I am affirming fearlessness strengthened by a mature consciousness. Without courage one cannot build. Without creative work one cannot approach the Chalice. Only the flame over the Chalice reveals the height of the arch. For Us, the Redeemers are not hidden behind golden vestments.

307. The Fiery Warriors are often called by this name because *Satya Yuga* begins with the approach of the element of Fire. Then those gather who are imbued with that penetrating element. The motion and striving of Fire lie at the foundation of light. Nothing can surpass light, because it is fed by the streams of omnipresent Fire. I affirm the stream of Fire as the most pure and swift. All unmanifest space is the ship of Fire. The ancient symbol of the fiery wall relates to the Fire of Space. The East knows of the Army of Fiery Warriors that will arise before the coming of the New Era.

Cataclysms result from conflict between the spatial fire and the flaming sediments of the planet. The planetary gases that are generated by the poisonous decomposition bring into action unbridled energy, *Kamaduro.* In other words, the physical nature of the planet is not in harmony with spatial fire. The luminous matter seeks to reconcile these disparate elements, but what we call darkness can paralyze the radiant matter, and then a cataclysm occurs.

The Fiery Host lives when the Fire of Space achieves victory.

308. Every wrongdoer is afraid to return to the site of his misdeeds. People realize that their previous conduct in the astral world often does not correspond to standards of spiritual dignity. Therefore, they are filled with awe and fear before the gates of the astral. They even try not to think about crossing, hoping that ignorance will relieve them of responsibility. But, by admitting this knowledge, they could make these crossings no more difficult than the ascent of the rungs of a ladder.

Ancient is the symbol of direct ascent. Besides the accumulations of consciousness, what can contribute to this ascent? Of course, fire, the element that transforms one's path. The fire of the bodies unites with and is fed by the Fire of Space. The manifestations of psychic energy are founded on fire. All phenomena are produced by fire, and fire illumines all entrances.

Certainly it is not easy for people of the fiery element to live in the body. But choose only these as co-workers, because there is no treason in them. Danger will not cause confusion in them. Duty is understood by them, and their striving ascends like a flame. Who, then, can more readily manifest the rays from the shoulders? To whom is creation nearer if not to those of Fire, the All-Penetrating? It is difficult for people to understand the characteristics of this element. Earth, water, air—these are evident. But that fire penetrates through water will seem like a jest. One must understand penetration by fire, otherwise one will not enter the Fiery Gates.

309. Of all manifestations We value the absolute and dominant pervasiveness of spirit in one's life. Mistakes are as naught when the seed of fire has grown stronger. Action is like the unfurled banner of the warrior. Like a crown is his decisiveness. Like a pearl is the flame of his spirit. Flaming spirit, you burn away delusion and pierce the darkness! We value, above all, the fire of the spirit.

310. Imperceptible are the steps of the growth of consciousness. Such steps do exist, but their boundaries are not easily determined. It is difficult to determine them by any formula. Especially regarding the lower steps, evaluation must be careful, in order not to cause harm.

How can one make everyone turn in the same direction? Looking in different directions, people will see differently, but without undermining the General Good. Let them look in all directions. Let them observe all points of starry space. The eye must learn to observe. Let them utilize all of humanity's accumulations, but with respect for the General Good. Permit the use of all sources, and the one who grasps more will gain more. The burning of spirit is manifested in many ways. It is by the burning of their spirit that people will be recognized. It is preferable to err by exaggerating the possibilities for good in them, than to underestimate them.

Do not pluck flowers needlessly; every flower should be allowed to grow. Consider that even the most clumsy co-worker can contribute a useful stone for building. It is not proper to reject anyone unless the line of treason has been crossed. Judge by this black sign.

311. Our co-workers, in action, are distinguished from others by their flexibility and striving, and by their open-mindedness. The cosmic life is built on attraction and repulsion, in other words, on rhythmic explosions and accumulations. The activity of Our co-workers is not free from the laws of nature. It can be observed how activity builds the consciousness, and there should be no fear of destruction by its explosions. One thing is unknown to Us—rest in inaction. Our co-workers, like Ourselves, generously lay the foundations.

This sowing is needed by Us and We know that these seeds cannot be lost, for whatever exists cannot be destroyed. We are not greatly interested in the changeability of form, for the seed is unchangeable. Such an unchangeable seed lies in each being. Even negative actions do not prevent Us from remembering that the seed is the same everywhere. And this awareness makes Us tolerant. It is evident to Us that discordance is usually simply the result of conflict of rhythm. Of course, this lack of correlation prevents the unification of psychic energy within groups. It is precisely the group energy that makes possible the utilization of the rays without the annihilation or burning of forces. Vampirism, to a considerable degree, can be attributed to a conflict of rhythm, which results in devouring instead of cooperation. Therefore, learn to recognize those whose waves are not harmful to you, even if superficially they appear to be from the soul of an alien race.

Two who sit at one table, opposite each other, cannot be opponents if they follow the same Teacher. Inclusiveness and tolerance are one. Only treason cannot be tolerated.

312. One must distinguish between objective difficulties and those caused by lack of skill. Objective difficulties are caused by external obstacles on the higher path, but lack of skill results from one's own mental blindness.

One should know that the laws of life are of unlimited flexibility in their application. You may speak about laws as they apply generally, but you also know their broader range of application.

Explain always that rapid reincarnation can be impossible to endure. Only the indefatigable travelers dare frequent sea voyages. For this, I teach you how to endure in spirit, without need of a permanent home.

Neither one's understanding of the subtlety of the Teaching nor one's wisdom of judgment depends on age.

313. The accidental is pre-laid in the consciousness. Even the worlds can be molded by the accidental, with no evident cause, because creation issues from the accidental. We are Guardians of the laws but We respect the accidental, because motion is inherent in it. It would, however, be wrong to direct everyone to the extremes of possibility. In other words, not every foundation can support a heavy roof.

314. One should know that the time for change is different for every formation of matter. If matter is changed in one place, that does not mean that the entire group of planetary bodies will be changed at the same time. Properly speaking, if *Satya Yuga* were to begin on one planet, it would take a very long time to spread and unite the entire group of planets, though the signs of such spreading would soon appear on some planetary bodies. One should never limit one's thinking to a single planet.

315. The Mother of the World has ordained: "Winds, gather ye! Snows, gather ye! Birds, hold back! Beasts, stand back!

"No human foot shall put its mark on My Summit. The audacity of the dark ones shall not last! The light of the moon shall not endure! But the sun's rays shall touch the Peak.

"Sun, guard My Summit, because that is where I keep Vigil. Never shall beast ascend, nor human power prevail!"

The Mother of all that exists keeps Her Vigil with a fiery shield. What glows upon the Summit? Why have the whirlwinds gathered to form a resplendent crown?

She, the Great Mother, ascended the Summit alone. And none shall follow Her.

316. Having an earthly home should not diminish the importance of maintaining the fire of the heart. Understand that establishing an earthly home should be as the offering of a flame. The labors of creation must be as the lighting of altar lamps. One hundred and eight flames and as many works. A thousand flames and as many works. A myriad flames and as many works. But should the flames die out, it will be because the eye of man has died.

317. Upon the highest summit the Mother of the World stands effulgent. She came forth to defeat the darkness. Why are the enemies fallen? And whither do they turn their eyes in despair? She has cloaked Herself in a fiery veil and encircled Herself in a wall of fire. She is our citadel and our inspiration.

318. One must not be concerned with the barking of dogs. One may carry a staff, and remember that just one well-timed thrust will frighten the most vicious dog. Do not waste energy with a premature stroke. But aim well!

It is difficult for most people to understand the saturation of space. They accept the saturation of water and even of earth. They discuss the metalization of roots. But space to them is not a living substance. Hence, the element of fire terrifies them, and the joy of cosmic motion is unrealized.

319. Whither to direct one's courage? Whither to direct the will? Whither to direct oneself? To the same spirit-fire. We shall find strength and not become exhausted, because on our path we gather the words of knowledge.

Let us recall the known saints of various lands. By what marks are they distinguished? By showing humility or obedience to their rulers, by taking vows of silence, or by obeisance? If so, they would be unworthy of the name. When We regard saints, We see among them warriors, highwaymen, condemners of kings, builders, and leaders of people. By the fire of the spirit is their level of ascent recognized. Laws inscribed by people cannot extinguish this fire. Therefore, let us be careful about judging the approaching ones. Like fragments of heavenly bodies, diamond-bearing, those approaching from afar may carry within themselves signs incomprehensible to others.

One cannot expect too much from the crowds. The Stone from the far-off star carries a message that few can accept.

Attraction multiplies force. And the special language of fire will inscribe the signs of the future. Again let us show care, because the fire of the spirit is imponderable.

320. Each era has its own methods. To depend on old precedents is like wearing one's grandfather's boots.

321. Invocations and incantations can of course help in attuning oneself to the spatial rhythm, but the law of evolution presumes a more direct contact of the human consciousness with the cosmic one. Instead of the rhythm of magic formulas one should comprehend the fiery seed of the spirit and silently build the bond linking the fire of one's spirit with the Fire of Space.

322. He who acquires knowledge only for himself is not Our builder. When the structures are about to collapse, who can sit calmly? When even the most remote cataclysm sets the organism atremble, then all must become masons, laying the new foundations. I say this because the undeferrable work requires all forces.

323. How to start on the path of Agni Yoga? Primarily, one must realize the existence of psychic energy. Then it is necessary to realize that fire is the essence of the spirit.

There is no doubt that abstinence from meat is beneficial. All vegetables are good as foods, but a few, such as asparagus, celery, and garlic, are mainly medicinal.

One must take precautions against fiery sickness. The first remedy for this purpose will be the understanding and mastery of psychic energy. But, as an external purification, one may apply the essence of *moru,* or, as it is also called, *balu.* When you are asked, provide the precise formulas. Indicate *moru* as the primary remedy, to be added to the bath water. One can prepare a powerful extract from the juice of its leaves and roots. If this first formula is judiciously applied, you can then give the next one. The same plant may also be taken internally, with milk. But it should first be tested externally.

Also, do not hesitate to stress that valerian can be a powerful protector when one is suffering from the fiery sickness. Think about psychic energy as simply as possible. Indeed the finer energies are not manifested like thunder. They penetrate the remote layers of the atmosphere, and are manifested in especially subtle ways.

324. I must advise you to banish fear for the future. One who is bound by fear does not create a suitable atmosphere for action. We need those who strive for victory.

325. In giving Agni Yoga, you perform a work of inexpressible importance.

326. Every structure has its outer walls and its unseen foundation. No structure can exist without walls, and walls cannot stand without a foundation.

There are two ways of manifestation in everything: one is the walls, as a symbol of the Teacher, and the other is the foundation, as the manifestation of the Mother of the World. Which is of greater importance? Ponder!

327. The walls and the pilings of the foundation are equally necessary for any building. But, just as a foundation is not seen from afar, so does the image of the Mother of the World remain invisible. It is the walls that withstand the assaults of the gale. In the same way, because Our Name is known to multitudes, We must take upon Ourselves the assaults of the hostile currents.

You will often be asked, "What is the difference between those two paths of service?" Say, "There is neither difference nor advantage. Two sacred rivers replenish the ocean."

They will also ask how to know the current to which one belongs. Naturally, the knowledge of the spirit directs one toward a certain current, according to the rays under which one is born.

One can imagine the intensity of striving stimulated by the rays of the spatial bodies. Our followers are exceedingly sensitive to these rays, but no one should fear this sensitivity. Ordinary people shudder at any nearby sharp sound. How, then, could a developed spirit fail to react to a distant earthquake? Even an electric pole hums with the energy it carries! It is time for humanity to value properly all abilities inherent in the body.

How can we fight against the waves of flame?

328. It is useful to speak about the Teacher. It is useful to speak about the Teaching. It is useful to speak of life. It is wise to understand the upward spiral of motion, because the application of energy directs the

stream upward. But at the same time the law of gravity lowers it. Thus are the steps laid together.

Speak according to your listener's understanding. Intolerance is an outworn garment that must be discarded.

329. The illness called neuritis has a certain relation to fire. Much that is attributed to rheumatism or nervous disturbances should also be attributed to fire. These pains can easily be eliminated by locating the material crystals of psychic energy. When these deposits obstruct the nerve channels many painful developments can be expected. Like stones in the inner organs, the crystals of psychic energy can be injurious if the energy is not utilized. Especially dangerous is the conflict of the crystals of psychic energy with the deposits of imperil. Often, organisms with highly developed nervous systems are sickly. Experimental research into psychic energy is urgently needed. Whatever can be measured physically will be more easily accepted.

330. Observe the symptoms of ailments that seem incomprehensible. Locate and observe those centers near which the symptoms and pains appear. Perhaps there is an aching of the shoulders or elbows or knees. Perhaps three signs appear near the center of the Chalice, or burning occurs in the larynx. Each such symptom indicates the activity of that center. As if inscribed in a book, the personality of each individual is written by the sign of his essence, constantly flaming above his head. One can read it even with plain observation. But people are accustomed to cruder manifestations. They expect deafening thunder and blinding lightning. Yet, they themselves often perform the most important actions in silence.

Just as the effect of a powerful magnetic current can be observed only on certain bodies, even though it acts upon everything, so also are the most penetrating energies invisible. But for now We beg that attention be paid mainly to evident manifestations.

By studying the characters of people and their physical pains, one can arrive at valuable conclusions. We should know how the centers affect the surrounding organs. Why have lung ailments been seen as a complication following upon a cold, or anemia, when the centers near the lungs indicate related peculiarities of the organism? Why has swelling of the shoulders and elbows been attributed to rheumatism when the centers of the shoulders show tension? It is Our task to help people understand that it is time to discard old formulas and turn to the path of universal law.

331. How to know which are the best co-workers? Only by their irreplaceability. It is right to value one who has become irreplaceable.

Only to Urusvati can I entrust the Teaching, without fear that it will be distorted or diminished. Only centuries-long experience provides the needed degree of devotion together with the understanding of the essence. I can entrust to Fu. the earthly deeds, because through him I can act.

I can provide to My disciples all that is needed, but I expect the development of experience. Affirm the work in practice, because the seven years' duration of the first period is coming to an end.

332. What is the nature of the Bodhisattvas' compassion? Without coercing the will, They invisibly and patiently direct each suitable force toward good. It is not difficult to conduct oneself according to the Guidance of the Bodhisattvas, for all characteristics of the spirit are allowed for by Them.

Work is felt as a burden only when the forces are distributed incorrectly; but when co-measurement of a direction and its execution is maintained, then even a complicated task will not be beyond one's capabilities.

Most harmful is the belief that though one is giving all, there is no reward. One can undermine the most brilliant achievement by such demeaning. Let us not forget that, knowing the goal, one can always proceed. But to count the stones upon which one's precious foot treads impedes one's steps. Let us consider that when birds fly they do not count each flap of their wings.

Not a single Teacher ever thought that His work was completed, or that He deserved reward. This is the quality of the self-sacrifice of the Bodhisattvas: creation by the labor of each sweep of the untiring hand, because the eye knows the distance to the goal. Such will be the labor of the Bodhisattvas—like Fire—omnipresent, self-sacrificing, and inexhaustible in its essence.

333. It is most important to speak of the concept of the Teacher. It is necessary to point out the hierarchy of Teachers, each of whom is the disciple of a Higher Teacher. One must become accustomed to the fact that the Teaching in its wholeness is without contradiction. The landmarks may be far from one another, but they are signs on the same path.

If someone insists that incarnations are always three thousand years apart, he will be as correct as the one who claims that they are three months apart.

The happiness of the realization of possibilities is the happiness of the future. Manifesting possibilities without violating the essence of the laws means approaching perfection.

If, in the second race, a far-distant date was needed for incarnation, in the sixth race the coming together of physical and astral conditions reduces the need for such lengthy periods between incarnations.

One must also accustom oneself to the overlapping of these races. The third race will scarcely have developed fully when the seeds of the sixth already will have appeared in space.

He who follows the Teaching of Fire must understand the perfecting of matter. The worlds of the physical and of Light are increasingly united. This is an indication of the transformation of so-called death. It is the fear of death that shuts the Gates of Knowledge.

It is useful to teach about immortality in the schools. Religion that teaches about death will pass away, as will all those who believe in death. Our consciousness determines our future state. Those who understand the real power of Fire, which is invisible, also understand the meaning of death, which, though visible, is but a superficial manifestation of disincarnation.

334. To the question of the realms of the worlds, one must point out that heavenly bodies can be part of a particular solar system or can be intersolar bodies.

The condition of Earth is grievous. Earth is sick.

335. One should not think that one's work can be measured by one's earthly dwellings. If Ramakrishna's bed burns up, is the truth of his word diminished?

Is it important to the shepherd to know which of his sheep will give the better wool? Is it important to the gardener to know how much fruit each of his cultivated trees will yield? No, the shepherd's care is for his entire flock, and the gardener's love is for his whole orchard.

336. No name will provoke so many attacks as that of Maitreya, for it is bound up with the future. Nothing

172

provokes so much fear and irritation in people as thinking about the future.

Striving toward the future, be ready for battle. Do not hide your striving, for fire strives upward and only a high degree of striving will strengthen our union.

The Teaching of Agni Yoga must transform one's inner life. And externally, neither horns, tail, or wings, nor pompous condescension, superstition, or malice, shall be your traits.

It is essential not to fear to broaden your labors, for this is the best way to co-measurement. Sitting under one particular tree, one may think that it is the center of the world. But, expanding the essence of one's spirit through the entire world, one becomes like Fire, all-pervading.

337. Consciousness is the measure. Beauty leaves no room for ugliness. A lie cannot be concealed. Conjecture is the cookstove of lies. The growth of values is life. Consciousness is the judge of motive. Karma provides the means, but often they are in repayment of old karmic debts. There are so many aspects to life, and only consciousness can be the judge. Therefore, develop consciousness.

If we limit ourselves by dead laws, it would be better to move to a cemetery.

Anything ordinary will not invoke the Fire of Space. Sacrifice is accepted by the consciousness. But how precise must be the chisel inscribing justice, and how subtle can be the wiliness of self-justification!

338. A time of happiness—thus We call that step in the development of consciousness when, without turning away from life, Our co-workers are given the opportunity to join Us in Our Abode. But why has not one of these chosen ones made immediate use of this opportunity? Because, although the degree of development of their consciousness has unlocked the gates to Us, their same consciousness tells them not to abandon Our work when it is needed. Self-sacrifice grows from the developed consciousness, and the defense of Our Abode is a radiant task, a stone of salvation. The development of consciousness deepens one's understanding of the correlation of the laws of life and permits help to the consciousness of one's co-workers. But We do care that Our chosen ones, even physically, should not too distantly separate themselves from Our mountains.

One should understand that it is not lack of devotion that temporarily holds back Our co-workers from Our Abode. On the contrary, it is devotion that causes them to postpone their comfort and their joy.

It should be remembered that there are very few developed consciousnesses. Therefore, cherish each such consciousness, even with its faults. The ability to correctly evaluate both faults and virtues is a sign of an ascended consciousness.

Remember, Our works are not always the most urgent. A sower must first finish scattering his handful of seed and only then will he answer to the call of the Master, "I come, Lord! Kalagiya!"

339. People love manifestations to be no smaller than an elephant, and sounds no softer than thunder. But the action of the fine energies is performed in stillness.

340. Most important, learn to think in solitude. And remember the responsibility for thought. Truly, thought levels the strongest walls. I advise that one observe oneself carefully, and consciously eject doubt, irritation, and self-pity. Remember that no one but the Teacher can help. I advise that the Teacher be regarded as one's only stronghold.

341. Proclaiming the New Era of Fire means that it is necessary now to master this element. The reality of Fire must be embraced by the consciousness. But long ago I told you about the necessity for this exercise of accepting ideas into the consciousness. Can one presume that the Teaching has been applied in life if even one's thoughts have not received a new impetus? Do not seek for new seedlings where all remains as before. Where the old dominates, the New Fire will scorch, and life will not receive its new blessings.

Let Our words about Fire not be regarded as abstract symbols. I speak of Fire truly existing. This is not the first time that the planet will experience the effect of this element. During each change of race Fire approaches as a purifying stream. Humanity remembers the devastation caused by the fusion of the Fire of Space with its subterranean fiery precipitates. Why repeat the destruction of Atlantis if it is possible to attract the beneficial aspects of the element of fire? But in order to approach Fire without fear it is necessary to learn to think about it and to assimilate it in the consciousness.

When it becomes possible to see the emanations of the human body, you will discern with clarity the hideousness of duplicity, when the face shows benevolence but the thoughts are sharpening knives.

One must learn to accept the Teaching simply and to fill one's life with it. Fire can be a great blessing.

342. In analyzing matter, many elements have been identified, but there are two that are not yet discovered or named. The first is the deposit of psychic energy, and the second, the substance of Fire. As long as the crystal of psychic energy is not found, the substance of Fire will not be identified. Just as the deposits of psychic energy can be found through imperil, the substance of Fire will be found through observing the tension of psychic energy.

The Fire of Space, in rare cases, can be observed by the naked eye where it is more dense, near the protective purple border of the aura. Space becomes, one could say, filled with small tongues of flame. But for this manifestation a strong aura is needed, which will not suffer from the proximity of the intense flame.

On ancient images one can see tongues of flame encircling the auras. But now this physical phenomenon has been forgotten. You know the full reality of what is being said. But let the scientists not complain if, prior to their discovery of Fire, We suggest that they first discover the crystal of imperil. Besides, it has almost been discovered by them already. It is easier to deal with the poison of irritation than to seek the superior psychic energy.

343. The manifestation of fire is rarely discerned, because its speed is too great to be perceived by the naked eye. However, fire will sometimes be steadier when in proximity to the aura. The waves of fire have their own rhythm. You are already accustomed to the fact that manifestations do not depend on external conditions as one sees them.

344. In mirages you can see the lie of evidence and the truth of reality. I repeat, you see reality, but it is a reality that is not where your eyes indicate. And this is true of many phenomena.

Often people will not look at reality, but insist on their own misperception. People will ask why demonstrations of the subtle energies are so rare. Tell them that on the contrary, they are continuous, but the human eye and ear do not care to recognize them. When the human eye does glimpse them, it is usual to convince oneself that they were imagined. This is the attitude of an undeveloped consciousness.

The ability to observe with clarity should be developed in the schools. In the schools it is necessary to test this ability. And the best way is in silence and in darkness.

Understand once again that the time of changes of continents is approaching. Maitreya is coming, in the vanguard of science, addressing its new frontiers. All the problems of science and of the evolution of all that exists are of concern to the Teacher.

345. It is not so easy to learn to think. It is difficult to develop intensity of thought, and even more difficult to attain thought of high quality. A person will often mentally repeat to himself, "I will think purely." But his being is accustomed to egoistic thinking, and a most undesirable form of thought results. Two birds, flying in different flocks, cannot become united as one. It is necessary to exercise thought, not mentally, but with the fire of the spirit, until all disunity of thought disappears. Thought can have power only if it is monolithic. But each crack diminishes its power and also causes cosmic harm, by inducing dissonance into space.

It is necessary to devote the needed time to the mastering of thought, but at the same time repeatedly remind oneself that all thought has one essence. We rejoice at diversity of thinking, but each thought must be pure as a diamond.

346. I already told you about the divisibility of spirit. There is no need to be astonished if a developed spirit generously manifests itself, even at far distances, where it is attracted by the spiritual quality of those present. One should not think that the effects of such projection of the spirit are always invisible. One gives out coins almost without noticing, or even knowing, to whom they are given. How much more generous is our spirit when, as the finest energy, it hurries toward the best application.

Therefore let us develop self-sacrificing fullness of spirit.

347. People often talk about untiring labor, but in their spirit, they fear it. One cannot name anyone who, without broadening of consciousness, can find joy in endless labor. Only Our people will understand how life is fused with labor, drawing from it strength of achievement. It can be understood that, just as fire is inexhaustible, so also is the energy that is derived from labor. The fulfillment of Agni Yoga begins from the moment of realization of labor. But if the energy to sustain the fire is insufficient, cloudbursts will begin to extinguish it. The tension of energy does not come from a command of the mind, nor does it increase by a command from without. It grows only from within. However, only a free consciousness can transform labor into a festival of spirit.

Also, avoid coercion of another's will. Like fires let your calls flame, filling space. But the path following these fires of the spirit must be built by each one for himself. The labor of saturating space is similar. An ignoramus considers the forces of space to be outside his regal personality. He expects that all he is will die with his body. Actually, the crystal of ignorance will remain indestructible until the knowledge gained by spirit breaks down its lifeless substance.

Seeking the Yoga of Fire, people must understand that the inner fire must be ignited by labor. The interaction of energies nurtures the fire, intensifying it so that the channels of fire will reach the spheres of the highest worlds.

We say that Agni Yoga is the most applicable to life, because life is based upon the interplay of energies.

348. It should be understood that meat is not desirable for the organism, because of the harm of ingesting dead tissue. One may permit some smoked meats, but only while traveling. But in general, I would advise abstaining from meat. It is useful to have apples on the table. The fundamental quality of this fruit is beneficial for one's breathing, as long as the fruit has not yet spoiled.

349. The Teacher is ready to accept every sign of devotion. Devotion and readiness forge the bond between the worlds.

350. One may understand self-sacrifice as the most rapid way to gain admittance.

Think about why, for any physical effort, a deep inhalation is needed. Is there not in this a connection to the transmission of energy, of which we have spoken today? Among physical manifestations how can there be anything supernatural?

351. You know Our attitude toward the astral world. You know how much the astral world must change in the process of evolution. But, while pointing out the imperfections of the astral world, we cannot reject it, because nothing that exists can be rejected. One must build knowledge, not according to one's personal desires, but according to real meaning. People thus can learn about the astral world, and, even more, can bring it closer to the borders of visibility. In this way, they can aid Our experiments in the densification of the astral.

When people read about the tangible manifestations of the astral world, these phenomena may seem to be quite extraordinary. It would be insufficiency of thinking to reject what is undeniably near. It would be helpful for people to accept this and establish a new point of view. How can we fight for improvement in the conditions of life if we fail to properly observe life?

You may speak to those who approach you about how the densification of the astral will affect life, and also about experiments in making changes to the physical nature of one's locality and of nearby objects. You can point out that an experiment based on natural laws cannot be called supernatural. But of course a consciousness covered with age-old dust cannot quickly grasp the reality of things. For example, when I speak of patience it is necessary to understand it as a fundamental part of daily life. Who would turn a tarrying guest out into the rain? Such attacks of the elements are not lengthy, and it is necessary only to use the time as wisely as possible. It is necessary to understand that now spatial thought is tensed in the direction of the unification of the spheres, and human thought is advancing laboriously along the path of broadening of consciousness.

352. The fear of astral manifestations is based upon other things than ghosts. It is necessary to understand that the cold of the astral world provokes a chemical reaction in people.

353. If they ask about reward, relate this parable:

A man gave much gold for good works, but then awaited his reward. Once his Teacher sent him a stone with the note, "Accept this reward, the treasure of the far-off star."

The man became indignant. "In return for my gold a stone is given to me! What is a far-off star to me?"

And, angered and dejected, he cast the stone into a mountain stream.

But the Teacher came and said, "How did you like the treasure? In that stone was contained a most precious diamond, sparkling beyond all earthly gems."

In despair the man rushed into the stream. And following the current, he was carried farther and farther downstream. But the ripples of the waves forever hid the treasure from him.

354. By renouncing fear, prejudice, and hypocrisy, one can become linked with the invisible life. One can observe how, without these three enemies, clairaudience and clairvoyance can more readily be developed.

355. Those who would study Agni Yoga must direct their attention to the rhythmic pulsation of the elements, because by this natural phenomenon the various elements are united. The psychophysical experiment that took place yesterday showed the rhythm of energy as a pulse of elements. Activity alternates with silence, just as a *Pralaya* alternates with a *Manvantara*. While it would be absurd to attribute to spirits the action of the elements in all physical processes, there is undoubtedly a link between certain spirits and the moments of influx of energy. You may be astonished to see how disincarnated spirits can densify themselves by using the ectoplasm of space, and, on the other hand, how physical bodies can acquire subtle properties. Indeed, it is a true bridge between the two worlds!

Consider that the ectoplasm is projected precisely with the help of the fiery element.

356. It is not idle curiosity that prompts you to investigate the pulsating rhythm of the elements. All knowledge is useful. The importance of rhythm has long been known, but the rhythmic pulse of the elements is of particular importance and has a special effect.

357. *Mahavan* and *Chotavan* are the most characteristic rhythms of Fire. Mastery of these rhythms permits one to more easily approach the element of fire. This is not artificial forcing, such as by invocation, but is simply a conscious entering into the sphere whose meaning you consider essential.

One must understand rhythms, for how else do we bring effectiveness to our actions? If lifeless sand arranges itself into special designs in response to rhythmic vibrations, then how much more is humanity influenced by rhythm! Not sorcery but knowledge will show the way to transformation. This path is an urgent one. Thus was humanity exhorted in the days before the end of Atlantis.

It is not right to think that if today has passed unchanged, then tomorrow will also pass in the same way. Each hour can bring transformation for the advent of the New World.

Find a way to make the Teaching a part of your everyday life. The busiest people can devote an hour each day to their approach to the Teaching. We cannot believe that there is not a moment available for the most essential, for that for which we live. Daily we partake of food, and without it regard the day as miserable. But our spirit also requires nourishment of thought, and it is a crime to pass one's day without it.

Let us magnify our thoughts, and let us think of the fundamentals of Yoga as our bread and milk. This should not be forced, because the Teaching itself attracts by taming all that impedes growth.

358. It is correct to understand the eagle in the old writings as oxygen. Phosphorus, sulfuric zinc, and platinum are also often encountered as symbols in the old formulas.

359. It is difficult to force fast-flying birds to fly slowly. There is no greater sacrifice than when a consciousness, already expanded, must consecrate itself to physical life.

360. Once people realize psychic energy, the New Era will affirm itself.

361. There are two kinds of logic: the logic of external reasoning, which one attempts to learn from textbooks, and that of mental synthesis, by which one collects and links the sparks of spatial thought. These sparks may seem to be a happy accident, even though this "accident" may have been ripening in space for an entire century. The broadened consciousness provides the best possibility of grasping the nodes of spatial thought.

Of course, from the point of view of external reasoning, apparent lapses in the processes of mental synthesis can always be found. As rings of the spiral show to the observer the outer turns and conceal the inner turns, so mental logic proceeds according to the limits of the outer turns while the inner turns are still merged in the streams of collective thought in space. Hence, We take such care about the broadening of the consciousness, in order that union with spatial thought may be approached.

This must be accepted as simply as is the vital importance of oxygen. Equally simple should be the idea of the spiral nature of all that exists, and of creative explosions. Thus the breath of the Cosmos will be realized as an ascending spiral.

The pure fundamental essence, which might be compared to oxygen, emerges with the help of *Materia Lucida* from unmanifest space and, encountering the refuse of life, produces a series of creative explosions. Of course it is necessary to understand that without the Fire of Space these explosions would have no rhythm, for Fire is the regulator of the pulse of Cosmos.

We all rejoice if you are applying the rhythms indicated to you. Of course the rhythms vary with each individual, and the current condition of one's organism determines the results. One should accept the transmissions from space into the open Chalice. This is the guarantee of synthesis. Likewise, one must follow one's inner rhythm, because the developed consciousness cannot be without rhythm.

The combination of two dodecahedrons is useful for promoting the rhythm of fire. When enough energy has been accumulated, I shall demonstrate it, because this fleeting rhythm is necessary for the approach to Agni Yoga.

362. Whoever knows a grain of Truth is mocked as an occultist. And the one who resists the foundations of true knowledge is praised as a rationalist. It is easy to imagine the degree of perversion of earthly thinking that comes from such assumptions.

It is bad when the concept of the Teacher is not realized. But it is still worse when, after realization, one demands of the Teacher what should be performed by oneself. It would be better to combine reverence for the Teacher with the self-reliant application of one's own entire force.

363. People love to speak about ebb and flow, about waves of light and sound, about magnetic currents; but psychic energy remains overlooked, although psychic waves are far stronger than all others in space. It is a scientific fact that the waves of psychic energy act like astrochemical rays. Regions of action and counteraction can be observed at the greatest distances. The accumulation of the waves of space, as the consciousness of Cosmos, affects all sensitive receivers more than do either the personal will or the consciousness of the astral world. One can imagine the power of these waves, sweeping over the world, bearing in their wake countless joys or terrors.

Why do we measure the pressure of the atmosphere, but never pay attention to other factors that affect the moods of people? Life is built by such moods. Enough people exist who are sufficiently sensitive, but instead of benefitting from them, the world too readily treats them with disdain and superstition. Sad ignorance impedes the application in life of these other energies, which are knocking at the window. It is time to understand the true source of collective striving, by which people find upliftment or downfall.

Earlier races paid attention to the action of psychic energy. But our race, though departing, is still unwilling to leave this beneficent heritage to its descendants.

364. If, after the passing of these seven years, I shall say, "All is possible," will it then be understood? Will not people, as antagonists, still rush to act against reality? Following to the letter is dangerous; but is the consciousness ready to understand that creativeness has ever-expanding possibilities?

365. Most especially, do not frighten with the Teaching. Truly, into each life can be brought a blossoming branch. The Teaching should be like the light of morning.

366. Why should Our warranty be understood narrowly? The treasure should be carried in daily life more wisely and applied more broadly than is customary. Searching for a broad application of the Teaching will give experience to the hand. But one can easily destroy an expected result, for Our voice from afar is like a whisper of the reeds. The free will that rebels should not be opposed. We may regret and once again whisper, but the law of free will, as an inalienable characteristic of man, guarantees his dignity.

When I say, "Do not coerce," I have in mind precisely the law of free will. Who would bend a sapling that is tensed with its own will? And would not the recoil be worse than the bending? Thus, find ways to attract people without molesting their will.

Self-sacrifice cannot be coaxed. Self-sacrifice cannot be commanded. When the spirit, unmindful of itself, aches for others, it acts by free will. Even a hint of coercion would be improper where sacrifice is freely offered. Is division of the spirit possible where there is coercion?

See, how the ever-ready flame flares up! No pain can divert what has already been sent by the will of a pure spirit!

367. Dogs, as we know, will quarrel; do not emulate them. Consciousness obliges one to understand the consequences of a quarrel. Unwise words rise like black whirlwinds. It is dangerous to pollute space. It is dangerous to provoke a return blow upon oneself and one's near ones.

It is said that the monkey is easily offended. What is that to us? The panther can be very irritable. What is that to us? It is said that the hen clucks without reason. It is said that the vulture endlessly nurses his ire. What is that to us? A parrot repeats slander. What is that to us? It is said that a duck cannot control its nerves. What is that to us? Let us not emulate them.

368. Not discontent, not irritation, but the sensation of happiness is necessary. It is truly happiness to build the works of the Teacher.

369. For the last time I shall speak of irritation. Discern its harm—not only personal but also spatial.

This worm, concealed by a smile and politeness, ceaselessly tunnels through the aura. Its harm undermines all works.

For the sake of creation, stand firm against irritation. When, like a blood clot, it closes the ear, can one then hear? When it clouds the eye, can one then see? When the curtain falls on the consciousness, where then is achievement?

One should guard fire as a treasure. The phosphorous of the nerves can be consumed like a wick; is a lamp fit without it? One could add the "oil" of ozone, but with no wick, the fire cannot be kindled.

The symbol of fire reminds us about the most sacred substance, which is accumulated with such difficulty, but can be lost in an instant. How can we expect results when photographing our physical emanations if we are sinking into darkness?

Thus, untiringly warn all friends.

370. Tell to Oriole, to the golden birdling: "When you fly to the High Tower, remember the past. Remember how you destroyed treasures and how afterward you strove toward the creations of the spirit, but by then could not find the way to them. Yet striving does not vanish; it is transmuted into life. You have accumulated the treasures of the spirit. How many others have their path so well defined? The one who has overcome all obstacles will more easily conquer space. Wings are given to birds only for flight." Thus, remember!

371. Studying the subtle energies, you can see that close attention should be given not only to major manifestations, but also to the small currents of tension, because they give powerful results. It is necessary to give first place to the tangible accumulations and combinations.

Only recently has the study of the somatic structure of the organism begun. Recently, also, the purple protective auric net has become known. Both phenomena are related to the domain of Fire. The first is a result of the work of phosphorus. The second represents the power of fire, which is attracted from space by the healthy emanations of the bodily organism. Thus, one should safeguard the fire of the body, so that its effect may be powerful. Our medicines are intended to strengthen these fires. It is not the muscles, but the fiery wave of nerves that requires attention. It must be restored and nurtured.

The plant brought by you from the mountains can be used in many useful experiments. The intensified energy of its sap nurtures the power of fire. But one should also study other uses for it. The warmth-producing essence of the leaves and the oil of the bark will be the best strengthening remedy for the protective auric net.

Between the two Origins—Light and Darkness— the protective auric net shines like armor. Truly it is the boundary between Light and Darkness! We shall thus approach the Buddha's Teaching of the Golden Mean from a different angle. A line divides the Origins. Like lightning, it emanates from the one principle of the Primary Source. As both a defense and a bridge, fire unites the opposites. People should value the power of this union! Whoever masters it is a conqueror of Darkness.

Physicians should study the significance of the somatic structure and of the defensive auric net.

372. It is important to understand the interplanetary battles. One cannot describe in any other way the clash between sick and healthy atmospheres. The currents mentioned yesterday protect the planet against

poisonous emanations. The human consciousness in its present state adds greatly to these destructive conditions. The extent of the danger of these emanations cannot be imagined. Only through mastery over the Fire of Space is relief possible. But this Fire must be brought into life.

It is not enough to observe the signs of Fire near the human organism. One must observe the ways in which Fire affects the consciousness. These experiments are simple, and will help to develop techniques that cannot be obtained from textbooks. Fire touches life more often than one would think.

373. Agility of consciousness is a quality of the Higher World. One should understand why royal incarnations may alternate with those of shoemakers, without debasement. It is difficult for those on Earth to grasp this idea of changeability of external forms, because the ascent of the spirit is little understood. Agility teaches one to understand things from different angles. And the formula "by human hands and feet" ceases to be an abstraction.

You should also understand the infallibility of the general plan. Therefore, you must continually search, and not cling to any notion. If the enemies close off one road, by that very action they leave open another.

374. He who follows the Teaching loses the passivity so cherished by people. But he who does not follow receives the full downpour of karma. Judge for yourselves who has chosen the right path. When you follow the Teaching, can there be failure? The Teaching brings refinement of consciousness as a great happiness. Where, then, to find a power equal to that which results from the Teaching? Thus, follow Our Teaching with great care.

375. Wherein lies the success of a yogi? It is not in the attraction of crowds, not in the conversion of multitudes. But, near the works of the yogi, one can observe how others emulate him. Consciously or unconsciously, voluntarily or involuntarily, people begin to do the same thing. Even his enemies, while cursing him, are drawn in his wake. It is as if a special atmosphere had gathered about the actions of the yogi. This is a true success, when neither money nor fame, but the invisible fire kindles human hearts. Desiring to emulate him, these ignited hearts enter the yogi's atmosphere and bear away with them some drops of the creative dew. Success does not come only from without. It is created by the collaboration of human hands with spatial thought.

For them the yogi is the primary channel, the primary receiver of the energies of space, luminous as a beacon fire. He builds that which should be built. He lays together the intended stones. And his enemies may shudder, but still feel compelled to repeat his words. The yogi is not a preacher. He seldom speaks to the crowds. But the works entrusted to him grow with a special bloom. Others do not even acknowledge the flourishing of these works, whose intended purpose is not to capture them, but to ignite their hearts. Whither will fly the spark of fire? Do they not see all the lighted fires, and all the travelers warmed by the flame of an Agni Yogi? His fire burns the brighter because it burns not for itself.

376. How do We define success? Truly, works are successful when their very trail is followed by friend and foe alike. Examine the deeds of those who follow, and say to yourself, "All comes from our fire." All mistakes are burned away by the fire of following. One may traverse life with courage when the beacon-fires light the way, when the dangers themselves are part of the design of the Veil of the Mother of the World.

The Mother of the World does not fear the Great Play.

377. Truly, guard the Teaching as a pearl. Hold high Our Books, the joy of your day and the labor of your ascent. Extol the Teaching as a sword of vigilance. Can carelessness be permitted to creep around the Teaching of life? By what other means can we transform our lives? How else can we find application of the realm of spirit abiding within us?

Let us count the days we spend unworthily and be stricken with remorse. Let us count the hours not given to the Teaching and bewail. Can the hour given to the Teaching be sold for a sack of gold? Can one be satisfied with a garment of ignorance after beholding a chiton of beauty, adorned with the flowers of the Mother of the World? How can we devote our days to ordinary routine, when treasures are strewn along our path? One must become accustomed to the unusual manifestations of life.

Just as a magnet attracts iron and then magnetizes it, so is sustenance given to the magnet of the individual spirit. Without nurture the spirit will not see how many doors are open to it.

According to the law of the interchange of matter, it is necessary to create a steady current of receiving and giving. One should not think that whatever is read once stays in the mind. The gardener is not worthy who visits his garden only once. It is necessary to understand the signs, but for this one should accept them as one's own. One's own Book lies at hand. Wondrous is the realization of reverence through which one's life is transformed.

We send Our wish that the Teaching be treated with reverence.

378. We were able to demonstrate the dodecahedron, but this was not easy. Let us note all the signs of Fire and of psychic energy. Thus we shall affirm an understanding of the connections between these supreme concepts. And thus, gropingly, we shall discover evidence of the action of the subtle energies in everyday life.

It is dreadful that the most remarkable manifestations of these energies attract no attention. People often see and hear extraordinary things, but they bury them with their mind's refuse. How powerful must a manifestation be for the human eye to notice?

When a man sees and feels a fire, self-igniting and unconsuming, he decides it is electricity. When he hears the vibration of a string in the air, or the ringing of a bell where none exists, he thinks vaguely about sound waves. When he sees colored stars near him, of course, he rushes to an oculist. When he sees formations in space, he thinks of meteoric dust. When he receives objects from space, he only suspects his neighbor—his imagination can work no further. Almost never does he pay attention to manifestations within his own organism. Yet it is from just these small observations that a great experience is built. Opinions must not be imposed by command, but should pass through one's own channels of psychic energy. Let us watch closely.

379. The membranes and the somatic structure of the glands open them to fire, therefore sensitivity of the glands is beneficial.

380. It has been truly said that manifestations come first in thunder and later in silence. It is impossible to hear the Voice in silence without having first experienced it in thunder, which is much less difficult and exhausting. But after thunder, silence follows; and it is in silence that the Essence is found. But then, can darkness exist for the eye that has attained light? Or silence for the ear that has heard the birth of sound? How could *Materia Matrix* be soundless or without light?

It is well-known that one can open a tightly closed vessel either by breaking it or by sounding a most delicate rhythm. Similarly, in all other realms of matter, one should become accustomed not to expect important manifestations to come with an elephantine tread, and to sense even the flight of a butterfly. This is not easy to learn, for life is full of hammer blows. Subtle energies are not accepted in everyday life. And the farther humanity goes, the more crudely does it abuse those lower forces that it conquers.

In daily life we must refine the keenness of our understanding of the subtle energies, for in them lies the future.

381. It is especially difficult to discern behavior that is not accompanied by the usual nervous reactions of ordinary people. This is the self-control of the yogi.

382. The stream of life produces a continuous inflow of energy. When one's receptive centers are open, nothing can impede this inflow.

It is neither age nor illness, but prejudice that severs the threads of happiness. And irritability is the offspring of prejudice. One cannot free oneself from irritability without first uprooting prejudice. Continuous striving can help one to properly evaluate life's manifestations. Not renunciation, but a clear understanding of life is needed. One's pledge, like a sword of justice, should define a correct attitude.

The Teaching should be read daily, because each day provides new opportunities for its application.

383. In one's future striving, special attention will have to be paid to coordinating the development of both the spirit and the body. It is difficult for the body to keep up with the spirit; attacks of anguish can occur when the spirit races ahead to the heights.

There is another circumstance that is of no less importance, and for this reason I have asked you to refrain as much as you can from pronouncing personal names. People addressing themselves to someone at a distance impose a burden upon the person if his spirit is highly sensitive. You have noticed that yogis often change their abodes and avoid pronouncing names. This is because of their knowledge of the Teaching, which provides an understanding of the effect produced by sending names into space.

Only in the most urgent cases may one impose oneself upon other living beings. It must be understood that the growth of the spirit affects the body, and by overburdening the spirit of another we cause adverse bodily reactions. Therefore, one who is ascending in spirit should be treated with solicitude. But others show little discrimination in this. They are ready to burden the one who is growing in spirit with their most petty requests, not realizing the harm of their lightmindedness. Those who are ascending in spirit are often not in very good health.

384. It is necessary to learn to properly manage the development of one's psychic energy. It is easy to see how lack of coordination of one's forces impedes achievement. And if, at the same time, one is impatient, the achievements can then be lost altogether.

385. The Blessed One pointed out to His disciples a fakir who was throwing a ball with great skill. He hit the target every time, and two boys then hurried to pick up the ball and bring it back. The Blessed One said, "This man has attained perfection in passing on the ball; each ball that he throws is at once returned to him. So it is with each act of giving, but only when it is perfect. Therefore learn to sacrifice perfectly, for art should be present in every sacrifice."

The Blessed One also pointed to a silent man, saying, "Who can define the boundary of silence? A right word is difficult to find, but it is even more difficult to find the beauty of silence."

Thus did the Blessed One teach silent sacrifice.

386. Psychic energy needs exercising, and you see how challenging is its proper application.

It is difficult to define in words when and to what extent the disciple may make use of the Teacher's forces. Only a refined understanding will bring about the right co-measurement. There can be no precise rules defining the relationship between the Teacher and the disciple; life itself points out the necessary ways in which to follow the one path together. I can send My Ray only to those who are united.

387. Among the experiments with psychic energy there are simple and useful ones. To exercise the energy on other human beings and on animals can be dangerous, because if the object is strong it can easily return a counterblow. And if the object is weak, it is wrong and harmful to subjugate it. But there is a third group—plants—which are especially useful for experiments. An experiment with plants may require several months, but it will give the best results for the mastery of one's psychic energy.

Take several plants of the same kind and of approximately the same age. Any species can be used. Place them in the same room and observe them yourself without showing any preferences. After two months separate the plants into three groups and place them in different rooms. Be indifferent toward the first group, send your good will to the second, and send your will for destruction to the third. These transmissions should be performed at a short distance and the rhythm of *Mahavan* should be used.

It is helpful to have the length and intensity of these transmissions alternately increased and decreased every seven days. Three times daily is sufficient: morning, noon, and at sunset. In the morning the plants should be watered, adding a pinch of soda to the water. At sunset they should be watered with a solution of valerian. One may continue in this way, testing the plants but also conditioning oneself to the performance of rhythmic action. Poisonous plants should not be used for these experiments, nor should any of the families of lilies or ferns. In this way the emanations of psychic energy will be increased.

Afterward, one can demonstrate with interesting results the effect of psychic energy on water and on currents of air. But this requires the next, higher degree of tension. Thus, in daily life, without departing from Earth, many useful results can be attained.

388. Stones are no less useful than plants for experiments with psychic energy. Rhythm compels sand to form various designs. Psychic energy can produce vibrations with similar results. The ancient proverb that the will moves mountains is based on knowledge of the power of vibration.

389. Of course, imperil is the main destroyer of psychic energy. But one should not forget three other violators: fear, doubt, and self-pity. When it becomes possible to physically measure psychic energy, it will be instructive to see how these darkeners work to disrupt the flow of energy. But the flow of energy can be supported by countering efforts based upon self-sacrifice and achievement. These seemingly abstract concepts affirm the reality of the Life Principle, whose energy is cognizable and measurable.

I affirm that the fires evoked by these indicated rhythms can be intensified and also can be of service in the strengthening of one's psychic energy. The Fire of Space, like a sword, smites the darkeners.

390. The power of psychic energy will not be destructive if it is controlled in a co-measured way. Recognizing that psychic energy is a measurable substance will give rise to new thinking throughout all life.

391. Recently I sent you a Tibetan coin, and it was placed in the middle of the table under a notebook, in order that it might be found more easily. But no one thought to pick up the notebook. In the morning the maid happened to move the coin to a more noticeable spot, but even then no one noticed it until evening, when it was found by following a new Indication. Similar things often happen in accordance with the action of karma. Something is sent, but it must be recognized and accepted. So many small things clutter one's view that sent gifts remain unnoticed.

The results of karma are of two kinds—they may be connected with a particular time or they may be linked to a personality. Sometimes the karma connected with a particular time can also be linked to the personal karma. In no case, however, should one ever blame the Teacher for the karma. How can anyone have complete knowledge of all surrounding circumstances? For example, the Teacher may foresee the future of both types of karma, but if external circumstances have determined the form in which the karma will act, He cannot dissolve what has already been born in space. Its forms can be altered, but it cannot be destroyed. Here, also, a disciplined use of psychic energy can be of help, reinforcing the link between the time-related karma and the personal one.

392. Mastering one's inner fires is an effort fraught with danger. It is not easy to awaken one's inner fires; but, even after one has accomplished this, it is even more difficult to gain mastery of the multi-faceted, all-pervading fiery element. One who has realized the fires becomes responsive, resonating to the call of the flame. The earthquake that occurred yesterday provided an example of this. The heart of Sister Urusvati suffered a dangerous tremor, for earthquakes are a result of Fire. Precisely, the entire being is shaken by its encounter with fires of a quality different from one's own. But so important is the realization of Fire as a step in evolution, that I advise you to be especially careful when striving to master this element. This mastery is necessary, however, for the experience of cosmic communication.

The path of Fire is the path of attainment. This process should be carried out in calmness, without haste or irritation. We will of course help, so that outer circumstances will not be disruptive. But take care not to take signs of progress as signs of loss. Humanity prefers to see the discarding of refuse as destruction, and the beginning of construction as disorder. Therefore be careful, and act without haste. We shall point out the right times.

393. There is no obstacle that cannot be overcome by the human will. I do not say this as a consolation, or for encouragement, but as a thing immutable. People have long sharpened their wills; but they do not understand that they must attain the stage of consciousness that gives the will full authority to act, when one may say that all is permitted.

To whom can this great power be entrusted? Only to the one who will neither distort nor misuse it; to the one who is strong in consciousness; to the one who knows the Teaching. How many boast of their knowledge of the Teaching, yet do not know it! It bores them to reread the familiar words.

Just as the hunting falcon is recalled from the sky, sharpness of understanding should be summoned with a fiery call. The falcon is lured and obediently speeds down onto the gloved hand. Thus will true understanding descend upon the fire of consciousness. One cannot pass through darkness without carrying a light. Some may mockingly say, "This trivial advice is nothing new!" Yet they themselves make no attempt to light their fires. They do not even look around to discover the source of fire. They scoff at those who have found the fire. They do not even know that the fire is found not for oneself but for humanity.

But to you who have found the fire, I say, "All is permitted! You know how to leap across the abyss. Dangers are joys to you. In the words of the Teaching, fiery signs, embodying the inexpressible, flash out for you. Fire is not an abstraction, but is perceptible to the eye. This is a great treasure. Fire is the measure of the all-permissible. Fire is the sign of all-embracing trust."

394. Zeal is a necessary trait. Acceptance of Hierarchy is a precious quality.

The fog surrounding humanity is dense, but thoughts can be pushed through it in unexpected ways. It is much easier to build the structure of the Teaching out of separate pieces, like a mosaic. A direct, linear sequence of ideas should not be demanded. The fragments are added according to changing circumstances.

One should not coerce others, nor should one even try to persuade them. One may only suggest, strengthening it with the cement of feeling. But of course fiery feeling may not always be present.

395. All people have their particular gifts. Out of these often contrasting elements, a picture of special importance emerges.

396. In the West much is said about the transmission of thought to a distance, but the application of this action is absolutely unknown. For instance, in order to prove it, two stations are established that must work simultaneously; and the distance between them is calculated, as if the power of thought could be affected by miles! The most essential part of the experiment is overlooked, namely, the effect of the thought.

You know that My answers take different lengths of time to reach you because of the influence of magnetic and atmospheric conditions. Can a difference of a few minutes have any influence on the effect of a thought? Yet, according to the Western approach, the experiment would be considered unsuccessful.

The West ignores the effects of thought because it seeks only statistical calculation. But scientific research will in the future note the correlation between dissemination of thought and surrounding physical conditions.

The development of thought will permit many new methods, depending on the various waves. One may notice that thought can seem to leap, like a stone thrown flat that glances off the surface of the waves. In this way, the thought reaches unexpected places. The dissemination of thought places responsibility upon the thinker.

When we have learned to find joy in the new breadth of this responsibility, we will appreciate the importance of thought and will learn to investigate its laws. Many sensitive apparatuses will make it possible to determine the effects of thoughts. Thus, one more treasure will be extracted out of chaos.

397. In studying thought transmission, humanity will pay attention to all attendant manifestations, both beneficial and negative. Then people will see that the effects of thought spread beyond imagining. They will understand how much harm they can cause, weakening and overburdening one another's forces. One of the purposes of going into a hermitage was to hide, in order to preserve one's psychic energy. One of Our good co-workers had himself reported dead, in order to escape the attention of others. As though unburdened, he used to say, with relief, "It seems that I have been forgotten."

Under these circumstances, one is able to observe how thoughts—other than the impersonal thoughts of space—fly past. But impersonal thoughts usually contain no harm. I do not say that one should renounce personal thoughts, but full responsibility for them must be accepted. A more strict life for children would be an outward way of teaching such responsibility. A knowledge of reincarnation would also be helpful. But existing conditions of government and religion severely impede the development of such responsibility.

Without prejudice, and observing all one's surroundings, one will reach the conclusion that Our methods are quite different from conventional ways. Life must be directed towards the element of fire, but this cannot be accomplished by the conventional methods of government. You know that introducing the "supernatural" into the ordinary does not mar life, but adds beauty and vastness to it.

398. A proper relationship between the impulsiveness of the individuality and the infallibility of natural law is the golden mean, which gleams in the depth of each expanded consciousness.

How many useful observations can be conducted even without advanced apparatuses! Will not a comparison between atmospheric conditions and the condition of humanity provide a key for the reasonable deliberations of rulers? Will not magnetic storms provoke changes in social order? Sunspots, the full moon, the passing by of heavenly bodies, and many other powerful conditions affect the basic functioning of sensitive organisms. Even plants and animals react to cosmic phenomena. Is it possible that humanity, the ruler, is not worthy of attention?

Even the effects of earthquakes and meteors on human behavior are not studied. In addition to an investigation of the physical composition of meteors, is it not important to observe their effects on the psychic energy of masses of people?

Know how to discern the influence of subterranean gases, of which there are far more than is usually believed. Unfortunately, the policemen of science pay attention only to the crude and obvious occurrences, while more important and widespread effects are disregarded.

Observing the psychic energy of humanity is more important than measuring humidity or temperature. Human mental power deserves more careful consideration.

399. Our way of teaching is usually attacked from two sides. The adherents of the old cannot forgive Us for Our interest in contemporary Western science.

Those who follow only Western ways cannot forgive Our reverence for the Ancient Wisdom of the East.

The language of symbols has been forgotten by the West. When the West hears about a heavenly dragon it smiles. But when we speak about the Serpent Solaris, or the solar plexus, then the smile fades. When the Serpent Solaris manifests itself as the serpent of the solar plexus, a fiction becomes a physiological fact. When the serpent of the solar plexus awakens, all four realms of heaven become accessible. The symbolism of the Ancient Wisdom is based on the correspondences between Macrocosm and microcosm. Therefore, look for the human being, with all his possibilities, in even the most abstract images.

In the West can be encountered many conventional expressions, but this does not prevent one from knowing their true meaning. For this one has only to expel narrowness of thinking.

Often We hear complaints that the Teaching is impracticable. Usually those people complain who make no real attempt to apply the Teaching. Can a medicine that is still sealed give relief? In any case, not many can claim a deep knowledge of the Teaching. Either their understanding is limited by their antiquated way of thinking, or they read it in bits and pieces without connecting them. One should first apply the Teaching before judging it. Light-mindedness is a world-wide failing!

400. Why does support of the Teaching often come so timidly and apologetically? Of course, because the problems of existence are of no interest to most of humanity. The questions of existence have no place in their everyday life. Anything unusual is seen by them as an aberration of nature. Their understanding of nature's laws is forged by cowardice. Fetishes and taboos, as before, still stand as overseers of humanity, and teachings of life are constrained by conventional science or are suffocated by the incense of temples.

Attention should at last be paid to all that surrounds us, especially now, when cosmic processes are in a state of extraordinary tension. The sensitive apparatuses of our own organisms are in an equally tense state. The tension of the atmosphere prompts people to turn with care and sincerity to the cosmic forces. One should not mock when one does not know enough about what one is mocking. One may as well laugh at the formulas of higher mathematics because they do not help one to cook dinner!

We do not regret wasting time repeating truisms, for even truisms can be useful for the turning of humanity toward psychic energy. It is absurd that man must be persuaded to utilize a power that has long been his. It is the mentality of a savage, who fears everything that was unknown to his grandfather. In spite of all this, spatial thought has its effect!

401. Soulless repetition destroys the Teaching. Also, the quality of rhythm must be understood. Of course, every crystal functions according to the principles of attraction and pulsation. But pulsation—or rhythm—is characteristic of the living principle. However, any given rhythm may be more or less alive or dead. Living rhythms, spiritualized by the power of consciousness, will produce varying combinations of subtle energies. But the rhythm of the lips' soulless repetitions results only in a dead beat that violates the wisdom of silence and brings only harm. Beware of repetitions devoid of spirit! Truly, they dissolve the most precious gems of the spirit. If one's action is based only on fear or greed, then even a skeleton or a military drummer could rap out a more useful rhythm.

Can one expect a manifestation of fire from the raps of the tail of a dog awaiting a bone? Remember this when you are dealing with the finest energies, when you intend to approach and awaken the manifestation of Fire.

When I taught you the rhythms of the Fire of Space, I of course had in mind the application of a spiritual consciousness and a striving without base motives. Long ago it was told about the two fires: the creative fire and the destructive one. While the first shines and warms and exalts, the second sears and reduces to ashes. But I directed you only to the creative fire. You have seen for yourself how the perception of fire occurs. Even daylight could not prevent you from seeing the messengers of space. And the stars were surrounded by signs. One must treasure these fiery signs and learn to collect the best offerings of the consciousness.

Not blows of a fist, nor threats, but light-winged ascent carries one to the Gates. Beware of soulless routine!

402. Still another enemy threatens the Teaching—distrust, which destroys the almost-achieved, the most important. It is astonishing to see how unable people are to cope with what is new to them! Their self-respect is so limited, and their imagination so impoverished, that people are usually afraid to even think that something out of the ordinary could exist. It is always easier to deny than to investigate. Be destroyed, all ye who deny! Without your narrow thinking the sun will shine the brighter and the stronghold of knowledge will be raised the higher.

How offensive it is to see petty, grey distrust, with not even a sign of daring! Distrust thrives upon refuse. We always insist that knowledge be gained through experience. We affirm how slowly abilities grow and positive results accumulate. But We consider it inadmissible that a rational person would discard opportunities for gaining knowledge. How often people base the acquiring of knowledge upon material rewards! This is the way little children under seven tend to act.

One may occasionally see how a person who has come close to the Teaching and gained wonderful possibilities still continues to dream about some meager reward.

Let us preserve the Teaching as the greatest joy of existence!

403. It is essential not to mislead newcomers into thinking that the Teaching of Agni Yoga is easy. Truly, it is not easy, for there is much tension and danger in it. No one should be seduced by the idea of honeyed ease. Gaining mastery of the fires is a slow process. Premature and hasty steps threaten the striving one with conflagration. What seemed to be a high achievement is later seen as low, when one is on the next step.

You know how difficult it is to see *Fohat*, how the cumulative efforts of many years are required for one to be able to see this energy. But what will a weak spirit say when he learns that beyond *Fohat* is *Para-Fohat*, which in turn is nourished by *Pan-Fohat*! These energies can fill only the strongest consciousness with rejoicing and with love.

Few are the trusted builders who with self-denial accept the thoughts coming from space into the chalice of their hearts. They are not frightened of being scorched by the fires of the far-off worlds. They do not resent bearing the burden of anguish caused by surrounding imperfection. They are approached by the super-radiant fires of space and exchange thought with the sparks of spatial consciousness, silently kindling thoughts and answering questions. Weighty is the protective canopy of blessing, but it alone provides entrance into the highest Abode.

The ancient teachings use symbols of construction to represent the entrusted task. Their true meaning should be understood. Around an Agni Yogi you will always find construction, whose very difficulties are stepping stones in the overcoming of imperfection. Manifestations of Light are not easy to achieve, but then the Fire of Space illumines the far-off worlds.

Do not bring weak ones near, for they cannot hold on to the treasure. It is better to entrust the task only to those few who will be able to make right decisions for correct action. They will learn to love the difficulties and will not betray.

404. In the West there have appeared many self-proclaimed yogis, magicians, teachers, hypnotists, and occultists, who make use of phenomena produced by the will. Brilliantly multiplying their coins, they teach people, for a fee, how to improve their material condition; how to induce others to trust them; how to win influence in society; how to gain success in business; how to compel others to obey their orders; how to turn life into a rose garden. In teaching others to develop the will, some of these teachers may seem to be following a good path, but because they do not indicate any goal in this journey, they serve only to worsen the already ugly conditions of life.

Is not a powerful will that works to reinforce old prejudices a true horror? How much energy will have to be spent on these neo-occultists in order to counter the harm of their corrupted spirituality! The imitators of Hatha Yogis are the least harmful of them.

First of all, the Teaching is never sold; that is a most ancient law. The Teaching offers perfection as the goal; without this, it would have no future. The Teaching pays no attention to personal comfort; otherwise it would be egoism. The Teaching advocates the beautifying of existence, which otherwise would be submerged in ugliness. The Teaching is always self-denying, because it knows the true meaning of the Common Good. The Teaching reveres knowledge; otherwise it would be darkness. The Teaching is manifested in life not through invented ceremonies, but on the basis of experience. I consider that the way of the Teaching has nothing to do with the husks of outworn ways.

Joy is a special wisdom.

405. Psychic energy must not be used for performing miracles, but should be for the highest manifestation of pure reason.

406. Think about the meaning of danger. So-called danger is nothing but fear for one's present condition. But if we know that every condition is created by the consciousness, which is inalienable, then there can be no fear for one's well-being. The dangers that one customarily fears are dispelled by a broadened consciousness. Therefore, the growth of consciousness is the essential foundation for progress. Then there will be no dangers, there will be only obstacles. Overcoming obstacles is a means for the developing of energy. If the mountain is perfectly smooth, one cannot ascend to the summit. Blessed are the stones that tear the sandals of those who ascend! Assure yourself, therefore, that dangers do not exist.

Each step in the growth of consciousness is an explosion. But out of explosions is built the pulsation of the Cosmos.

Poor is the consciousness that has no control over passing emotions. Invulnerability is Our Shield. Each speck of fear is a target for an enemy's arrow. After washing away these shameful specks, we become as invulnerable as are the far-off worlds. The development of Agni Yoga becomes a shield of thought. The all-penetrating Fire, when realized, endows one with supremely pure strength and replenishes the source of renewal.

407. Do not give in to thoughts of sorrow. Such thoughts are like rust on a conqueror's sword. There can be no sorrow near the fiery crucible of life. If you read the *Puranas* in their dead letter, even this book of great wisdom will seem like a cemetery to you. But where there is fire there can be no sorrow.

To observe the life of space is to gain knowledge; it is a partaking in the life of the Cosmos. Human life cannot be separate from the laws of psychic energy. It is equally absurd to suppress one's own consciousness. One cannot remain without water even for a day. It is likewise difficult for the consciousness to survive without the light from far-off worlds. Thinking about the grandeur of life can become as necessary as food or drink.

The Teaching, based on experience, brings to each thinker the joy of application. Do not limit that which is immeasurably great and close to the active consciousness. Do not constrict within preset limits that which comes down to us as the Breath of the Mother of the World. Let us say how joyful it is to serve the cause of renewal without fear of taking the wrong path. Beginning with the most obvious and tangible, following the immutable laws, let us apply our best efforts to the Teaching of Life.

Neither a day nor an hour should pass without applying the Teaching. Safeguard the Yoga as the way of Light, knowing how bountiful are the sparks of its Radiance! We will not sever the bond but will sustain it.

As the sun is untiring, so shall Agni be inextinguishable!

The fire of Kundalini permits no indirect ways!

Consciousness is the divine energy!

408. Three mice approached a hermit, encouraged by his motionlessness. He addressed each one in turn:

"You live in the flour. It provides enough food for all your tribe, yet you did not become more generous.

"You have chosen to live amidst many books, and have gnawed through great numbers of them, yet you did not grow wiser.

"You have lived amidst sacred objects, yet did not become more spiritual.

"Verily, mice, you could be human. Just like people, you debase the treasures that are given to you."

Three lions then came to the hermit. He addressed each one in turn:

"You have just now killed a traveler who was hastening to his family.

"You have robbed a blind woman of her only sheep.

"You have destroyed the steed of an important messenger.

"Lions, you could be human. Brandish your terrifying manes and wage war, but do not be surprised if you find people to be even more cruel than yourselves."

Three doves came flying to the hermit. He addressed each one in turn:

"You have consumed grain not your own and have considered it yours.

"You have consumed a healing plant, yet are revered as a sacred bird.

"You have wrongfully nested in a temple and, taking advantage of the superstition of others, have enticed them to feel obliged to feed you.

"Verily, doves, you could be humans. Making use of the superstition and bigotry of others will plentifully feed you."

409. The Teacher instructs you not to condemn people for their vices, but to point out their similarities with animal behavior. This can help those with insufficiently developed minds.

Admittedly, many animals are more sensitive to psychic energy than people. People pride themselves on their intellect, but why does their intellect not stay their vile deeds?

410. It is most important to explore untried paths. One should not avoid palaces and limit oneself to old hovels. It would be equally narrow-minded to stay in palace chambers, avoiding the hovels. Do not limit yourself.

411. Each leaf safeguards the well-being of man. Each stone stands ready to ensure man's safety. Kindle the fires of unlimited knowledge. Find the wisdom to courageously strive.

412. I value each of your good moods. One can build only with good stones.

The Teacher rejoices when He can provide a new set of circumstances. One has only to remember that a new beginning will sometimes seem disorderly. People see little difference between happiness and unhappiness, success and failure, joy and sorrow.

413. Placing the Teacher's seat in the most revered spot in the home is not a superstition. This is the place for the One invited to the Holy Supper. He may arrive at any moment, and it should be made clear to Him that He was awaited. This constant mark of expectancy and readiness is like a call through an open window. Amidst constructions and battles, let us spare enough time for a fleeting smile.

The Teaching grows spirally, just as does all that exists. Blessed are those who understand the spiral nature of the Fire. The tip of the flame was represented by the ancient ones as a flattened spiral.

The element of Fire expresses with special vividness the principle of motion. Can you affirm that you are practicing Agni Yoga if you have not even realized the birth of the inner fire?

Pure striving produces flashes of fire. One has to observe these beginnings and the conditions that accompany them. For this purpose a true ability to observe keenly should be developed. It is not easy to achieve the ability to observe. The conditions aiding these fiery manifestations are different for each individual: cold or heat, sound or silence, light or darkness, all such opposites can produce equal results.

A multitude of circumstances must be examined. If people who have achieved the kindling of the inner fire would write down their observations about it, they would greatly help many beginners. The common work for humanity requires first of all the protection of individuality. And when all the many ways of kindling the inner fire have been found, the simplest way proves to be the quickest. It is astonishing to see what supposedly insignificant circumstances can help to ignite the flame. One such, which is always present, is a sensitivity to shocks. A straight position of the spine is also of great importance in this. But in the case of chronic curvature of the spine, musk can be used to help ignite the flame. The absorption of musk interacts with phosphorus, which restores the impeded flow of fire.

414. The Teaching of Agni Yoga demands continuous ardor. Sometimes respite from outer fiery manifestations is needed, but the inner flame is never extinguished. The ever-burning inner fire is pointed out in many Teachings as a step on the path of realization. One should accustom oneself to the manifestation of ever-present fire. An indication from without can never provide a true impetus. The inner flame burns like a bonfire. It is unworthy to suppress it.

The igniting of the fire will call forth a multitude of small phenomena and evoke an interest in fascinating experiments. A teaching can indicate the direction, but should not bind one with lifeless ritual. Remember that the decline of the most significant mystery schools began when their rites became overly complicated and lost their spark of life. A true teaching must live as freely as the Fire of Space.

415. Refine, refine the co-workers! Stagnation is the greatest danger for productive human work. A broad consciousness is needed to maintain the rhythm of action. When the moment for action arrives, people are distracted by irrelevant thoughts, and as a result they send against a tiger an arrow fit for a sparrow. This is not only a lack of goal-fitness, but also a loss of concentration. Is not one who has deprived himself of the power of concentration lower than a beast?

He who is spiritually inert cannot be an Arhat. The Teacher sometimes speaks of the need for rest, but never says that rest may become equal to that of a moribund spirit. One who imposes such limitations on himself can neither hear nor see.

We are told about motionless Arhats, but you must know that their stillness is only external. Many people are pleased when they can find excuses for their inertia. Any call to action disrupts their leisurely state of mind. Can such people be allowed to approach the element of fire, which in its very nature requires vigilance? Fire is like a scherzo, a fugue. But glowing embers are like an andante. Of course, the many kinds of flame all have different rhythms, but an Agni Yogi will never be an unresponsive sluggard.

416. Each era chooses its new, corresponding Teaching, when all previous Teachings have become distorted. People tend to cling to these twisted distortions of the faith of their forefathers, yet no new Teaching ever excludes preceding ones. Little attention is paid to this fact, for the followers of every Teaching like to build their success on denial of the previous Teachings. But it is easy to prove the continuity of what people call religion. In this continuity is sensed a single stream of one energy. Calling it psychic energy, we speak of the Sophia of the Hellenic world or *Sarasvati* of the Hindus. The Holy Ghost of the Christians manifests signs of psychic energy, just as do the creative Adonai of Israel, and Mithra of Persia, full of solar power. Certainly, no one doubts that the Fire of Zoroaster is the Fire of Space, which you now study.

Psychic energy is both Fire and *Materia Matrix*, and the Teaching of Agni Yoga is nothing other than an explanation of today's application of energy, the stream of which is approaching with *Satya Yuga*. This is not a new awakening of heretofore dormant possibility, but an enlightenment spread over time. I say, the Teaching cannot be given for money, nor can it be imposed; it heralds the New Era. One can ignore it or deny it, but its heralding is inescapable.

The coming era can be understood properly or in a distorted way, but its approach is undeniable. One can destroy in an instant what took centuries to build, but such madness can only beget madness. And are they not mad who would try to live without a mind? What mind is not nurtured by psychic energy? Why search for the source in the darkness of unconsciousness,

214

when one can easily ignite the inextinguishable spark within and approach the source in full consciousness?

417. The Teaching about the Redeemers is relevant to everything that exists. For example, it is possible to influence and approach others by use of teraphs, and in a similar way, but by use of the consciousness, to take upon oneself the karma of others. During simple experiments in this, you observed that you were able to take over the pain of others when their nerves were afflicted. Similarly, it is possible to take on oneself someone else's karma, and ultimately, one could take upon oneself the collective karma of a people. Thus would the concept of a Redeemer become a reality. It would of course be necessary to determine the goal-fitness of such a responsible task.

Karma is a most complex process. From the most casual, superficial action to the deepest level of motives, everything is varied in form and color. One should firmly ponder when it is possible and deserving to interfere in the karma of others. One can imagine cases of self-sacrificing and beneficial interference in the destiny of others. By the fires can the goal-fitness of interference be determined. The fires are the best indicators for this decision, since in them the inner consciousness is combined with the spatial consciousness. And nothing is equal to them in vitality; they are many-colored milestones, the product of a full understanding of surrounding conditions. You see how two abstract concepts, the Redeemers and the Fire of Space, become real for you!

418. The Teaching does not exist outside of life. The Teacher does not come from outside of life. In order to treat different problems of the spirit in the co-workers, We apply various methods. It is not appropriate to apply one remedy for all sicknesses. Also, We do not reject something of evident value just because of one not yet eradicated ugly trait.

419. We know about teraphs. We know that a teraph can be astral or material. The astral teraph is higher than the material one, just as the astral world is higher than the material world. Only very developed beings can have an astral teraph, whereas material teraphs can serve any conscious spirit. The teraph is a model of an actual event or thing. A navigator can more easily understand the behavior of his ship by studying a model of the vessel. Looking at the image, people, in a way, come into contact with what is absent. Even humble fortunetellers request first of all an image or an item closely connected with the subject. These objects direct their psychic energy, in order to increase its effect, like a beacon or a milestone.

With material teraphs, one must have a special image for every need. But the astral teraph has the advantage of serving all needs and of taking on different appearances as required. Therefore it is like a milestone, marking one's steps in the development of consciousness. The astral teraph is a product of the crystallization of psychic energy, just as the material one is a product of physical effort. The chief action takes place during the creation of the teraph, for it is then that the psychic energy is most tense. Even though the astral teraph is superior, We can describe the technique of creating a material one.

420. The material teraph was usually made as a sculpted image, by using any object to which was added something belonging to a person referred to in the ritual. Often, after the death of the owner of the teraph, it was put into the tomb, as in ancient Egypt and in the burial monuments of the Mayans and Etruscans.

When the funeral rites required cremation, the teraph followed into the fire.

In the Temple of Israel there was a general teraph for all uses, but for each ritual something belonging to the subject was placed under the teraph. Eventually, in the various countries there were scattered a multitude of teraphs, each one filled with the accumulations of many psychic transmissions. It is curious to observe the continued vitality of these accumulations of psychic energy. One can truly see that teraphs retain their power over thousands of years, like a seed that lives, manifesting undying power.

Of the experiments with psychic energy, the test demonstrating that it cannot be dispersed or destroyed is very important. The teraph is the best proof of this, especially if the aid of clairvoyance is available to the experimenter.

It is possible to make a teraph that carries an instruction whose effects will be known only in the future. The teraph can carry the message either to a particular person, or to someone else who will later own the teraph. Two things should be known—that the preparation of the teraph requires much time, and that much time is also needed for its effects to be revealed. The teaching about teraphs comes from great antiquity, when the Atlanteans knew about psychic energy.

How to make a teraph? A place must be used where the maker's psychic energy has saturated the space and has accumulated upon the objects in it. In this place a chosen image is molded out of wax, clay, or plaster. When the image has been created, it is then covered with a silver, crystal, or glass dome, or a leather cover.

421. During the rituals of saturating the teraph, as you know, chants were intoned, combinations of strange words often devoid of meaning. However, it is not the spoken form, but the rhythm that is important. The music of the spheres consists not of melodies but of rhythms. When the developed spirit knows the sounds of the spheres, it will understand the power of rhythm. So, while saturating the teraph the will and rhythm are the most important. It matters not with what words the mission is entrusted to the teraph. Important are the succession of the layers of meaning, the sincerity of the direct transmission, and the rhythm, which corresponds to *Mahavan*. Only the lesser consciousness needs ready-made commands. The developed consciousness can improvise words in accordance with the flow of psychic energy.

It is unnecessary to constrain oneself with memorized words. It is better to be imbued with rhythm, when each muscle merges in striving with the nerves. One vibrates as an integral whole, and the power of command is transferred by laying the hands upon the teraph. One should be imbued by a single-minded striving when creating a teraph. One should charge the teraph not less than three times daily.

In order to better invest the teraph with the power of your will, do not make its surface too highly polished. It is effective to cover it with a fabric and to burn resinous essences near it. Eucalyptus is good for this.

422. To simplify or to complicate? Even a child will prefer the former. When dealing with rituals one could choose the complicated way, utilizing all the finest shades of meaning of sound and color, but this way would be old and inflexible. The techniques of accumulation of sound and color are many. But when the most complicated mechanisms are invented, do not their creators then search for ways to simplify? So it is with the application of psychic energy. The majority

218

has completely forgotten about this energy; the minority has taken its use to the point of cold fanaticism. But Fire, as the foundation of psychic energy, has no relation to cold!

Agni Yoga directs humanity to the simplest ways. One exalted impulse of a Bhakti outdistances the slower Jnani. So also does the kindling of fire impel one to the correct destination. Fire refines the centers and develops a sensitivity that knows the right direction, just as the finest vessels are shaped in fire. In the casting of the best images the old mold is destroyed. And these images will be loftier than those made with the old form.

Therefore We bid humanity kindle the fires of striving and achievement simply. This panacea deprives no one of anything, and it can be discovered through study. The manifestations of light are embryos of fire. They are the rudiments of forms that often remain undeveloped.

423. What is the relation between physical musk and the phosphorus of spirit? Musk is also the product of fire, but of an unconscious fire. Yet, even the crystal produced by unconscious fire contains the treasure.

Is not the pure Fire of Space a living link with the higher worlds? Will not this simple question arise in the unprejudiced consciousness? And if we see the teraph as a repository of psychic energy, this concept, though ancient, will be easy to understand. So let us not be afraid to open a Pandora's box; for the enlightened traveler its gifts may appear quite different.

424. The measure of success is the degree of necessity. You may be sure that one would not leap across an abyss without absolute necessity. The more unavoidable the necessity, the nearer is the step of victory. Let the most dire necessity arise!

The measure of understanding is the degree of love. One can memorize lines word by word, yet one remains dead if the knowledge has not been warmed by love.

Truly, when one learns to discern the emanations of feeling in others, one will perceive that precisely love above all attracts the Fire of Space. He who said, "Love one another," was a true Yogi. Therefore We welcome each outburst of love and self-sacrifice. Just as a lever sets the wheels in motion, so does love inspire powerful responses. Compared with the radiance of love, hatred is only a hideous blot. For love is the true reality and treasure.

I do not speak about love abstractly but as a physiologist. I consider that as necessity is the impetus, so love is the enlightener.

425. Whence come the application and the action of the fire of *Kundalini*? From the same source—the fire of love. The image of the essence that is projected on Our screens reveals the truth. How joyous it is to see the waves of growing fire! It is like an enchanted garden.

I love it when the fire of love radiates so much that one can overcome any obstacle!

426. Humanity has often needlessly remade its garments. It either shortened them to an extreme, or lengthened its already dragging trains. Sleeves trailed on the ground or disappeared entirely. Either upper part was exaggeratedly large or the lower part was made immense. As if it mattered in what style of sleeve one seized one's neighbor by the throat! The change of fashion was in vain.

Let us take things as they are. Let us remember not to destroy enthusiasm, no matter whence it comes. Let us not hide the truth, but let us find a place for each exaltation. Can exaltation hinder great measures? Everything will find its place. To build upon exaltation is easier and more lasting. As does love, so also does enthusiasm kindle the fires. Let us gather all those who carry the fire, and remember how precious is each spark. Light and darkness—let us not forget anything created of Light!

We offer life-givers from the plant kingdom, but do not reject all that lies ignored within yourselves.

427. As little as people have gained from changing their clothing styles, so little have they gained from acquiring the comforts of life. The basic requirements for comfort necessitate an improvement of physical conditions and a simplification of the details of everyday life. But quite the contrary, people try to complicate things and reject each possibility of expanding the consciousness. It is no exaggeration to say that society does not tolerate any growth of consciousness. Families are destroyed and kingdoms perish when consciousnesses expand and manifest themselves. The Teaching of Life, like an orphan, seeks shelter in some out-of-the-way place, while the parades of death thunder in the public squares.

Let them not think that We are spouting outworn metaphors. Even the most narrow-minded people can see danger in the specter of an overabundance of objects. Of course, if one continues life according to familiar ways, then material overconsumption is inevitable. Only goal-fitting simplification can bring dignity to life and safeguard natural resources. One has no right to destroy the results of millenniums of cosmic effort, light-mindedly expecting some new, undeserved energy!

One has to prepare oneself for each new energy. Every expectant mother thinks about her future child.

How then can one not think about the energy that lives within each of us? One has to think about one's innate possibilities.

428. Following the time of Atlantis, in the rites of the Druids, while all the rest walked in a circle following the dawn-to-dusk movement of the sun, the chief priest performing the rite walked in the opposite direction. In this was contained the symbol of lesser and greater knowledge. Lesser knowledge is developed by following the flow of known energies, but great knowledge, facing the current of cosmic forces, extracts previously-unknown energies from what appears to be chaos. So in the cults of the sun, the steps of human ascent were wisely indicated. As you know, these were not abstract symbols but a reflection of reality; for example, the centers rotating against the sun produce special fiery energies.

429. It is astonishing to see how people spoil their own lives without reason or sense by depriving themselves of possibilities that are theirs by right. It is astonishing to see how readily people diminish boundaries expanded over lifetimes.

We say that it is better to act in error than to commit the error of inaction. Daring in action contains in itself its own justification; it applies pressure that multiplies the energy. Is it possible to ignite the flaming spirit through inaction? By pointing out the necessity for joining with Us in action, We draw you into the spiral of this special pressure. Truly, in this spiral one can only ascend; it must be protected as a dynamo of the most precious energy. We call you to come with Us, not out of desire to control you or to make you feel less important, but out of desire to strengthen and uplift you through beneficial actions.

Fire, Fire, descend on those who out of space draw thy streams! For them the firmament above is as substantial as the depths of Earth. For them air is as substantial as stone, and stone is a conduit as transparent as air.

Those who are with Me, walk with Us through the waves of Fire. They will not scorch you, but will serve the Good!

430. Just before the most significant events, people are particularly prone to deny the possibilities of the future. One could write a curious history about the precursors and thresholds of events. Thus one can trace similarities in the tendencies of thought connected with the cyclones of disturbances. The blind deride the advice of those who see, and the earthly know-it-alls point out the impossibility of change in the existing order, saying that all is stable and unchangeable, and that those who are more sensitive are nothing but liars. If one points out to them that no good can come from torpor, they become one's enemies. But it is necessary to know such enemies.

431. The recognition of Hierarchy is not a formal discipline, but a conscious cooperation. Once the spirit realizes that it has joined an endless chain of "dynamos," it receives a special right to move onward. However, just as oarsmen must follow the directions of the helmsman, so must the admitted co-workers follow the call of the Teacher. One must think in every way about economy of energy.

Our own Leaders have entrusted to Us the vessel to quench the conflagrations of evil, and We relay this mission to chosen emissaries, entrusting to them the task of further transmission. Recognition of Hierarchy facilitates movement into the Infinite.

The laws of matter are immutable. Just as the pump and the fountain are bound to work together, so are the two worlds, whose boundaries are transcended and illumined by the omnipresent Fire.

It would be a mistake to see My words as poetic hymns. One must accept them as the call of the Builder, to whom it is not important to be the Highest One, but to whom it is important to fulfill the mission entrusted by the Lords.

432. The Teacher knows the best hour. A special knowledge is needed for Us to provide an understanding of the flow of outer currents without violating your karma. The Indications, like arrows, must surround the target, not piercing the center of the circle, which belongs to each of you. The lack of clarity is like a mist. However, it is not a sign of ignorance, but of Our caring. We wish you to be successful, but this is possible only with your cooperation.

433. One can strengthen the effect of one's actions by saturating space. This can be done by projecting one's personal will; but an expanded consciousness will intensify one's sendings by linking them with the consciousness of the Teacher. The expanded consciousness never regrets the past, because each new moment is broader than one's entire past. Likewise, such a consciousness does not yearn for places visited in the past, because each new place, illumined by consciousness, is more beautiful than the old. Thus, the realization of a new and beautiful place, together with knowing one's Teacher, is a guarantee of new creation.

Can there be any path more beautiful than that of building the foundation for the stronghold of the Teaching of Life? The Star shows the way. Walk unwaveringly!

Urusvati saw the so-called Wheel of Buddha. This is actually the teraph of the far-off worlds. Its essence is contained in the foundation of the Universe, which may be seen as a pestle. At its ends are the spheres of polarity corresponding to the two basic laws. At the center is the swastika-like wheel of psychic energy. And the circle of the whirling rainbow is the manifestation of all stages of Spatial Fire. Knowing this is a step toward the mastery of fire; by visualizing this structure the approach of fire can be evoked, and its dangerous essence transformed into a healing property.

The teraph from the far-off worlds has been made real by Urusvati; this required a great expenditure of energy. The main aim was to bring it to life, for it to become a harmonized part of her aura. After this was accomplished, a short rest was needed. Then, the inner tasks could be given to her immediately. Urusvati is Radhastana, who has breached the boundary between the two worlds.

434. One is told in all ancient Teachings, "Do not turn thy back to the Teacher." This command can be understood either slavishly or reverently. Conscious reverence is like a flower of light. One cannot order it; only an expanded consciousness will enable one to experience reverence for spiritual values. How to describe to the blind an entire stony slope? How to alert the deaf with a warning call? Only the experience of life will show the meaning of the command, "Do not turn thy back to the Teacher."

435. The joy is not in the traditional order of things, but in the finding of new ways. The sensitive eye discerns the benefit of the new. It is not a mistake for the one who is perceptive to be rewarded.

It is instructive to observe how people fight

225

everything that is unusual to them. We possess remarkable records of how people destroyed all unusual signs. What selfless dedication to destruction! Such signs, prepared with care, are the salvation of humanity.

All followers of old ways have even outwardly the same uniform nature, like the sands of the desert!

Our Rays can strongly restrain this human destructiveness. But how few are those who recognize the urgency of conditions!

436. There are many co-workers, but it is necessary to evaluate the extent of their devotion. Striving toward Us is often tainted by a proportionate expectation of reward. But how can one ask for reward when participation in Our work is in itself a reward?

From intensification of one's forces comes their growth. From alertness comes the light of experience. From pursuit of one's goal comes increase of energy. Observe how conditions are molded so that at moments of extreme need unusual new circumstances appear. The inexperienced will call them accidental, but those who know will recognize the spiral of creation.

I believe that consideration of Our Rules can be helpful in any undertaking. There is no venture that cannot be embraced by the Teaching of Light.

Striving toward Us should be expressed in the quality of every action. One should not ask for Our Advice if it has already been given. One should not make confusing any Advice that can be understood simply and be made a customary part of everyday life. Become firm in your desire never to be separated from Us.

437. Each new condition of the body is like a new location in which one has not yet found one's proper place.

People think that there can be times without danger; but even those who sleep in a field can be hit on the head by a meteorite. One should understand all the danger of earthly existence.

Today We looked into Our mirrors. I saw surface agitation in the disciples' auras. Let us be firm in the coming new year, because all is growing. Yesterday's measures are too small for future problems. The pure heart produces a clear picture, but surface agitation indicates a new growth in consciousness. The period of shaping new conditions must be gone through, without confusion, desire, or irritation. There is much tension in space, and it can be oppressive for the human aura.

438. The so-called command of the will is a sending of psychic energy, which, as a product of the fiery element, strikes the weaker radiations by fiery encirclement. This means that for the strengthening of the aura not only a pure consciousness is needed; one must also attract the Fire of Space.

The dove was considered the symbol of purity, the serpent the symbol of wisdom, and the lion the symbol of the fire of fearlessness. The Fire of Space fills man with manifest courage, free of attachment to any passing condition. The element of fire is the most impelling one. When it is realized, one finds no joy in reliving the past. One who has realized the all-penetrating Fire will easily see that We commune through fire.

The Teachers never had many disciples. One can remember the small number—sixteen, or twelve, or even fewer. This confirms with what difficulty the Fire of Space is approached and assimilated. But, for the saturation of space, Fire is a vital necessity. He who can think about psychic energy must know about the

Fire of Space. It would be foolish to assume that the element of fire is somewhere outside of us and that its realization can be lazily postponed. No, fire rages around us! One can have it as one's friend or one's enemy.

439. It will not be difficult in the near future to achieve projection of the astral body as a common ability. It will not be difficult to learn to control random projections of the astral body, which occur more often than one would think. The Teaching assumes full use of all one's available abilities. Why, then, do people ignore the possibility of utilizing the subtle body in life? The teaching about the subtle body is very ancient. The activity of the subtle body is not thought about in the physical life, but its projection nevertheless does take place. This means that all progress will depend upon the level of understanding and experience. Of course, as in psychic experiments, one should not be hasty where two states of being are involved. For many thousands of years people have separated these two states; therefore, their harmonization should be worked out goal-fittingly. In life itself one should develop a feeling of connection with these two different states. Man himself should realize that he can annex the subtle body to his daily physical life. Gradually, then, he will observe the manifestation of the astral body. When the physical body is kept immobile, it should not be touched or disturbed, and should be left in silence. When the sight is directed inward one should not bring light near or change the temperature. These conditions are not at all difficult and can be established by common agreement. For a long time the subtle body will be independent of the intellect, but then it will enter into harmony with the higher consciousness. This is not just an experiment; it is a re-attraction of those forces that have been driven away by the intellect. But the intellect, too, must take the next step of ascent. One can thus quite simply direct oneself toward higher levels of existence.

There is no doubt that narcotics and meats are obstacles to the harmonizing of the physical and astral bodies. But certainly there is no room for coercion in this, for all harmonizing efforts must proceed in co-measurement.

440. The chief obstacle is that people insist on choosing uniform methods for achieving particular results, whereas it is precisely the means of achievement that must always be individual. The easiest way for one is the most difficult for another. A nation's structures are based on uniformity of execution, and this is why its best possibilities perish. The desired results must firmly be insisted on, but their attainment should be left to the individual.

One can note in the history of humanity a few short periods when the course of events took a happy turn. One may be certain that just at such times individual ways of action were encouraged.

441. Experienced sailors look at the sea in two ways. They distinguish two currents: one, visible at the surface, is of no importance; the other, below the surface, and not easily discernible, has real power and offers either safety or peril.

It is difficult to turn one's attention away from the foam of events and to perceive the most important currents. How much energy would be saved if we looked past the illusions of the surface! It is not difficult to train one's discernment upon the manifestations of nature. Our Teaching directs one towards seeing man as an integral part of nature.

You could have observed already that Our Indications relate to the very heart of events. I often speak of trust, not because I doubt it, but because what is obvious hinders one from seeing the inner currents. Everyone can recall having mistaken the incidental for the fundamental, and thus having forged mistaken notions about physical nature. But this also can be said of ideas about the element of fire. Someone may narrow-mindedly muse, "Our ancestors lived without fire, yet journeyed to the grave as honored citizens. What have I to do with fire? Let it be the concern of my cook!" But the wise one thinks, "Whence come the unexplainable epidemics, withering the lungs, the throat, and the heart? Beyond all the apparent causes there is something undetected by the physicians. It is not the circumstances of life, but other conditions that wipe out so many lives." This way of unprejudiced observation leads to right conclusions.

The Teacher works to reconcile contrasting conditions into one flow. Bringing together conditions that differ produces a dynamic picture. Thus, one can see success and failure as siblings.

442. Certainly, the wisest course is to partake of food only when the body has need of it. Also, food taken just twice daily is sufficient. But in view of the circumstances of present-day life, this is difficult to follow. Therefore the stomach can be given its work at specified times. The most harmful is consumption of food at any time with no real need. An orderly life is not something shameful, for one must carefully protect the apparatus built through the ages.

It is correct to suppose that one needs very little food, but it must be of sufficient quality. One should avoid acids and artificial preparations. Rancid butter is even more harmful than dried-out cheese. We vouch, and you should keep in mind, that it is easy to avoid burdening yourself with food.

443. You will be told of places where there are many gods. You will be told of locations where there are subterranean fires. Make use of this information.

What does a site of the gods mean? Does it not signify that this is a place with special conditions for the astral? Where the streams of fire are near, there may be found vivid manifestations of the astral that astonish the human imagination. Is the subterranean fire not related to the Fire of Space?

444. Are not the difficulties that arise preferable to dead silence? Is not the whirlwind the product of motion? The teaching about the overcoming of difficulties is the teaching about the striving toward good.

445. You should relate the discussion of the astral to the future experiments in densification of the astral body. Amidst earthly conditions, the psychic energy is trained to accept into the consciousness a new kind of body. These changes are made up of unnoticeably small steps of assimilation, manifested by few.

I have already pointed out the experiment with the astral body that must take place in the process of evolution.

446. In order to be able to perceive the broadening of consciousness as a success in life, one must already possess a tested spirit. People are so accustomed to basing their lives upon things of material value that even foundations of existence cannot be understood as long as humanity remains bound to customary ways. This means that new conditions of life have to be shaped by unusual means. There is no rule for this unusualness, in which the life of the spirit will shape everyday circumstances. The main cause of unhappiness in families is that the life of the spirit is not a part of their daily existence. By introducing improvements, life can be adorned and the flow of spirit uplifted. There does exist a certain manner of living that becomes like a beast's lair.

In losing the bridge to the Higher World, people harm not only themselves but also their surroundings. Their dogs develop harmful habits, and their livestock, their fowl, and their crops become unfit for evolution. It must be pointed out to man what he creates around him! Whether the spiritual foundations of one's life are dead or living is determined by the conditions of one's entire life.

One can see that the main Plan is unvarying. When it is necessary for Us to take some time to recoup Our forces, do not assume that We are about to retreat. It should be understood that We will accelerate events as much as Our forces allow. You must just help Us with a right attitude. Understand that no orchestra conductor can properly produce a symphony if the musical instruments are not tuned. Besides, irritation is but a step back into lower matter. It is better to engage yourselves in useful work. Thus, you will be able to bring closer the predestined events. Indeed, there are certain paths on which one can proceed only with Us.

447. The level of one's psychic energy can be determined according to its quality, not its power. Generally, the lowest quality of energy is possessed by mediums; it is susceptible to all surrounding conditions, even atmospheric ones. The Teachers are greatly concerned about this.

The next level produces partial, spontaneous manifestations of psychic energy, but without synthesis with spirit. One can see or hear psychically, without having merged with the Teaching.

Certainly, the type of psychic energy most needed for evolution is that possessed by mediators. Possessing true sensitiveness, they always maintain synthesis with the Teaching. This quality of synthesis, accumulated by the experiences of ages, protects them from dark influences.

Mediums may spark one's interest, but mediators must be esteemed and appreciated.

448. In the dark the yogi places a strong magnet or a chip from an object from the far-off worlds above the crown of a pupil's head, and asks, "What do you feel?"

Usually the first answer is negative, "I do not feel anything."

The yogi says, "It is not true; there cannot be in you such a lack of alertness that you cannot feel anything."

The pupil insists, "I cannot feel anything."

"It is not true; you are simply afraid to express the sensation and relate what you experience."

After a long silence the pupil says, "Perhaps I do feel some cold and see something like a flashing of stars."

Why do people say "seemingly" and "perhaps," when they see and feel? Only by decisive affirmation does psychic energy grow. Thus one can increase one's receptivity, because above us there are always magnetic currents and the radiance indicating the flowers of space.

449. The tension of eternal vigilance, the tremor of striving and salutary toil, demand a special adaptability of the organism. We value this vigilance.

450. One may regard a chain of incarnations as a sequence of separate lives, but it is better to look upon the entire chain of incarnations as one life. Truly, life is one; from the moment of mastering the human consciousness, life with all it involves does not cease, and the surrounding cosmic currents evoke the same sensations in all phases of life. This is one of the most binding conditions of life, proving the innate oneness of all principles. One could call the time of incarnation a sleeping dream or a waking day, depending on one's point of view. In the past perhaps it was a sleeping dream, but in the future it will perhaps be an awakening. This depends upon the success of one's evolution.

One can observe the way in which, in every life, over many centuries, similar vibrations provoke similar sensations. These observations are useful in learning to understand the wholeness of life. If people could grasp the wholeness of life, they would sooner learn goal-fitness and responsibility.

In the most ancient scriptures the day and night of Brahma are indicated—this seems to explain the various states of life. But after Atlantis a wrong understanding of death appeared, and earthly life was locked in a shell of narrow-mindedness. Denial replaced knowledge. However, the day and night of Brahma exist in everything, even the throb of the pulse. First, the intervals of the pulse; then, the intervals of the body's sleep; and then the intervals of the physical and subtle states; and so on, until the pulse of *Manvantara*.

Man must transform his consciousness, including himself in the unbreakable chain of consciousnesses. The path of expanding the consciousness provides a higher level of understanding of each step of life. This creates the unusualness of which We already have spoken. This unusualness is truth!

451. Once a French nobleman said to St. Germain, "I cannot even begin to understand the nonsense that surrounds you!"

St. Germain answered, "It is not difficult to understand my nonsense if you will give it the same attention you give to your own, if you will read my reports with the same attention you give to the list of dancers at the court. But the problem is that the order of a minuet is of greater importance to you than the safety of the planet."

In these words is contained the tragedy of our times. We find time without limit for all kinds of petty activities, but we do not find an hour for the most vital.

452. I do not speak casually about the full understanding of service, which dispels the atmosphere of the commonplace and leads to the harmony necessary for the fulfillment of one's tasks. One can cure nervousness through outward discipline, but embracing service in the consciousness is the best discipline.

Fire requires caution. One should develop this, and service is the measure of one's solicitous vigilance. Just as the petals of a flower curl and droop from a clumsy touch, so does the protective lotus close itself when a violent threat pierces one's space. As a solicitous worker I commission the co-workers to carry the treasure.

453. The cherub was depicted with wings, but without human extremities. This was perhaps a symbol of non-human evolution. Buddha was human, and was depicted as such, but with rays from behind the shoulders. Thus, to the full scale of human nature was added the symbol of mastery of the elements, and in this lies attainment. But people cannot accept the idea of attainment in the human state. When they are told about the rays of the shoulders, they begin immediately to demean the importance of other parts of the body. Thus is created the caricature of a cherub as a lifeless sausage—a complete and senseless isolation from life. Therefore We adopt a tempering procedure, first with a flow of unexpected events, then by uprooting the sense of personal property, and afterward by assigning a mission of particular danger. And after these purifications, We turn your attention to everyday life on Earth, where in the midst of seemingly ordinary conditions, extraordinary challenges occur.

One can imagine the quality of wings when the body lives surrounded by imperfection. The wings then expand with full radiance under the blows inflicted by others.

When a bird of paradise was asked from where its brilliant feathers came, it answered, "Many poisoned arrows glanced off me and the most virulent poison gave me the best hue."

Therefore, let us thank these archers!

454. When the astral world is near, many small, illusionary phenomena become evident. We dispel the enchantment of the astral world so that Maya may not impede, and once a right attitude to the astral world has been established, We can again direct your attention to it. In the name of evolution, We always consider the subtle body objectively, with neither rejection nor enchantment. The physical body contains the astral one just as the thick bark contains the sap of the tree. But if the astral is given the possibility of developing and becoming stronger, it will reclaim from the body its balanced conditions.

455. Like a boat with sails taut in the storm, so is Our ship propelled forward. One can see that the past was simpler than the present. This does not mean that the present is burdensome and bad; it means that there has been progress. During preparations for ambushing the enemy, the command given is, "Silence!" Then only the ignorant one will raise his voice; experienced warriors keep silent, for they know that an outcry brings destruction.

I affirm that although an achievement may have been brilliantly planned, it is the disciple's subtle refining of the details that crowns the creation. The Teacher rejoices at every move in the right direction, but can My Teaching prescribe for you each footstep? Only main points on the path may I set—such is the law.

456. Bodily pain is a natural fact, and cannot as such be banished. Of course, pain can be lessened by narcotics or by power of the will, but it also can be assumed by another conscious being. From ancient times there has existed the practice of groups of people assuming another's pain; for instance, in Egypt during the sickness of a Pharaoh. But the full effect was not often obtained. For this, outward agreement was insufficient—a spontaneous upsurge of inner unanimity was needed.

457. One can sometimes notice in children strange and fleeting glances, as if they see something unexplainable. Sometimes they may speak of a fire, of stars, or of sparks. Of course, adults usually attribute this to illness or foolishness, but attention must be paid to just such children. As is known, younger children can easily see astral images and, furthermore, especially sensitive ones can even see the fires of space. Such organisms should be carefully observed from their early days. Be assured that in them lie the promises of Agni Yoga, and if placed in pure surroundings, they will freely fulfill these promises in an exemplary way. Chiefly, their minds should not be polluted with outworn ideas, nor should fear of the unusual be instilled in them.

We have spoken sufficiently about the urgent importance of Agni Yoga, and of course the sensitive organisms should be prepared not for display, but for real life, as guides on the predestined path.

For a mother these observations are not difficult; she has only to know what and why she is observing. I am not speaking about harmful indulgence, without correct evaluation. The observer assesses the child's abilities unobtrusively, offering seemingly casual impressions of guidance. It can be noticed how joyously the eyes of a child open when its movements and its exclamations about things that are most dear to it are lovingly supported. Derision is the worst educator. Sensitiveness reveals a degree of culture. One cannot make Agni Yogis, one can only open the path for them—the cosmic manifestation does not permit any forcing. But where the flower of fire is ready to blossom, do not hinder.

458. Craftiness and resourcefulness are different qualities. Craftiness is defense, cunning, a clinging to the old. Resourcefulness is the future, mobility, devotion. No one can criticize resourcefulness. When the ship speeds towards its destination, does it matter if it tacks to port or to starboard? We are not astonished at the zigzags of its course as it sails against the wind, because it conquers obstacles all the same.

Craftiness, on the contrary, provokes only disgust. One can see that craftiness does not aim to the future, since it stands in defense of only the way things are; it is an example of valueless existence.

One has to value the fire of resourcefulness. If we pay attention when the fire is ignited, we will see that much finer flames appear when courage and resourcefulness are manifested.

459. I affirm that the joy of labor is the best flame of spirit.

The manifestation of joy is accompanied by intensified activity of the centers. Many great achievements come through the manifestation of joy. Joy is fire!

460. One has to properly understand the relationship of the timing of a predestined event to the essence of that event. People will generally relate to a coming event in terms of the surface details that they expect to see, and if they do not see those details, they are unable to think about the essence of the event. What then should we care about—the surface or the fundamentals? Remember how often too much attention to details undermined the essence. People would rather cling to trivialities than follow a foundation of universal significance.

461. Attainment, synthesis, and vigilance are expressed by the tri-colored flame. Attainment is silver; synthesis is green; vigilance is yellow. This triad is developed by training one's consciousness in the many conditions of life. One can point to this triad as the sign of one's having mastered the necessary conditions for self-sacrifice.

462. A part of an ancient mystery is called the "Chalice of Attainment."

The inner surface of a four-sided chalice was covered with silver and its exterior plated with red copper. The chalice was filled with pomegranate juice. The affirmation of attainment was signified by the raising of the chalice. Then the juice was poured out to all four sides, as a symbol of unconditional readiness to serve the General Good.

463. Satisfaction is not welcome in Our house. Who among Us could ever be satisfied? The onrushing task of world creation cries out against satisfaction. Can there be joy in completion? We gain impetus from the joy of new beginnings. This is not an abstraction. Beginnings correspond to motion, whose line of continuation is determined by inertia. The stroke of the beginning is Our bell. If We were to take back from the world all that We have begun, the greater part of the world's texture would crumble.

Who can change destiny? Where is the power? Only in thought. People do not trust thought sufficiently, and the power of their will is fettered seven times over. A man says, "I have gathered all my will power," yet at the same time he is afraid, and doubts, and hates, and hesitates. The will does not act in this way. It can send its arrow only when all fetters have been removed. This state was called dispassionateness, but this is not correct; it is better to define it as liberation. Let us take the example of an archer. If his arrow is weighed down with any objects, the flight of the arrow can only be spoiled. If people could learn to compare their inner actions with their physical activities, they would greatly enrich their consciousness.

464. Even if one gathers all the power of will, one still cannot evoke the Fire of Space. Those manifestations of the fiery element are not subject to command, they grow naturally from the expansion of consciousness. We call the human consciousness Our garden, where grow the fruits of labor. The work on the expansion of consciousness proceeds on two planes. These two planes are separate from the manifestations of life, just as a subterranean passage does not touch the vegetable kingdom and just as the fall of a meteorite is independent of the weather. People understand with difficulty these stratifications of two planes. Vigilance of the consciousness is required, but few are those who possess it. Each phenomenon of fire not only requires certain physical conditions but also depends upon the state of consciousness. The unexpectedness of phenomena is not so difficult to explain: it is enough to look into one's own consciousness without prejudice and to discern the physical conditions that preceded the phenomena. One will perceive a kind of short circuit of the current, which produces the manifestation.

465. Urusvati experienced the opening of the third eye. It is not easy to attain the ability to perceive the radiance of psychic energy. We make use of the tension in the atmosphere to help make manifest the development of the consciousness. That which exists in the depths of the consciousness must be called forth. There is no step of spiritual growth that is easy. One should not force progress in the mastery of psychic energy. The circle of the third eye is difficult. Its union with the Fire of Space takes place near those glands that are filled with the conduits from the centers.

Three flames, then the Chalice of Attainment, and then the third eye—this is part of Our Mystery. Afterward a rest of at least four days is needed.

466. I advise noting what actions and thoughts are accompanied by the appearance of stars, and what are the colors and dimensions of the stars. These indications are like the bliss of the worlds. The Fire of Space is seemingly metalized, and life becomes filled with the radiance of the *prana* of reality. One should simply watch the signs without prejudice, and observe to what thought they relate. Certainly they may seem familiar enough to the psychic vision, but one should not lose attentiveness and let oneself think of them as familiar. Only for weak ones can the everyday work on the Teaching be tiresome. The sparks of Cosmos are unique and unrepeatable. We could provide an entire chapter describing observations of these stars.

467. "And with His staff He wiped away all the designs in the sand." In this action we see all the generosity of the Teacher, all His riches, all the dismissal of the past and the striving into the future. But people, as I said, turn everything into the ordinary, so that all their actions, whether personal or national, whether material or spiritual, are deprived of enthusiasm. But if our daily labor is consecrated in the Name of the Teacher it cannot be ordinary or tiresome. If we forget for what we labor, boredom will cover us with its shroud of decay, and all the jesters of the world will not be able to provoke a smile in us.

How is it possible to describe the daily work of the Teacher when He scatters His creation in space, and the whirlwinds carry away the designs? But with a smile the Teacher scatters the signs, for He will never tire of sowing the sparks of attainment.

468. Multicolored sparks connect us with the spatial consciousness. But the Fire of Cosmos cannot be manifested in its full power, for the human essence would then be reduced to ashes—except in the case of one who has consecrated himself to Fire, passing in his own flesh through all the stages of approach to the fiery element.

Similarly, when teaching the foundations of life, one can provide varicolored signs of the fundamentals, but the complete Teaching must not be, and cannot be given. No book can contain the entirety of life, and it is not the purpose of the Teaching to turn students into wind-up mechanical robots. Truly, no Teacher has left a final and complete exposition of the Teaching. This would contradict the principle of Infinity and would assume limitation in the consciousness of the followers.

We can point out the direction; We can invite you to fly; We can affirm labor; We can indicate the light; but the ways and means should not be enslaving. The expanded consciousness always will point out where karma must remain inviolate. The inviolability of karma is the responsibility of everyone who transmits the foundations of the Teaching. To burden with an excessive load is unforgivable. To overlook possibilities is unworthy.

The Teacher directs the flow of consciousness. The pupil may not even notice the touches of the Teacher. Thus everyone should enter the domain of the Teaching as into life, unwaveringly. But for this purpose one has to read the Teaching repeatedly, while in different states of spirit. It would be a mistake to devote to the Teaching only one's times of rest or of upliftment. The best symbol of the Teaching is the all-pervading Fire.

469. Three centuries after the departure of the Blessed One, His disciples were already infected with religious strife. After only a century, Christianity manifested extreme intolerance. The last utterances of Mohammed were immediately followed by fanaticism. Religious controversies always destroy the sense of the true Teaching; therefore We now call for special tolerance and We reject controversies.

One may ask how to guard the Teaching, yet not respond to false accusations. The best defense is to strengthen one's labor in a non-hostile way. One can disarm hostile accusers by strengthening one's reserves. You know that We do not avoid enemies, but one should not waste one's strength on them.

When you are with Us, surrounded by Our blue sparks, all is attainable. But Our Rays must not be violated. There is a special time when unity of your power with Ours is needed to traverse the abyss.

470. Everything heard and seen through the *Brahmarandhra* center deserves especially sensitive attention. The highest faculty of psychic energy connects with the fires of space. One rarely can see these fires in great measure. Just as the heavenly vault

243

is filled with the radiance of the far-off worlds, so do the fires sparkle above the crown of the head. By this the quality of psychic energy is refined. We should rejoice at every sign of refinement of psychic energy. Indeed, it is here in the earthly incarnations that one crystallizes the psychic energy. When one passes to the astral plane one must retain cognizance of the future, and also ignite one's striving with the crystal of psychic energy. Otherwise those who pass into the astral plane will submerge into the twilight of carry-overs. That is why one's accumulation of psychic energy is precious.

471. It is the quality of the psychic energy that is most important. Truly, psychic energy exists in full potential even in its lower manifestations. In the lower organisms, it is expressed in instinct, but not consciousness. The lower quality of psychic energy corresponds to the lower layers of the atmosphere and circulates in them. And in humans, it functions in the lower centers of the organism.

One has to know how to control the psychic energy and direct it toward attainment. Psychic energy is refined through a proper way of thinking. Striving toward the heights is the best task for the *Brahmarandhra* center.

Of course, one cannot force oneself to direct one's thought upward. This direction of thought becomes natural, but only after long experience. Alternately, the psychic energy uplifts us, and the next level of consciousness created by it in turn refines the quality of energy.

The Great Serpent, again seizing its tail, completes the circle.

The degree of refinement of energy can be seen in one's radiations. The ability to perceive these radiations will be a token of the victory of consciousness.

472. Not seeing any possibilities, people often fall into despair. Usually they forget that one of their main allies is the flow of events. We do not say that one should passively await the unknown, but sometimes anticipated possibilities simply do not appear when expected. And sometimes they are outlived and have already ceased to exist.

473. In the same way that we study the nature of the astral world, let us clarify our attitude with regard to Rosicrucian, Masonic, and other organizations devoted to the General Good. Many Mahatmas have participated in them. And when we remember the original altruistic principles of these organizations, we must not turn away from them. When it concerns sincere motives, then all workers for the General Good must accept one another, especially when the spirit is developed and the consciousness is awake.

Why should we listen only to condemnations? Only on the lower steps are words of condemnation uttered; they are out of place when the seed of striving falls into the Chalice.

474. The culture of harmful micro-organisms is useful only for studying their nature, with the ultimate purpose being their destruction. Precisely, one must learn to destroy them. They harm the best secretions and may be considered the enemy of psychic energy. Just as rust slows the wheels, so does the waste product of physical processes obscure straight-knowledge.

475. The Teaching follows its own path without resorting to coercion. It can be pointed out how freely the Teaching spreads when the time is right.

476. The astral plane frequently reveals itself in the physical plane. But how senselessly beings of the physical plane react to any phenomenon that is beyond their known laws! Equally shocked are those who enter the astral world while ignorant about it.

477. Most people have completely lost the understanding of and ability to apply psychic energy. They have forgotten that any energy propelled into action will continue by inertia. It is almost impossible to stop such action. That is why each manifestation of psychic energy pursues its action, sometimes quite continuously. For example, one could already have changed one's thought, but the effect of a previous thought will nevertheless continue to pierce space. In this lies not only the power of psychic energy but also its particular quality, which deserves special care. Only through an enlightened consciousness can one control psychic energy so as not to obstruct one's path with thought-projections from the past. Often an accidental and unfitting thought can disturb the surface of the ocean of attainments for a long time. One may have long since forgotten about a thought, but it continues flying before one, lighting or obscuring the path. A luminous ray will attract small lights, which enrich it. But dark and dusty particles will adhere to rubbish and impede one's motion.

When We say, "Fly with light," or "Do not scatter dirt," We warn about the effects of one's actions.

All that is said about psychic energy applies to every action. There is nothing abstract in it, for psychic energy is contained everywhere in nature and is especially expressed in the human being. Much as one may try to ignore it, it reminds one of itself, and the task of enlightenment is to teach humanity how to use this treasure.

If the time has come to speak of the physically visible accumulations of psychic energy, it means that the reality of psychic energy has become evident. It means that people must strive without delay to master this energy. The Fire of Space and psychic energy are linked and are the basis of evolution.

478. We divide harmful micro-organisms into direct and indirect destroyers. What was said previously concerns primarily the first category. At the merging of the astral with the physical body, these are the most harmful.

479. L. is important for the deposits of psychic energy, because the essence of L. helps to preserve its crystals. The substance of L. also shields the nerve centers, where the psychic energy is deposited. The priestesses of old used to wear plates made of L., covered with wax, to protect their centers of the Chalice. These protective plates of L. will be a panacea to humanity. I spoke long ago about L.

480. The salts of L. are useful not only in treatment of gout but also against all kinds of harmful deposits. By alkalizing the accumulated debris, they clear the way for psychic energy. These salts are utilized for this clearing power, and may be prescribed for inner consumption.

It can be noticed how certain needed substances are introduced into life when the time is right.

481. The student who is not afraid to continually reassess the foundations of the Teaching for the purpose of refining his knowledge is on the right path. The one who is not afraid to be misunderstood by others is with Us. The one who is unafraid to build links among the great currents of the teachings is Our friend. The one who is not afraid to see the light has an eagle's eye. The one who is not afraid to enter the fire is of fiery birth. The one who is not afraid of what he cannot see can pierce the darkness. The one who is not afraid to travel the world is ready to strive to the far-off worlds. The one who is not afraid to know the teachings of wisdom is with Us.

We renounced and thus acquired. We gave away and thus received. We deprived ourselves and thus freed ourselves from temptation. The one traveling the path of knowledge walks like the lion of the desert. Who will respond to the roar of a lion? Only another lion, free of fear.

Where then are the bonds? Where then are the chains? Knowledge of the far-off worlds will forge the crown of achievement.

482. It is correct not to drive sickness inward. This truth is known to the physician of the body and ought to be known to the physician of the spirit. As hidden decay harms the whole body, so does that which has not been outlived by the spirit impede the growth of consciousness.

It is not wise to proclaim, "Tear out thy corruption." It is better to say, "Let benevolence fill thy being." Morning will replace the night.

483. One must observe in a simple manner the different ways in which psychic energy is manifested. It can be either a liberator or an enslaver, depending on the impulse that directs it. For its direction no special formulas are needed; only sincere striving is necessary. But recognizing sincerity is not easy, because what people call sincerity is often quite a different quality. They can justify any wrongdoing as having a sincere motive. But where is the self-denial that purifies the action? Evil is connected with hypocrisy and the personal ego.

No magic formulas are needed; the purifying of consciousness alone will propel the psychic energy in the right direction.

484. The most base of all feelings is that of self-satisfaction. Any feeling has its consequences, but self-satisfaction brings only death. It is not easy to think of self-criticism as a blessing, but one can train oneself to persevere on this endless road to achievement.

If you imagine your highest attainment, even it will be ugly when compared with perfection. Our labors primarily have dissatisfaction at their base, it is the impetus for Our searching. But to the newcomer the most difficult question will be, "Brother, can you contain eternal dissatisfaction?"

485. Some people are called bearers of happiness, some of unhappiness. Many examples and much evidence can be found. Let us assume that something like this exists, and let us look at it from a psycho-physical point of view. In addition to karmic effects, there is something that attracts or repels happiness. By a series of physical experiments, one can demonstrate that certain combinations of elements will determine the degrees of attraction and repulsion. The stronger the presence of the basic energy in people, the more positive will be their effect. If this main element is fire, then the other needed elements will be drawn like moths toward the light. This means that even success can be revealed and measured in physical terms, and it is useful to know one's own essence.

Where is the boundary of the action of fire? Are not the magnet and fire related? What nourishes the essence of the magnet? Even now people do not possess an apparatus for measuring the tension of the Fire of Space. But metals can be found that are sensitive to the fiery waves. Many reactions which until now have seemed to be of the most rare and refined quality will soon astonish by their primordial nature. People always notice the most evident elements first. As yet they have not tried to distill the all-penetrating energy.

Advise your friends to think in this direction. This experiment was begun by primitive man with just two pieces of wood. But energy is far from being fully utilized. Fire, like light, strengthens the human substance.

That which is most wondrous and sensitive is tempered in fire.

486. At present, people are not aware of the action of metals upon psychic energy, but in antiquity there was a great understanding of this. Magnets, and also alloys made of seven, eight, or nine metals were studied. As you know, many images were fashioned using alloys of metals, and instructions were given to worshipers to touch them with their hands. Thus, under the guise of a reverent act, a beneficial effect on the psychic energy of the worshiper was obtained. These primitive practices are no longer followed, and they have not been replaced by anything rational. Astrochemistry is recognized, radioactivity and magnetism hold the attention, but these are all directed only upon the body, whereas the most essential, psychic energy, is forgotten. Notice how colored glass, used as a filter, acts on the psychic condition. Metals and their combinations will act still more strongly.

However, psychic energy does not depend on metals; in its nature it is closer to light. Metals are conductors of psychic energy. Metals do affect psychic energy; they do not accumulate it, but act to regulate and protect it.

One will have to pay attention to psychic energy.

487. Some will say, "Why preoccupy oneself with Agni Yoga and psychic energy, when we already have wireless communication and all kinds of other inventions?" But wireless communication can carry only words, whereas psychic energy instantly transmits thoughts, and also impels the recipient to immediately respond in action. We do not err in saying that half the world responds to the transmitted suggestions, and that psychic energy knows no distance.

Others will say, "But then, cannot psychic energy be a danger to the state?"

We shall answer, "Certainly! All unmastered energies are dangerous; but they do exist, and the time approaches when we must learn to apply them consciously to life. Everyone has a reserve of psychic energy; but if it is unutilized consciously, it turns into an ugly sediment called sclerosis, whereas it could have been utilized wisely."

Do you remember the story of the one who questioned? Leaving the disciple on his own accelerates the development of his psychic energy, just as a plant grows best when left alone. So does one's psychic energy require independent and free development.

488. If you are given a piece of cloth sufficient for only one garment, you will not be able to make a complete garment out of just half of it. Similarly, if you accept only half the advice you are given, you will not achieve a full result. People like to extract a part of given advice and afterward complain about their unfulfilled expectations.

Wise advice is a medicine whose formula cannot be changed.

489. A well-known Rishi sat in silence, his expression one of striving.

He was asked what it was that absorbed him so. The Rishi answered, "At this moment I am building a temple."

"And where is this temple that you are building?"

"Twenty days' march from here; the builders are in great need of help."

"So even in your inactivity you build?"

The Rishi smiled, "Is action only by the hands and feet?"

490. It is very valuable when spatial thought can be summoned for cooperation—when fire accompanies actions, and stars participate in them too. On one step we intensify our will, and on the next we come in touch with the fires of space. Then spatial thought serves as a kind of semaphore and as an amplifier. In this state we do not need to depend so much on will power, for near us is found an inexhaustible source of energy that works with us if permitted.

If a spark strikes from your manuscript lines that ought to be erased, and underlines with blue light that which should be accepted, it means you have found a powerful co-worker. This cannot be evoked forcibly; only experience can bring you closer to spatial thought. Then, after fire and spatial thought, you will move toward the realization of the far-off worlds. We rejoice when someone enters into the ocean of space.

491. Asbestos, a few kinds of mica, manganese, and precipitates of soda are as yet not fully utilized in life. What sicknesses can one now cure on soda fields? What preparations can asbestos yield? What trans-mutations does mica offer? About manganese I have already spoken.

492. Agni Yoga approaches just in time. Without it, who could say that epidemics of influenza should be cured by psychic energy? Who would pay attention to the new kinds of mental, brain, and nervous illnesses, such as sleeping sickness? It is not leprosy, or the old forms of plague or cholera that must be dreaded; for them, preventive measures already exist. But one must ponder over the new enemies that are created by the conditions of contemporary life. One cannot apply old treatments to them; a new approach will be found through the expansion of consciousness.

One can trace, how, over the last thousand years, waves of sicknesses have swept over Earth. By these records one can compile a curious tabulation of human failings, because sicknesses clearly show the negative aspects of our existence.

I hope that alert minds will think about this in time. It is too late to start making a pump when your house is already on fire.

493. One must thoroughly realize the future. Labor does not end in the works already determined, but continues endlessly.

Reaching toward Infinity is the most beautiful striving.

494. I rejoice if you understand that obstacles are really opportunities.

Failure is proof of recognition by the dark ones. We must treasure such recognition, for it is always useful for the growth of the work! Just as compost fertilizes the earth, so does darkness decay to the benefit of the flowers of Light. The encircling rainbow safeguards, and shines all the brighter against the surrounding darkness.

495. Cancer is the scourge of humanity and will inevitably spread. The chief measures against cancer will be preventive ones. Those who do not use meat, wine, tobacco, or narcotics; who keep psychic energy pure; who from time to time undergo a milk diet; who cleanse the digestive tract and take the water of L., need not think about cancer.

During the early stages of cancer, surgery can be beneficial; it is pointless, however, if the patient after his convalescence returns to his former ways. Of course, ultrasound can break down the tumor, but of what use can it be if the cause of the poisoning has not been eliminated? Life must be made healthier. It is not wise to invent cures for corpses! One has to pay attention to the conditions of life and habits of those who fall sick.

How can cancer be cured? Of course, with psychic energy, whose crystal achieves the best healing. It is possible to utilize the accumulations of psychic energy, a true panacea for all illnesses, even for leprosy. The crystal of psychic energy can be obtained from musk, but this is a crystal of unconscious energy. Of course, there is the crystal of universal power, the Philosopher's Stone. Here, once again, the alchemists are close to the truth. The Philosopher's Stone, as a physical accumulation of psychic energy, is at the foundation of all life.

It is customary to think that cancer is hereditary. Of course it must be accepted that a poisoned organism gives birth to a similarly poisoned one. One should protect children immediately, for among them there are already many special ones.

496. Very sensitive organisms can sense an extreme tightening of the strings. This permits true cooperation. Indeed, there are moments when the shield of the world becomes incandescent, and at such times no life-giving substance can draw close to it. The one with developed psychic energy can know when it is necessary to wait out the storm. This ability does not come suddenly; therefore, sensitive and able co-workers always should be valued.

We rejoice when We find one whom We can call "the full chalice," for such a one can be trusted. There are many instances when, even after many signs, the ones who were called turned back. They sank into mediocrity, they decayed alive, and retreated into darkness.

497. Realize how useful it is to follow Our Counsel with striving, without regret, knowing that the whirlwinds of the storm intensify the centers. But under the umbrella of *Dukkar* you can wait for the storm to pass; for the Teacher has many sentinels. Lightning serves, in its discharge, to set ozone free.

498. The light of *Abhidharma* is the combination of the fire of higher spheres with the radiant emanations of the consciousness. We demonstrated by example the protection that the light of *Abhidharma* provides against the poisoned emanations of the lower earthly strata. The dark flame of the poisonous gases can be pushed back by the light of *Abhidharma* and made harmless; but for this one must embrace in consciousness the Fire of Space and one's own emanations. More generally, for positive results this realization is always needed. The simplest truth needs repetition; otherwise it will be lost under a pile of trash.

499. Every action based on reason is an indestructible acquisition. Affirmation of the Teaching is an invincible armor. Knowledge is gained by mastering the sparks of Light. Space is filled with material bodies beyond counting.

The sense of time lies in the perception of rays. The protracted can turn into the fleeting. The structure of oxygen—the birthplace of the power of fire—is invisible.

500. You may have noticed that often telepathic transmissions are quickly forgotten. This is because of the method of transmission, which touches special centers not involved in the usual processes of hearing. One can train oneself to retain these communications in the memory, but the ability to transmit in this way is not so easily acquired. The sending of communications does not depend on a forced tension of the will but on clarity of consciousness in combination with the light of *Abhidharma*. Thus, the quality of transmission depends on the purity of the consciousness and on the presence of oxygen attracted by the Fire of Space.

One should observe the different chemical natures of human transmissions of thought. Customary experiments in thought transmission are useless. In these the sender mentally repeats, "I am sending," and the recipient, by thinking, "I am receiving," actually obscures his consciousness.

During sendings to a distance one should adjust one's communications to the psychic condition of the receiving one. It is better to employ expressions customary for him, in order not to fatigue him. Notice how much one's psychic energy is affected by one's physical habits.

501. In which household will psychic energy grow? Of course in the one that strives toward the future. This is neither simple nor easy. People are too attached to the present. When We speak against the idea of desiring reward, the one who is attached to the present will not be able to understand the vital importance of this advice. But the one who is striving toward the future will not even think about reward, and he will regard any reward that comes as new shoes for the next journey. In this way, the guiding fires are lighted and psychic energy grows. Everything is developed through experience. And gained experience is comprehended by penetrating into the future. It is opposed to purposeless vegetating.

The most valuable experiment that one can conduct is an experiment upon oneself. It is both centrifugal and centripetal. These simple truths must be repeated. It is precisely in the offering of one's own spirit for the sake of humanity that both sacrifice and acquisition are contained. Unconnected opposites will not form a circle, and without the circle there can be no rotation. Each turn of a spiral, seen from above or below, will appear as a circle. All complexities in the picture will vanish for us if we strive into the future.

Do not complicate the path of psychic energy. It will itself whisper to the sensitive ear when less sleep is needed, when less food is needed, and when less drink is needed. Indeed each kind of energy provides nourishment, psychic energy especially.

A temporary weakening of the extremities should not cause anxiety. The poisoned currents of Earth act first of all upon the extremities. But the natural growth of psychic energy can compensate for the body's weaknesses and help to establish a balance between the seen and unseen forces.

502. One can foresee that some students will begin conducting psychic experiments with plants, but will not achieve any results. One can also foresee that some of these will then blame the Teaching for its imprecise Indications, without giving a thought to the inadequacy of their own psychic energy.

One should not look for a lack of precision in Our Indications when I say that psychic energy must not only be strengthened but should also be refined. It will be strengthened under the waves of fire, when the aura begins to take on a purple color due to tensity. It will become refined from alertness, sharp-sightedness, and subtlety of thinking. How can one more exactly term the refinement of the current of thought when the formulas for the future resound in exaltation?

Many people choose to pass these formulas by and thus avoid the spiritual stigmata brought on by the painful striving of the spirit. Truly, these stigmata are the best signs of sensitivity. Not coarse, startling manifestations, but wings of cosmic thought fall with the lightest touch upon the crown of the head, awakening the striving of the *Kundalini*. These thoughts may fleetingly leave intangible traces, but they sharpen the centers, so they become like needles gathering electricity. Are not our centers like pine needles?

Whoever has entered upon the path of refining psychic energy will not speak of a lack of precision in Our Indications.

503. Whither may one direct thought? Whither to project the will? Toward space, whence comes the life-giving energy.

Let us strive toward it.

504. The full moon usually is favorable for telepathy. But there are other factors that affect it too. Most important, it is influenced by certain phases of the sunspots. You may yourself have noticed that telepathic manifestations grow stronger with the increased chemical activity of the lunar and planetary rays, but sunspots also affect many other aspects of existence. Cold, which can reach disastrous extremes, the heat of volcanic eruptions, and earthquakes follow changes in the solar aura. One must keep this in mind, because the cold may increase and the earthquakes become more powerful. Thus, a transitory solar manifestation can be terminal on Earth.

505. The student of Yoga must become accustomed to one thing—the inevitable suspicion in other people. One should not blame them for this attitude. If the student were an ascetic, in the customary sense of the term, they would more easily accept him. If he were to have the appearance of a magus, he would also be accepted, though out of fear. But his essence cannot be defined in simple words, and his work for the evolution of the world has no place in the customary ways of the world. How will people accept the renovation of their lives, when that is what they dread above all?

Happily, he who has entered upon the path of Agni Yoga does not worry himself about suspicion. He labors, devoting himself entirely to the cause of evolution. He walks without doubting, knowing that satisfaction is not his lot.

506. Besides cosmic conditions, emotional disturbances also influence telepathic communications. This instability, fully understandable because of personal and surrounding concerns, intrudes itself into the line of communication. Likewise, an eagerness to anticipate the communication causes tremors in the fiery conduit. But still, no physical apparatus compares to psychic energy. The waves produced by a physical apparatus can overburden certain layers of the atmosphere and cause new calamities, if psychic energy is not used.

It is wrong to assume that the waves produced by physical apparatuses do not affect one's nature. The invisible and inaudible waves can act more powerfully than deafening explosions. But a multitude of such dangers will disappear when the inexhaustible source of psychic energy is realized. However, even the idea of the realization of psychic energy is not easy for humanity to grasp.

507. Killing by undisciplined use of psychic energy is a crime equal to that of killing out of ignorance. Murders of this kind are countless. One should think about this! The fact that some are unaware of it does not mean that such crimes do not exist.

508. Intellect is not wisdom. Straight-knowledge is wisdom. Intellect is reason. Wisdom makes decisions that long ago had already germinated. Intellect is at the threshold of wisdom, and when sharpened it moves into the realm of synthesis. Reason and a mind trained to one specialty are only corners of the future house. Those with narrowly specialized minds can pave for themselves a brilliant future, but they must continue to incarnate until their minds lose their narrow specialization. Only when the intellect loses this can it become wise. Each specialty is meant for conditions of life on Earth, whereas the synthesis of spirit opens all spheres. Spiritual tension accumulates spatial psychic energy. Spiritual tension can lead into any sphere of the astral plane.

509. It is proper to ask how psychic energy can be accumulated. It is primarily through consciousness, self-sacrifice, and achievement. One cannot be deprived of psychic energy gained in these ways. Through the development of consciousness, it becomes refined; but, if accumulated in other ways, the energy can remain in a state of potentiality, awaiting the proper conditions for manifestation. In all manifestations of psychic energy it can be assumed that some good deed was performed instinctively in the past.

510. Consciousness is broadened by a slow process of gaining experience. It is possible to demonstrate by a simple experiment how this judge—consciousness—transmutes our actions. One can prompt some actions in a less developed person and observe how he fulfills them. Then, through suggestion by the will his consciousness is dulled and he is prompted once again to perform the same actions. The comparison will be astounding.

Great is the significance of the closed circle of the human will.

511. Not long ago thought was directed more toward phenomena, the so-called manifestations of energy. But now one can think of the renewal of life and steps into the future. One has to summon all one's courage to leave behind one's desire for miraculous manifestations and to turn one's idea of energy toward reality. This is difficult, but one must overcome the limitations of conventional ideas. It is difficult to resist sinking into the ordinary, for the impelling motion of evolution, which involves all aspects of existence, is always strangely unfamiliar and does not resemble the past.

Can one build life amidst the hatred that prevails at the end of *Kali Yuga*? But the complete task of the future *Satya Yuga* must be expressed now, amidst today's animosity and destruction.

512. With each experiment, resistance caused by the presence of lower matter can be noticed. By purification or expulsion one can eliminate this harmful lower matter. Human existence is subject to universal laws. Does not the dullest opposition appear with every progressive step? Is not one forced to destroy irrationality and decay through the tension of fire? Just as in laboratory experiments, one must separate and remove all dead by-products.

If you want to find out who is subject to lower influences, propose an action of General Good at a meeting. You may be sure that those who object have not been freed from dead matter.

It is easier to discern the inner qualities that people reveal by their speech and actions than to see the geological stratifications of the soil. Therefore, in selecting the fiery ones, observe the way in which they respond to the tests presented to them. With psychic development the revealing process increases, and one deepens the way already begun. Few are those in whom the true essence does not become evident. With the process of fiery development, one's ability to unerringly judge manifested events will grow. Out of the straight-knowledge, foretold so long ago, will burst forth the fire of intensified psychic energy. What can be concealed from it?

513. When We spoke about the International Government many were perplexed. When they learn that this is the Government of Knowledge, will they then understand it?

514. It is difficult to distinguish between a desperate act and one of impetuous desire. The flame is similar in each.

515. How can the blue fire be transmuted into purple? The tension of psychic energy will send out ruby-colored arrows, and their growth will pierce the blue of consciousness.

516. *Uru* and *Svati* are found in cosmogony. The signs of approaching Aquarius and its combination with Saturn are again being repeated. One can see once more how the cosmogony of the Atlanteans was on the right path. Not only was the chemism of the rays known at that time, but also the actual cooperation of the luminaries. After long wanderings, humanity again approaches just that. But still one more simple thing has to be realized: that the forms of those who populate Earth need not be repeated elsewhere in Cosmos. People cannot imagine themselves in different forms, but what joys could arise from the realization of cooperation with other life forms! One should be able to approach easily such all-embracing circumstances.

517. In studying the process of accumulating of psychic energy, one can observe that the energy acts similarly to the pulse of Cosmos—a gathering of power gather through ebb and flow. It is not wise to expect only an incoming tide, for no power could then be accumulated. Like a fine weaving, a web of cooperation of the centers is created by uniting them with a fiery thread. The fires of psychic energy glow, forming the complex radiance of the Universe. This energy can be called *Atma*. *Uru* and *Agni* are needed to bring about the *Svati* of consciousness.

Someone will ask, "If the realization of psychic energy leads one to the infinite recesses of the Universe, is it possible to live without realization of this complex energy?" It is impossible, truly impossible, to avoid that which itself draws closer to us, all-pervading.

518. People lose much by expecting fulfillment only according to their own ways. How then will they be able to think about the far-off worlds? Only by outgrowing their many lists and tables.

519. You notice that at times We speak briefly, with hardly a mention of even important circumstances. It means that at the present time the waves of space must not be made more complicated than they are. This necessity is little observed, and as a result irreparable harm follows. Let us respect the significance of the crystal of thought.

520. In the Mysteries of ancient Egypt there was a ritual called "The Sharpening of the Sword." The one to be tested was placed in deep darkness. He was approached by the Great Hierophant, who disclosed to him some of the Mysteries. Light illumined the Hierophant, then again everything sank into darkness. Afterward the priest designated as Tempter approached. Out of the darkness, the voice of the

Tempter asked, "Brother, what hast thou seen and heard?" The tested one answered, "I was honored by the presence of the Great Hierophant."

"Brother, art thou convinced that this was the Great One Himself?"

"My eyes have seen and my ears have heard."

"But the image could be deceptive and the voice could be false."

Then the tested one either became confused and was rejected, or he was filled with firmness and spoke, "The eyes and ears can be deceived, but nothing can delude the heart. I see with the heart, I hear with the heart, and nothing impure will touch the heart. For the sword entrusted to me is kept sharp."

Once again the Great Hierophant approached and, pointing out a chalice filled with a red liquid, said, "Receive and drink of thy chalice; empty it to see the mystery at the bottom."

On the bottom was an image of a supine man enclosed by a serpent coiled in a circle, with the inscription: "Thou art the one who hast given all and accepted all." Thus reads the same Teaching at all times, but the darkness of ignorance causes one to forget its meaning.

521. The tasks that We entrust are always dangerous ones, for they are directed against a most powerful enemy. There is no truth higher than the truth. Only with this realization may one accept and carry the chalice to the goal.

One can find among objects of antiquity symbols of the path of knowledge.

Traveler, art thou free of fear?

522. We saw that psychic energy is closely related to fire and is an inalienable, cumulative acquisition. This means that the energy can be accumulated in

objects, which can then be used for concentration of the will. A considerable accumulation of energy can even make objects radiate, or transmit a suggested thought. This is a scientific explanation of the nature of sacred objects. One can find in them accumulations of psychic energy, unless improper transmissions have erased these accumulations.

People who have stored psychic energy should be considered as treasures of the nation. Not of its millions of citizens should a country be proud, but of its store of psychic energy. For the sake of even one individual with a store of energy, thousands of average ones must be spared. Like a magnet, each one with an intensified store of psychic energy attracts the embryonic energies buried deep within people. This means that each possessor of conscious energy is himself an embodiment of the General Good. Therefore, let us treat with care every accumulated store of energy.

523. In the process of the conscious development of psychic energy, there will in the future be apparatuses for the accumulation of this energy; but of course it is the human energy that must be its conduit.

For experiments with psychic energy a patient and steady process of accumulation is needed. It is harmful to send out energy without co-measurement, for impulsiveness can undermine the quality of the accumulations.

524. An old proverb says: "The bridle of Satan is strong." Another: "He who has seen the face of Satan will never forget it." Even in ancient times, people knew about the inertia of human consciousness. Our advice is to develop the needed agility of the mind.

What treasures a pure, free, and dauntless consciousness can give to humanity! But the inertia of habit holds the inexperienced one in fetters.

We could even now provide an apparatus that accumulates psychic energy, but who would be the conduit? And how many could appreciate the application of this energy in life?

Fire cannot be bridled by the will; it gains strength through straight-knowledge.

525. Let us speak today about labor. Intense labor leads to a conscious development of psychic energy. The results of one's many years of labor can be manifested rapidly.

526. It is right to think that psychic energy, properly utilized by people, will uplift human dignity. The mere focusing of thought in this direction is already a blessing.

527. If someone comes to you and speaks of his desire to approach Agni Yoga, ask him what led him to this decision.

He will answer, "I am looking for proofs." You will think, "He is not one of us."

Or he will speak of his sad life. You will think, "He is not one of us."

Or he will speak of his intention to defeat his enemies. You will think, "He is not one of us."

Or he will speak of his desire for riches. You will think, "He is not one of us."

Or he will speak of gaining earthly advantages. You will think, "He is not one of us."

He will speak of his desire for repose. You will think, "He is not one of us."

But if he says, "I wish to perfect myself," then ask, "What reward do you expect?" He then should say, "Only to come close to the Teaching."

You will rejoice, for his spirit has chosen correctly. He is ready for a life of self-examination. He is ready to rid himself of his faults, without regret. He will understand that it is not suffering that is needed, but liberation. He will understand that it is not miracles that are needed, but straight-knowledge. He will understand that it is not dead scholarship that is needed, but realization and application.

Exultant on the first day, he will not tire on the next. He will proceed like a joyous elephant, bursting through the brush. He will see his successes as the smile of the sun. He will drive away the scorpion of fear. He will accept the gift as the light on the path. He will understand the realization and development of the fires of the centers as an attracting magnet. And he will understand that the fires grow imperceptibly, just as plants do. He will understand that the fires burn away the past and illumine the future. And he will understand what *podvig* means!

528. We would prefer to avoid repetition, but sometimes We are compelled to return to a previous subject. Pay attention to these repetitions; they are usually provoked either by a disciple's misunderstandings or by cosmic complications that demand special attention. For example, We must repeat about the proper attitude toward psychic energy. Of course psychic energy is always present, but it can become dormant, and then it will crystallize and become inactive. That soil will have to be turned again with the plow of self-sacrificing labor. Certainly, not a grain of psychic energy can ever be lost, but its accumulations must be stirred. That is why the Teaching so condemns immobile self-satisfaction and conceit. Truly, it is better to be aflame than to be dormant.

529. It is true that the power of thought has been spoken about for ages, but nothing has changed because of this. People generally do not pay attention to their thoughts in order to determine their causes and consequences. Yet what remarkable experiments could be conducted even now, in the midst of everyday life! No special conditions are needed for such experiments. Attention and mobility of consciousness are all that is required. For instance, in experimenting with telepathic communications, one can observe the outer and inner conditions that influence the quality of the communications. Drowsiness or alertness, irritation or joy, lethargy or striving—each reacts strongly upon the quality and intensity of communications. The personal character of the participants also has its effect. Is it not important to take attentive notice of these things?

Indeed, it is known that various defects in the character of the participants are often reflected in physical flaws. Some of these may be overcome, but others, often karmic ones, are irreparable, except perhaps, in particular cases, through a special tension of the will. But of course, one's will power can only be developed by one's already-developed power of thought.

I advise you to pay attention to all the telepathic communications that you receive. Note the immediate, first sensations without undue analysis.

530. It may be observed how outside influences affect messages. It may be seen how sometimes even the best surrounding conditions are adversely affected by intrusive distant calls. For example, someone in need in some far-off country can drag after him a trail of pleas and thus interrupt someone else's communication. By observing the circumstances, one can determine the best conditions that are needed and try to achieve them.

531. All the best inventions will not be enough to bring about the needed solutions. If lightning, or a magnetic wave, or earthquake, or hurricane, can destroy these inventions, is it not better to devote one's attention to the cultivation of thought?

When psychic energy has been cultivated, its action is indestructible. The waves of thought, when under control, will not overflow space, nor will they be affected by the lower layers.

How wonderful it is to observe the striving of thought, its origins and causes, the differences between thoughts of various times, the proximity of consciousnesses at different stages of development, and the eternal competition of the higher and lower spheres! All this creates an incomparable existence.

The realms of psychic energy encompass all obstacles. Nothing in the physical world compares to the subtlest energy, for the entire future, when coarse matter will return into the domain of light, is founded upon these most refined energies!

532. We avoid those techniques that involve mainly the use of the muscles. One's muscles must express the projection of one's own will. We do not like automatic writing, because it always impedes the ascent of consciousness. It does not lead to the perfecting of the subtle energy. The main task will always be the development of straight-knowledge. When straight-knowledge has been developed, the dangers connected with the mechanical means of communication do not threaten.

Thus should we always give preference to all that uplifts the cultivation of thought.

533. The traditional ways of automatic writing are imperfect, because a constant conflict is created. The action of automatic writing uses the center of the wrist, but the consciousness also uses the same center, and thus two activities are in conflict, and subtlety of expression is lost.

534. Most harmful of all are the so-called involuntary thoughts. Every conscious thought is to a certain degree organized, but the little vagabonds, without any sense, obstruct the ways.

When people are united in the acquiring of knowledge their thoughts gain a special significance. Unity in thought is stronger than any physical unity.

535. If you desire, by power of the will, to see parts of your own aura, you will find it impossible. It is necessary to desire it, but the law of psychic energy also requires suitable conditions. Such conditions are not established in an instant; they must be built on a foundation of higher influences. But the way to higher influences is not easy either, since they can be reached only through open gates. Each failure in communion with the source of the subtlest energies closes the gates. A proper understanding of the requirements for fruitful communion is needed. It depends not only on the intensity of striving, but also on the careful consideration of surrounding conditions.

Sometimes a short period of silence is the best accumulator. One's consciousness, according to the degree of development of straight-knowledge, provides an understanding of what action is needed.

Among the components of developed auras it is especially rare to see the emerald green and the noble ruby colors, which stand in contrast to each other. The first denotes synthesis and the second, the self-sacrifice of attainment. In clouded auras hints of both may be seen, but to see them pure is as rare as are synthesis and attainment themselves. Emerald is closer to the Chalice, and ruby to the Eye of Brahma.

536. One has to develop psychic energy steadily and diligently. The development of psychic energy depends on both the harmony of one's surroundings, and one's physical condition.

537. Churning and the spinning of a top are symbols of the creative spiral motion. What looks like physical immobility does not signify lack of power, and what is perceived as silence does not indicate a lack of voice.

538. When all books are read and their words have been studied, then it remains to apply in life what has been learned. If books are read again and again, and their words carefully noted, their application can still remain outside of life, and not even the strongest signs will compel one to change one's habits. Yet one has to find a way to develop mobility of consciousness. The heart can sense the shame of an unworthy waste of time.

We do not want to seem severe in Our judgment. We would prefer to see the joy of attainment, but for centuries it was necessary that the sword be held ready, for fear has always dominated people. Victory over fear will be the threshold of the new consciousness.

539. The conditions of the nerve centers of children should be studied. It is known that in each child these centers are developed in individual and uneven ways. In some children, there may be one highly developed center that can prompt spontaneous actions equal to those of adults.

At times certain centers cause sickliness, to the perplexity of physicians, since physicians do not think to seek evidence in the nerve centers of a child. However, according to such signs of sickliness and other unusual symptoms, one can judge the true condition of the body and the quality of the spirit. How much good could result from such observations! How many possibilities could be protected, thus enabling the development of psychic energy in the child.

For old spirits who have experienced many incarnations, the period after the seventh year is quite difficult, and the one after fourteen years even more so. After fourteen years the psychic energy has already come into action. The spirit has already torn itself away from its former existences, and the burden of the new unknown path overwhelms it. The accumulated possibilities cause a vague anxiety, and the core strives to return to conditions in which there were greater opportunities for the consciousness to act freely.

The proper care of the nerve centers of children is a necessity for the future. There has existed a mistaken opinion that the spirit cannot early on master its new body and that this is the reason for children's foolishness. But actually, when the centers do not work correctly, the deposits of psychic energy are not produced, and the spirit has no substance through which to manifest itself.

The care of children's nerve centers can be considered to be the care of the future race.

540. True, people make contact with many kinds of energy, but in most cases in a very limited way, and they experience only one aspect of the energy. Out of this limitation can arise many dangers. For example, universal electrification is of benefit to civilization, but since people approach it too one-sidedly, the artificial saturation of space by electricity may cause dangers. One can receive discharges of considerable strength in places highly charged with electricity. But if the cause is intensified so also will be the effects. Thus, instead of just a powerful discharge, mass destruction can occur. Likewise, one can envision the overfilling of space with currents of many kinds of energy, causing most unexpected disturbances in life.

Of course, you may be certain that We do not speak against the mastery and application of energies, but We are concerned and want to warn that it is urgent to acquire protection when making contact with new energies. All Our experiences indicate that psychic energy will always be ready to transmute the assault of other energies into something useful. We saw how psychic energy could, like inoculation, prevent the possibility of sickness. In the same way, it can transform the effects of all other energies into beneficial ones.

Do not confuse this statement with Our Teaching about the will, for will power is only one of the manifestations of psychic energy.

541. Did you ever hear of a yogi's being killed by lightning? No, but you have heard about the deadly eye of the yogi. It is not only the command of the will but the summoning of energies that provides the power for this phenomenon, for which it is necessary to have a sufficient store of the all-powerful psychic energy.

542. The so-called fourth dimension is a property of psychic energy. The properties of psychic energy will make possible the broadening of all understanding.

Under hypnosis, one's consciousness can direct the psychic energy to the site of one's ailment. This can be done, for example, in cases of herpes, tumors, or eczema. What is needed for this is that the store of psychic energy in one's somatic system be sufficient. Psychic energy is accumulated in the nerves, and its crystals activate the somatic system, which otherwise would remain dormant.

What can be the purpose of deep breathing, and why are certain fires related to it? Deep breathing affects the center of the Chalice.

543. You may meet people who reject the Teaching entirely. Do not try to persuade them. Our Teaching is not a campaigning one; it is an instructive one, intended for those who already desire to perfect themselves. Some may choose a favorite page for themselves, with which they will abide, but not with the full Teaching. Others will pretend that they respect the Teaching, but will just place the book under their pillow while they sleep. And still others will speak of their love for the Teaching, but will not renounce a single bad habit. Nevertheless, the predestined ones will come!

544. The ancients had a proverb: "Do not set free the tiger!" It is unnecessary to explain its meaning; its significance is demonstrated in life.

Thus, let us not set free the tiger!

545. Be assured that the manifestation of the New Era will penetrate even the simplest of souls. The best ones will carry the burden of controversies and battles. The lesser ones can be given the simpler ways. Let them keep their calm when the flames and explosions begin to rage.

Remember the symbolic event shown to you when, before the onset of a catastrophe, attempts were made to lead the people out of their halls of pleasure. Not only did the people refuse to leave, but new crowds tried to enter.

When you are spreading the Teaching, do not wonder why so few understand its urgent necessity. In immature thinking, one trait prevails—ideas about the future are distorted. The approach of something may be felt, but the undeveloped consciousness refracts the perceptions. It is unnecessary to cite instances of people's rejoicing before disaster and celebrating before defeat.

The cultivation of straight-knowledge requires careful striving; therefore both the best and the simplest ones will achieve an equal ease of understanding. But the more ordinary consciousness is obstructed by its own preconceived ideas, unable to separate the phantom from the real. It is intoxicated, not by narcotics, but by its own way of thinking. The fixation of ideas, inculcated in childhood by the conventions of daily life, weakens attempts at sensible thinking.

Examples of absurd behavior at times of catastrophe have become common, for the trend of thought has turned into the riverbed of unreality.

546. Fundamental and irreplaceable is the element of fire. Similarly without substitute is psychic energy. The most self-sufficient, the most refined, the most upthrusting energy is the true Daughter of Fire! Not without reason do We call you to the Fiery Conqueress. Every manifestation of enthusiasm precipitates a particle of the treasure. Each exaltation before nature and Beauty gathers the seeds of light and creates a ray of victory. Long ago I said, "Through Beauty thou hast Light." Is it possible that We say this only to give pleasure? Each Indication has undeniable and urgent importance. Thus, enthusiasm will be the shortest way to the accumulation of psychic energy.

More than once you will be asked where is the nursery that produces the beautiful garden of fiery energy. You will say, "In the joy of Beauty." But learn how to embrace this joy of Light. Learn how to rejoice at each leaf awakened to life. Learn how to respond within your centers to the call of joy. Learn to understand that such joy is not idleness but the harvesting of the treasure. Learn to accumulate energy through joy, for with what else shall we weave the threads of the far-off worlds?

Not in grief, not in madness, not in intoxication, but in the joy of realization will we become the happy possessors of the treasure. It is difficult to quench one's thirst from an empty well, but the mountain spring is ready to refresh each one who approaches. Rejoice!

547. Thoughts sent into space attract kindred thinking. How should one act if one's broad views do not achieve their goal? One must expand them still further. Beyond the boundaries of hostility lies the field of friendship. The traveler must know the geography of this domain.

Is attainment possible without exaltation? Is self-sacrifice possible without joy? Is courage possible without enthusiasm? Thus point out and remind others about these easier and more immediate ways to gain psychic energy. My Hand points out the treasure to the seeker.

548. To rejoice is good, but in this let us not be like the animals. In what lies the difference? Only in consciousness. Animals do not know why they rejoice; but we must know why. With our consciousness we see cause and effect. Thus do we construct the bridge of perfectment.

One can review a complete chain of events and evaluate their sequence. In this also do we differ from animals, who cannot connect the separate moments. The teaching about comparing events provides a new way of acquiring psychic energy. If people would learn to understand the events of their lives according to their consciousness at the time, they would be able to progress from the level at which they have been stalled.

549. It is correct to define the *Kundalini* as an abstract principle. When the conditions of earthly life

were crude, it was necessary to direct the spirit to higher spheres. At first, the symbol of the Eye of Brahma held priority; then it was followed by the triumph of the *Kundalini*. But with either, the attainment of *Samadhi* by some did not protect humanity from the horrors of slavery and treason.

Now is the time to insist upon synthesis of action. Straight-knowledge will provide this synthesis during earthly existence. The treasure of straight-knowledge is contained in the Chalice, therefore one should add to the two mentioned centers the blossoming of the third center. The rainbow of the *Kundalini* can draw one upward, but here on Earth, earthly construction is needed. One has to build a foundation for the pillar, just as writing does for thought. The long-silenced Chalice will again come to life, and humanity will tread a new path. Three Lords, these three centers, will lead to true cooperation here.

Whoever understands the relation of the Chalice to the *Kundalini* will understand how the father transmits the earthly kingdom to the son. The *Kundalini* is the father, the impeller of the ascent. The Chalice is the son, awakened by the father. Whoever knows the principle of the father will, at the change of races, embrace the son. The Chalice of attainment initiates action. Thus nothing is rejected, but only strengthened. The Eye of Brahma is the natural complement to this order.

550. Where can be found the refinement and upliftment of thought tempered in the holy fire? Is it possible to find it in the ever-increasing heaps of artificial and over-sophisticated reasoning? No, real thought will strive toward an appreciation of the best and the beautiful, and toward the search for the most useful. One can foresee that the accumulations of the

Chalice will permit a flow of clear thinking, with proper comparison of the past with the future.

551. The Blessed Buddha once said to His pupils, "Let us sit in silence and let our eyes behold."

After a while the Teacher asked, "How many times did I change my position?"

One noticed ten changes, another only three, and another insisted that the Teacher had remained still.

The Lord of Wisdom smiled, "I changed my position and the folds of my garment seventy-seven times. As long as we do not learn to see clearly we shall not become Arhats."

For a true understanding of psychic energy, one must first develop attentiveness. It is useful, therefore, for the teacher to ask unexpected questions, to request descriptions of occurrences, and to require the keeping of daily notes. It is known that even a very sluggish attentiveness will awaken through such exercising. The inattentive, the unobservant, cannot even notice the development of psychic energy. The advice to observe is the advice of a friend, for the future demands attentiveness.

552. During periods of physical weakness experiments with psychic energy are difficult. Fatigue can be overcome by a short but complete rest.

553. Only a body open to sickness can be infected. Only a spirit ready to accept psychic energy can receive it. If people would realize that an accumulation of psychic energy is needed not only for the present life but also as a constant and inalienable attainment and blessing, this realization would erase the perception of each life having a beginning or an end. Should not a true understanding of life promote care for the future along with the present? This is the immediate duty of every scientist. Until now scientists have dealt with life as finite—is it not now their mission to see life as extending into Infinity?

The teachings of the religions have always pointed to life in the hereafter, but those testimonies have lost their relevance. Formerly, miracles had importance, but now the consciousness is attracted to reality. The chain of incarnations is attested to by the ancient as well as by the latest teachings. In modern literature mention of the words *incarnation* and *karma* has become common. However, these truths have entered but little into human consciousness; otherwise it would have transformed the whole of life. The human mind prefers to burden itself with strange concerns, happily occupying itself with superfluous things. The human imagination has not been trained for fundamental ideas. However, just one hour of thoughtful talk can change the life of a child forever.

Immortal humanity—is this idea not worthy of the future? The rising of the Phoenix out of his own ashes has been taught since antiquity. But the Phoenix needs wings; does not psychic energy provide the best rainbow wings?

554. Many thousands of years ago it was said, "The time will come when people will open their hearts and offer their Chalices to the Supreme." The time has approached when humanity nears its sixth stage of perfectment, and the flame will soon begin to glow above the Chalice. How many images and prophecies have been accumulated in space! Truly, it is time to recall the image of the Chalice, when resin flamed within the chalices of the ancients, and the priestess, leaning on the sword of attainment, raised the Chalice to the Highest.

Truly, the manifestations of psychic energy are as manifold and intricate as the most delicate design. It is not reason, but the straight-knowledge provided by the Chalice that can discern them. Just as a mother understands the agitation of her child, so does the fire of the Chalice illumine the disturbances of the currents. It is advisable that humanity ponder why the Chalice is of such great importance for the development of the future race.

It is essential that refinement of thought be developed along with the advances in technology. What beautiful images will be perceptible to that enlightened eye! Indeed, everyone is responsible not only for himself but for the consciousness of all humanity.

555. How many dramatic events must there be for people to pay attention! They will happily place a wreath on any raised stone. But let them go by any road, as long as it leads upward!

556. In Agni Yoga, even the most abstract concepts become tangible and real. Sincerity, usually called honesty, becomes irreplaceable. Test the quality of sincerity in communications to far distances; and then observe the difference when personal feelings of impatience or irritation are allowed to intrude, or, worse, preconceived ideas or deliberate distortions. These deprive the result of its value, and can cause irreparable harm. But true sincerity is a purifier, bringing about a crystal clarity, which enlightens the consciousness just as fuel gives flame. Thus, one can contribute to success by applying what is called honesty.

557. I speak of psychic energy as though all of humanity has already accepted it and decided to improve their consciousness. However, the Teaching remains a wonder from the mountains. People are ready to listen to the Teaching only during their moments of leisure. People see the followers of the

Teaching as just lucky, not considering whence comes their happiness.

Some will say that the Teaching is too general, or too tiresome, but the Teaching, unseen, spreads in its own unexpected ways. Drops of the Teaching radiate in the words of people, both famous and unknown, in scientific laboratories, and in the glorious deeds of unforgettable heroes. Not recognizing each other, these seemingly unrelated co-workers carry the fragments of timely knowledge. Who will censure them?

He who has been tested by the Teaching will smile at his attackers, "Friend, bring me more! Your slander is nothing but a basket of offerings."

For carrying even the best fruit, baskets can be made from the bark of any tree. Is it not immaterial whether the bark is bitter or sweet? Whether the bark is yellow, red, black, or white? Useful fruit can be kept in baskets of any color. Why rail at nature as it is? At the hour of tension, the needed fruit will be there for us.

But those who have realized psychic energy and have accepted the urgency of the Teaching will understand how closely the time of gathering of treasures has approached. The manifestation of surrounding chaos is for them like the crowd at a festival. Few are those with empty hands. To those who carry, one may say, "Do not break!"

Where is the source to which one should refer? Who can set limits? There is soil enough for every seed, and each seed contains the needed psychic energy within itself. The ancients had the knowledge of extracting psychic energy at the time of the softening of the seed. This is an example of how softening gives birth to motion. Each one knowing the Teaching will be a softener and the keeper of the paddle of the Great

281

Churn. For the great teraph of Infinity is at work in the actions of each day.

Austerity brings order. Softness brings creation. Let us look into the empty basket too, to see whether a seed of life is not hidden even in the bitterest bark.

558. The Atlanteans and also the Egyptians remembered the energy in the seed. For the sake of this energy they placed seeds in the tombs. But wiser applications were forgotten. The force of this energy could have powered great ships and other machinery. Just as a touch of the hand can move a large object, so can the condensed energy of the seed produce prolonged power. Even people near the seed can receive healthful revitalization.

559. When people speak of death, they often, even without thinking, express things that are true. People sense that it is helpful for the departure of the astral body to be gradual, and that sudden death can cause problems. But the most important consideration is not talked about—that the quality of psychic energy is the dominant factor. Man can overcome all obstacles through his consciousness. When the consciousness has expanded, then transitory conditions have little importance. When the bond with the Higher World is strong, then all tasks become easy. But it is strange that people generally prefer to talk about details, and overlook what is most important.

560. I affirm that psychic energy can overcome all obstacles. There is no force that can block the path of psychic energy.

561. There used to be a belief that heroes were able to watch the grass grow. But did this not in fact express an understanding that they were capable of higher observation?

562. Sometimes the human organism resists accepting possibilities that are ready for manifestation.

This corresponds closely to the story of how they ceased to expect the messenger though the messenger was already at the door.

563. Independence of action is encouraged. But should one be criticized if sometimes the desire arises to reach out to the Teacher for advice and to merge one's aura with His? It was always said: "First the storm, then the thunder, then silence." In this absence of sound comes the so-called Voice of the Silence. But higher than this voice is communion. You know how the voice of the Teacher is transmitted; but there can be a coming together in consciousness, not using words but transporting one's consciousness instantaneously into the consciousness of the Teacher. One almost ceases to be aware of oneself; but the Chalice is filled to the brim with straight-knowledge. Such union surpasses words, for it nurtures one with straight-knowledge. Of course it is not easy to attain such a state; but with expansion of consciousness it comes by itself, if not hindered by ignorance. All forms of communion are made possible by such a consciousness.

Why must the Teaching be absorbed as the basis of existence? If one begins to apply the Teaching egoistically, one will begin to add structures without first attending to the foundation. Half-hearted striving causes inner discord and does not bring regeneration. All harmful consequences result from half-hearted striving. Because of this, people cannot perfect themselves and cannot purify their sense of beauty, without which the blending of one's consciousness with the Teacher's is impossible.

564. You know how during the tension of some centers a contraction of the muscles can be observed, and inversely, a contraction of muscles can cause a strong sensation in the centers. If this idea is approached just by the intellect, it can lead to Hatha Yoga; but the noble straight-knowledge will always direct one upward.

565. Psychic energy was sometimes called Teros. In the Hermetic teaching one can find this expression: "The warrior Teros raised his shield." So was indicated the protective role of psychic energy.

Did you ever hear of a yogi's being devoured by beasts? There was never such an occurrence, for no animal that possesses a particle of instinct would dare pit itself against the shield of Teros. The essential thing is to summon Teros out of the Chalice and into the extremities. The channels from the Chalice branch out to all the extremities, and some people can sense the light of the Chalice as a tension in the fingers and toes. Others can sense the light of the *Brahmarandhra* center with a corresponding feeling in the Chalice. All this is not metaphysics but a practical indication for application in life. Many are in need of protection; why, then, not utilize one's own treasure?

It is not difficult to accumulate the energy of Teros or to evoke it. And it is not advisable to lose consciousness at the decisive moment, for that would produce a condition not unlike that of the so-called deadly eye. A yogi does not kill an animal by his own will; it is the evil will that smashes itself against the shield of Teros. One has to understand that not a coercive will, but the accumulation of the Chalice, will provide protection and permit action.

566. Fear cannot coexist with attainment. But again We must point out that fear and caution are not the same.

567. Accumulation of psychic energy should be the most important goal, and all efforts must be directed toward this. Many insects—whether white or black—are drawn to the flame, for fire is psychic energy. One must understand that everything is attracted by psychic energy, and that all measures should be taken to utilize it properly.

568. The growth of consciousness is accompanied by attacks of anguish, which are truly unavoidable. A growing awareness of the differences between the conditions of Infinity and those of earthly reality cannot but provoke the sympathies of a fair consciousness. There is no way to Infinity without a sensitivity to one's surroundings. Be assured that the greater the consciousness, the greater the anguish.

Who, then, can sense the beauty of Cosmos? Whoever has heard the music of the spheres even once will understand the earthly imperfections caused by the present condition of humanity. One must consciously fight against these attacks of anguish, though understanding their inevitability.

569. The best protection not only against sicknesses but also against hostile attacks will always lie in the conscious application of psychic energy. Its development is the most vital task of humanity.

570. It is one thing to hear, another to remember, yet another to apply. The Teaching will help one to reach this third step. The Teaching will also help one to leave behind the limitations of one's earthly phantoms; it will help one to perceive the seemingly usual as unusual. When this simple truth becomes evident, one will then not be far from attainment and the next step of ascent into the supermundane spheres. Those who seek attainment will be told, "The most important is to give yourself completely to this task." The predestined hour will approach only through attainment. When the joy of attainment fills the Chalice, success will come. Of course, this joy is not that of the calf whose gamboling crushes the flowers. The joy of attainment knows all labors and all perils; it crosses the bridge only once and dazzles the enemy with its radiance.

Teros was called a warrior; surely he is not a harvester, or a shepherd. In his nature Teros is conqueror and victor; but the joy of attainment does not turn him into a tyrant. Four prescriptions given long ago are: Reverence of Hierarchy; Realization of Unity; Realization of Co-measurement; and Application of the Canon "By thy God." With these, the disciple provides Teros with a proper basis for understanding. How else can he find where lies the path of the Good?

571. Pay attention to sites at high altitudes, exposed to the winds from snowy peaks. At an altitude of 24,000 feet one can observe deposits of meteoric dust. Under the power of the wind and the rays of the sun, this dust settles into the lower recesses, and changes the properties of both the snow and the soil. It is especially instructive to observe this in places where the ground is rich with metals. The metalization from within and without produces unusual magnetic combinations. Not only psychic energy but also many other energies acquire unique properties in such places. One should value those places in which so many different conditions are united. Observations of the quality of the snow, soil, and plants are not difficult, even with ordinary apparatuses.

The dust of the far-off spheres, when found in the snow on the peaks and at lower altitudes when it has melted, provides the opportunity to learn about new substances. In order to approach psychic energy under earthly conditions, one must observe how the deposits from the far-off spheres influence the human organism. One can see that these influences are many and strong. Thus, let us be attentive to the manifestations of nature.

572. The experience of joy in one's work is a manifestation of a special aspect of psychic energy. Joyous labor brings success multiplied.

573. Nervous choking is often the result of an over-burdening of the Chalice when its accumulations are not used consciously. Children can suffer from this, which indicates that their former experiences were considerable. Of course, thoughtful care and quiet occupation will balance the struggle between spirit and body. The throat, teeth, and eyes may likewise remind one about the struggle of unmanifested accumulations. In the same way, one should pay attention to what can be called consumption, which also may be provoked by the center of the Chalice.

Long ago the significance of *Manas* was pointed out; it is impossible that such a treasury as the Chalice should have no importance for all that surrounds it. There can be palliative measures, such as ammonia, menthol, eucalyptus, and cedar resin. But these will only ease the symptoms whereas the real panacea will be the cultivation of psychic energy.

574. Once, people were assembled to hear the Voice of the Teaching. They had often before heard about a treasure predestined for them. But some could only imagine the treasure as precious metals, and one even sewed a long purse for his share. Time went by and the treasure did not appear. However, they were told that the treasure was near and came together to receive it, but their patience was shorter than the long purse.

All but one hired someone to listen to the Teaching for them, while they themselves went to the bazaar, regretting their wasted time. One had missed collecting his debts; one had missed his chance to marry; one had forgotten to convict an offender; one had failed to gather his profits; one had missed bargains; one had lost the favor of the rajah. In short, the Teaching had apparently caused losses to each one.

Resentful, they gathered in the bazaar, sneering, "Where is this proclaimed treasure? What we were promised is a cloud—but one that cannot even produce rain!"

The Voice of the Teaching addressed the only one who had chosen to remain, "Why aren't you afraid of missing your time in the bazaar? Everything will be sold without you, and your name will not be included in contracts. Who told you that the promised treasure will not be nebulous?"

The one who remained answered, "I will not leave, for the promised treasure is more precious to me than life. The foretold good cannot be a delusion."

The Voice said, "Do you not fear that I shall fall silent?"

"You cannot, for You have already proclaimed Infinity."

"Are you not afraid of treachery from Me?"

"No. Courage and Light are Your guarantors."

"Do you not fear that the word *treasure* may mean *trap* in My language?"

"Even without words, Space vouches for the treasure."

The Voice said, "Wisely do you tirelessly persist. There, where you have heard the Teaching, there is the Treasure. Rise, you need not go far. Raise the stone on which you sit. Accept the divine cloud of Benevolence, and also from the earth its gold. The one who has harkened unto the end receives. The one who is courageous cannot be deprived. The one who gathers acquires."

575. Tomorrow's flowers bloom from yesterday's seeds. Advanced minds do not refuse to eat yesterday's bread. One must learn to combine all the knowledge of the past with the striving toward the future. Usually people deprive themselves of their best advantages by remaining bound to one point of view.

How can one succeed if, while the fire is burning, the eye insists on peering only into the darkness? The fire of Teros will illumine all accumulated treasures. It will also, like the inextinguishable *Brahmavidya*, be a protection against the seductions of Maya.

As you see, I use the language of ancient parables as well as that of the modern laboratory, so that you may learn to love both and extend your respect for the seed as well as for the fruit. An end must be put to narrow-mindedness.

576. Sometimes you may notice peculiarities in the way We express Ourselves. One must say that, although perfect correctness of form can be attained, in a telegram one pays more attention to the meaning.

577. All one's surroundings are subject to the influence of Teros. One can feel the invisible benevolence with which everything responds to the touch of the pure flame.

578. The process of deepening and refining one's thinking enables one to conduct remarkable observations of distant communication. You know that a communication enters the consciousness as something separate, and therefore is easily forgotten. You also know that neither tempest nor hurricane can hinder psychic energy, though they can affect the centers, especially the Chalice. It is possible to observe how communications relate to the particular centers, and how the quality of the communications is affected by them. Briefly, the manifold ways of thinking and the varied properties of psychic energy will provide new opportunities for the individuality. Observations conducted under various conditions of locality, temperature, and weather will provide an inexhaustible source for new achievements.

579. One should remember that Our enemies make effective use of every spatial disturbance and try to inflict the most undesirable harm. This combination of physical and psychic conditions demands attention.

580. It is correct to presume that evolution is propelled at times of great cosmic reaction. But this does not mean that people should not prepare themselves for it. Each conscious, thinking individual seeks anxiously for the future direction of evolution. If this direction is sensed, then common sense will strive to approach the right path more speedily. Our Teaching does not coerce, but indicates the way. Not mysticism, but logic of mind, is offered to the seekers.

We say, let the books of the Teaching be published in a normal way. Let them be without an author's name, to exclude personal interest. In a few years people will understand that experience and deep study have produced these Teachings. Those who find the time for study of the books will enter the new world structures as welcome guests. Thus the mist of savagery will be replaced by refined understanding.

We always underline the concept of refinement, for it is bound up with the growth of spirit. You saw the slowness of accumulations of the spirit; similarly, refinement cannot be developed at once. The process of improvement of any machine shows how slowly perfection is gained. But realizing refinement of thought, we all must command ourselves to move with evolution; then every day becomes a day of victory.

581. Usually people think that these days are absurd with complexity; but if, without prejudice, we compare these times with others, we shall see that during the last ten years much has been simplified, opening the way to evolution.

582. We have already spoken about the rotation of the centers. Of course, any forward motion is a rotating one. The symbol of churning relates to everything. The accumulations of psychic energy can be intensified through the rotation of the center. The individual may prefer one center over another, but it would be better to choose the Chalice or the *Brahmarandhra* center.

One can promote the circulation of psychic energy externally by rubbing the body with an emulsion of seven vegetable ingredients, known from antiquity. This is the same emulsion used by yogis when leaving the physical body for a lengthy period of time. It also can be applied with benefit to treat various problems, beginning with skin diseases.

This emulsion when rubbed into the body, provides the energy needed to sustain nourishment for a long time. This is similar to the taking of musk, which, as you already know, reduces one's need for food. Give the formula for this emulsion only to those who have proved their devotion to the Teaching. There is little reason to feed the body of one who tries to deny psychic energy.

583. If people would only realize the consequences of their thoughts! It would be no exaggeration to say that even the greatest of crimes have been born of the smallest of thoughts. One may point out to people how material and alive thought is.

I do not speak only of yogis, for each one who has developed psychic energy is protected by it. People are afraid to assault one who possesses special powers. Common wisdom remembers how the blow that strikes the armor of Teros boomerangs. Likewise, common wisdom knows that some people can leave their influence on objects. This is true—psychic energy can, for example, be transmitted to objects through touch. Thus, one may observe the power of thought and the emanations of psychic energy.

Animals, especially dogs, sense the emanations of psychic energy. It is not just through smell that they can find their home and their master, but through something deeper.

One will ask how to begin to approach psychic energy. At the beginning, simply keep in mind that this energy exists.

584. Look for the close correlation between magnetic whirlwinds and manifestations of psychic energy. These whirlwinds were correctly termed in Hermeticism the thought of space.

585. It is right to desire to explore the foundations of Vedic medicine. In spite of the later changes, the essence of the Vedic medicine remains useful. To each searching investigator the very logic of this medicine provides new perceptions of the properties of plant extracts. Instead of a crude listing of plants and other products of nature, precise information about the properties of the various parts of plants and the conditions of their use leads to more exact conclusions. Attention must also be paid to the conditions of cosmic chemistry. Coming from the most ancient times, these conclusions can bring joy to the present-day observer.

586. One can easily strengthen the action of vegetable remedial substances by increasing the metalization of the soil. In this way, even slow-acting medications can be made more powerful and rapid in their effects. Instructive experiments can be performed using the fortified seeds over generations. With short-lived plants these experiments do not require many years. Even the third generation will show considerable change.

587. If I say that everything is good, it will be untrue. If I say that everything is bad, it will also be untrue. It would be better to say, "Battle, and victory." But how can one be taught the joy of battle?

588. Why is a tensed physical position sometimes needed? It enhances the radiation of psychic energy.

589. The wise one knows the spoken word, knows the written word, knows the thought, and knows silence—so says the old proverb. Let us examine this from the point of view of psychic energy. Truly, one has to distinguish when a spoken word, a written letter, a thought, or silence is most needed. One can achieve much by directing one's energy properly. Refined straight-knowledge will determine which method is the most needed at each moment.

590. You have noticed that sometimes physical tension activates one's psychic energy. This purely mechanistic and physical condition should direct one to thinking about the material nature of psychic energy. This materiality of psychic energy can easily be demonstrated by physical means. It is not difficult to observe the reflexive reactions to physical tension. Should one not search along these obvious directions? It means that spiritual manifestations are not at all abstract and can be measured. They may not be evident to all, yet the coarser actions can be seen by even an ordinary person. Unfortunately people often pass by without noticing even the loudest colors. Red may sometimes be remembered as green; this kind of distortion can be met everywhere.

I do not speak about straight-knowledge simply to repeat myself. This condition has been spoken about sufficiently. But pay attention to the material nature of spirituality, which can be observed from many points of view. Still, there remain two worlds—the apparent and the real. Knowing the meaning of these two ideas, everyone will agree that preference be given to reality. What perfection can be achieved upon cognizing reality! Once reality is brought to the foreground and affirmed as a completely valid concept, the surroundings will change beyond recognition.

Many truths are spoken of. Should not one break through their shells and strive to the One Truth? The most precise and objective observation of reality will broaden the consciousness. Indeed, the consciousness is that magic coffer in which all lost treasures will be gathered.

591. I rejoice when you realize the harm of false spirituality. Often a sickly distortion of psychic energy becomes a substitute for a properly expanded consciousness. Where there is fear, where there is self-pity, where there is conceit, where there is passivity, where there is avoidance of self-sacrifice, where there is lack of co-measurement, where there is irresponsibility, can there be service to evolution?

Those who avoid the labor of the harvest should be made to understand that their groans are less than the rustling of one blade of grass. Also, those who venture into the astral world without an understanding of ascent must know how responsible they are for the polluting of space. Only the consciousness can lead, and permit the discerning of the right direction. Also, those who consider service to evolution as an effort deserving reward may be repaid in coin, but not by expansion of consciousness.

Affirm that the refining of consciousness is the magnet that attracts all beneficial energies. The consciousness, an inexhaustible treasure, will lead to the summits, where victory is found. Is it worthy of man to let his consciousness be overgrown with weeds? It is essential to consider whither one wishes to propel oneself. The fire of consciousness will illumine the way.

592. It is correct to assume the inexhaustibility of psychic energy. The store reasonably used is replenished immediately from the treasury of Cosmos. It is good to project psychic energy; the new supply more easily produces its deposits, and then strives to the universal work. How can one set the wheel of law into motion? It is so easy to evoke the new power from space! That is why I speak about the circulation of psychic energy.

593. The word *I* should be kept only for special responsibility and testimony. The word *we* is for the whole of life and for cooperation. Then there is also the word *they*. But first one must accept the word *we* and realize cooperation.

594. The fundamental mystery of Hermes was contained in the approach of the astral world to our Earth. One can see these sparks in the Hermetic Teachings, although they are carefully veiled. But now We will from time to time recall them.

Crystals of psychic energy, when applied to one's body, draw one's own inner psychic energy, just as a magnet draws a needle from the body. One can imagine how powerful are crystals of psychic energy when used as medicines.

595. You already know that the crystal of psychic energy possesses the properties of a magnet. It attracts electronic particles of Teros from space. The emanations of the approaching waves surround one and color with their chemism the attracted particles of energy. This is the chemical basis of so-called colored stars.

The planetary bodies radiate with different lights. Scientists will see the sparks of psychic energy. The fires of the human body's centers also radiate differently depending upon the chemism of the metals in the human body.

596. Many people have observed the significance of the successive development of the centers. Incomprehensible labels often have been given to real things. Thus, when you hear the word *Abramram*, it will be a reminder about the center of the Chalice, where straight-knowledge predestined for the future evolution is concentrated. When you hear about "fiery wings," it will mean the centers of the shoulders. Likewise, the "treasures of the five summits" will be the centers of *Brahmarandhra*, the wrists, and the knees. When a sudden weakness is felt under the knees, or a strain in the wrists, this will mean the sharpening of the *Brahmarandhra*. Countless observations can be made that will reveal the inexhaustible qualities of the organism, so shamefully neglected.

597. Certain peoples have a custom of invoking their distant, absent ones by calling up a chimney flue that was purified by fire. Let us remember too the long trumpet of the ancient Egyptians, which also acted through fire.

Consider that the sending of thought was combined everywhere with an understanding of fire. Truly, for the sending of thought to a great distance, one has to evoke the flame of the centers. Not a forced strain of the will, but a combination with fire gives power to the sending of thought.

598. It is useful to remember all the legends about fire, for they contain much truth. The growth of understanding will make it possible to distinguish the fundamentals of reality from the errors of mistaken conventionality.

599. Certainly, one of the main tasks of the coming evolution will be to transform our view of the so-called abstract into a recognition of it as cognizable reality. The study of psychic energy will make possible a completely new approach to one's surroundings. The contrasting results of selfish versus altruistic actions have until the present been seen in an abstract way, but let us henceforth examine them from the point of view of the chemism of the various centers. Different thoughts and actions issue from different centers. Hence, their emanations are chemically different, as is their visible radiance. The effects react on the creator himself and on his surroundings. Thus, it would seem that the most abstract will become weighable and measurable. One of the simplest experiments will be the weighing of an individual under the impact of his different thoughts. A sensitive scale and sharpness of thought will provide clear contrasts. This is not a science for hermits but is knowledge for the improvement of life.

600. As light conquers darkness, as thought conquers chaos, so does the Teaching enter life.

601. Scientists speaking about the subconscious, about cerebral and nervous reflexes, about animal magnetism, about telepathy, certainly speak of one and the same thing—of psychic energy. But this term is somehow not uttered. These snatches of knowledge beg to be united into one current, but narrow-mindedness prevents the proper relating of these various fragments of knowledge. Pure science is not afraid of alleyways. Attention is being paid now to the study of secretions, and perhaps this particular direction, the investigation of glandular secretions, will call attention to the existence of other secretions. Glandular secretions have only recently attracted attention, although ancient medicine pointed out the importance of secretions long ago. This matter was avoided, although all of nature proclaimed it. Is it possible that dialectics and materialism are only limitations? The development of consciousness brings us into closer contact with the entire mighty energy. Is it possible to think as before, with only half one's brain, not caring about the locked-up treasures?

602. The forging of the sword in the flame under the hammer's blow is the best illustration of how one tempers one's psychic energy. Someone may ask how to endure unrest and agitation. But rest can be found only at the peak of unrest. There is no rest amidst the cosmic whirlwinds. The blind and deaf may dream of a rest that does not exist, but the ones who see, who want only to see clearly, prefer to endure the storms. There is no rest, as people understand it. One cannot step out of the turning spiral of creation. One has to evoke Teros as one's anchor, to link oneself to the proper chain of currents. The strong spirit rejoices in tempering his sword.

603. Notice that a deep sigh accompanies any application of psychic energy. Does not this indicate that this energy is something tangible? Point out the manifestations of this energy scattered everywhere. A path can be built with these milestones.

604. In the study of psychic energy, much can be learned about its properties. For example, you have noticed that astral beings can assume any form and produce any image. This has been shown sufficiently in photographs. What kind of energy helps them in this creation? Of course, psychic energy, if already cultivated while they were incarnate. But it is not so much the frightful phantoms that are evidenced as the reaction of our own organism that is important in our observations.

The ancient ones said, "The mountain of the Mother rises from the Earth to the heavens," indicating thus the unity of all that exists. Is it possible that in an era of culture people will agree to their own degradation, or to the conventions and distortions of their religions? When, along with mechanics, psychomechanics proclaims itself so mightily, can there persist a dull denial? People come together to fulfill the best tasks. But where are those tasks? We must continually repeat that the external conditions of life are a reflection of the consciousness. It seems that these words are already branded on the human forehead, but one cannot deny that humanity requires repeated shocks.

605. The mind vacillates, but the consciousness triumphs. This is not a contradiction, but a reference to surface and essence. Which way to turn? Even a child will say, "To the essence." Even a child knows to peel the fruit in order to refresh itself with the juice. Nothing should impede us from the task of regenerating our consciousness.

606. Some nervous diseases can be cured by a change of residence. One could regard this idea as a whim, but there are explanations for it. The air that surrounds one is as mineralized and magnetic as water. We make use of waters of different compositions. Why, then, should air not be similarly utilized for its effect upon the different centers?

Much is spoken about *prana*; but pure prana is inaccessible on Earth, except on the heights, where few dare to stay. At the lower levels the *prana* is mineralized and is subject to the influence of discordant magnetic waves. Certainly, a change of residence can lead one to more beneficial combinations of *prana*, and may have a healing effect on the condition of one's nervous system. Unfortunately, so far the air in homes is generally regarded simply, as either pure or impure. In fact, every change of air has importance, since it affects different groups of nerves. Our Brother who was a shoemaker occasionally changed his trade to gardening. This is wise, for the seed growing into a sprout radiates psychic energy of particular tension. One should remember this. After the *pralaya* of night, the morning sun acts with special vitality in calling forth the psychic energy. Similarly, the awakened life of the seed, like the dawn, sends forth its emanations of prayer. Let us note carefully all benevolent influences.

607. If, instead of having recourse to courts and prosecutions, people would apply psychic energy, the incurable disease of crime would become a mere matter of ordinary investigation. Physicians should look into this as a stage of obsession. Applying psychic energy without changing one's customary understanding of crime would be harmful.

608. Every motion has its own rhythm, just as any energy has its own pattern and crystal. The pattern of the rhythm stimulates an outflow of nervous energy.

609. Many illnesses can be prevented by means of psychic energy. It may be said that some organisms are predisposed or not disposed toward certain sicknesses. But what this protection or weakness consists of no one can say positively. Studies of psychic energy would provide the best answers.

610. Many think about worldwide peace. But if you dare to utter these words, you will be subjected to the most rude and hypocritical attacks. People are even afraid of peace, for their consciousness cannot accommodate this benevolence. But those who have broadened their consciousness, on the other hand, must untiringly speak about the opening of the gates of peace.

611. The Teaching is like prophecy in the world of science. Even skeptics will admit that the fate of humanity cannot depend upon the dissecting of frogs. The revealing of Our Indications at least will not increase the number of the bearers of ignorance! Accept enlightenment, the helper of humanity. Those possessing diplomas have overlooked the law of the Common Good. You, attracted by Maya, manifest understanding!

612. One plays on twelve strings, another produces the same tune on four, and a third limits himself to two, creating just as many harmonies on them. Does it matter how many strings one requires for harmony? The essential thing is that it be created. Let us not wonder at or criticize variety, for we shall not find even two grains of sand alike. On the contrary, let us rejoice at every unusual manifestation. Flowers choose for themselves whatever soil is suitable. Even stones are arranged in a relation one to another. Likewise in the domains of Teros, there will be combinations of elements that are related, despite their seeming differences. The consciousness refined by fire discerns the kindred foundations, and will not reject the true value by appraising only the surface. A countless variety can be expressed on but two strings. However, for this one has to realize how innumerable are the properties of nature, and how those properties are expressed in man. Such considerations are usually considered symbolical, and are not introduced into life. However, to know the Teaching and not to apply it is a sign of complete ignorance. Who has ever told you that one can wander over the Teaching like a fly on sugar, then just as easily dive into dung! One cannot turn one's horses recklessly when on the mountain paths. Knowledge leads only onward!

613. The resplendent world must not be forgotten. It is the link to the far-off worlds. As a subtle substance, it suffuses space. Reaching from dimension to dimension, it knows neither far nor near. The discrete layers can be penetrated by the disembodied consciousness. The consciousness will be the guide, for its substance is universal.

Mediators can be found in the Subtle World. Of course, our own consciousness should attract a refined consciousness, and the mediator must be capable of comprehending the tasks of the world. Not long ago I spoke of how impartially one has to think about the astral world. One must gain a proper understanding of the mediators through straight-knowledge; these are not guides, but simply helpers—telegraph poles, as it were. In time, their number will decrease and they will eventually become unnecessary. Thus, all elements and all conditions will be joined in the one work. How can one point out more clearly to a merchant that he can step beyond the limits of his account books? And how can one show that health and joy abide in the realization of Infinity?

614. The part of Agni Yoga that We now give calls attention to psychic energy, to the inception of the fires, and to the refining of consciousness. When these principles have been accepted, one can then begin the process of refining one's thinking. Thus, let us not think that the Teaching ever ends.

615. Why must the path of the Teaching be a path of accumulation? Can it not be offered in one dose, like a medicine? But the stomach is of limited dimension, whereas consciousness is not a measurable constant. Truly, there can be people almost without consciousness. There can be people who have deprived themselves of consciousness through excessive passions. There can be consciousnesses obscured by the conventions of their time. Like hothouse flowers, consciousnesses are in need of nurture. The foundation of consciousness is built by straight-knowledge, but the refining of consciousness is as slow as the polishing of a crystal. Not by one's opinion of oneself but by the quality of one's action is the expansion of one's consciousness recognized.

The Teaching is given as the stones are laid to build a tower. If one sets up all the stones at once, there will be not a tower, but a heap.

616. Attain and conquer. You do not conquer for yourself; your victory is important for the General Good.

617. The sacred fire of spirit opens the way to the Teaching, but the main aspiration of the disciple should be the kindling of his own fires. We shall affirm the Chalice of Aspiration, but the disciple himself must fill the Chalice of Achievement.

618. If people would only understand that the sending of sorrow returns as sorrow, but joy sent is joy increased. Such filling of space was known even to primitive man, when he said, "I will not allow sorrow to interrupt the stream of happiness." We will live through all, and attain all!

619. The power of the magnet is increased by the whirling rotation of the spiral, from the currents of *prana* of Infinity. By magnetizing Our thoughts, We send messages carrying thoughts and images that ignite the human consciousness.

620. I advise that the Teacher's Name be held up as a shield. Not a symbol, not an illusion, but a chain of consciousnesses provides the current of invincibility. We do not know the end of this chain, and you do not know its beginning. It is like a serpent stretched from the depths of Earth into the infinitely distant spheres.

The mountain of the Mother of the World does not know its summit. Shall we fear it? Shall we be terrified at its unapproachableness? Or shall we rejoice that *Amrita* is inexhaustible? Amidst all the world's measurable concepts, the Incalculable radiates its light. Shall we be displeased by the coolness of the far-off wind that comes from Infinity? In the sweltering barrenness, let us not turn away from a life-giving stream.

621. The joy of spirit is a pledge to the Teaching. Creative work is goal-fitting when the striving spirit, aspiring toward the manifestation of Beauty, realizes Infinity. I consider that the coiled spring of refined consciousness will be strengthened by the Teaching, when it is embraced.

622. Pledge with all your possessions. Pledge with complete aspiration. Pledge with all the power of thought. Thus new conditions can be created.

If yesterday you did not attain, it means that the accumulations were not correct. One should not repeat one's mistakes, for it is impossible to cross at the point where the bridge has been destroyed. Often people eliminate their minor faults, while their greater ones are kept, hidden in the dark. May the fires dispel the darkness! Therefore We ordain: Light the fires! Do not regard the Teaching as abstraction. Repeat to yourself the words of the Wise Ones!

623. A disciple aspiring to become an Agni Yogi must sense the full power of the flame of love for his Teacher. A disciple desiring to help in the building of the Teacher's works must safeguard the Advice of the Teacher. A disciple desiring to safeguard the Advice of the Teacher must protect His utterances as pearls.

I say that you must learn to affirm the Origin in the beauty of Cosmos by permeating life with the hymns of the Mother of the World.

624. What shall one do with those straying from the Teaching? Leave them, do not violate their will. Maybe the currents of life will again carry them to your shores. Each separation is painful, but the ways of consciousness are so varied that it is not wise to impede them. Let the spirit strive freely, taking responsibility for its own failures.

625. Remember that help is found in one's actions. The power of action provides the best armor, the best rudder, the best eye!

626. Just as the stream finds its way through the rocks, unconcerned about the structure of the stones, so does the Agni Yogi make his way through the customs of his own national culture. On one's way to the heights of consciousness, neither boundaries, nor limitations, nor prohibitions exist for the one who has ignited the light of his consciousness.

Ancient Israel, seeking the way to the Highest, and the Mayans, who gained knowledge about the boundaries of states of consciousness, remind us about the course of the quest. Just as fire knows no boundaries, so does the consciousness of an Agni Yogi proceed without obstacles.

627. Often we know a word, but cannot utter it. Its beginnings swirl in the depth of consciousness, but cannot be brought to the surface. The depth of the consciousness is strongly felt at such moments. Not in the fissures of the brain, but in some other repository are gathered the treasures of memory—indeed, it is in the Chalice.

I could remind you of times when the Chalice was physically injured, and the flow of memories immediately stopped. On the other hand, upon injury to the brain, images of one's entire life may speed by instantaneously, as if bursting from the depths.

Upon expansion of consciousness, cooperation of the centers is realized. One may cognize what can be obtained from the channels of the brain and what can be drawn out of the depths of the Chalice. Untold treasures are accumulated in the Chalice. The Chalice is one, for all incarnations. The peculiarities of the brain are a matter of heredity, but the properties of the Chalice are the result of one's own actions.

In the Chalice lies a winged child; thus does ancient wisdom remind us of the origin of consciousness.

628. I have already said that mysteries and miracles are no longer relevant. In their place an understanding of psychic energy must be affirmed in the consciousness. It is psychic energy that causes live-giving forces to be set into motion. Let us remember this.

Some obscure centers, as yet unknown to medicine, are revealing themselves as the source of power for our thoughts. Soon these levers will find their application and will merit chapters in books.

629. A properly paved road is laid with small pebbles. One cannot lay a smooth road with large rocks. When you study the ways of thinking, you will perceive a multitude of small thoughts, with which you can pave over the roiling surface. He who can be attentive to small thoughts will be able to control great decisions. The quality and sequence of small thoughts lay the road for great actions.

When we speak of psychic energy, we must first of all remember the causes and effects of our small daily thoughts. These worms weaken the higher energy. A disorderly heap of refuse will obstruct any work of building. Our enemies are small, annoying flies. Do not the torn fragments of fleeting images resemble them? When we point out the need for cultivation of psychic energy, we shall say the same about the disciplining of small thoughts. But we must know that the small can be forerunners of the great.

Let energy grow, without dust!

630. The human perception of reality is so misty that, truly, humanity is orphaned when deprived of the affirmation of the Teaching.

The irrevocable power, the valiant power, the essential power, the spiritual power, the downpouring power, the irrefutable power, the power of Our Ray, the power manifested from Our Summits! Denying ones, sense in your suffocation that light exists in the spirit! That which you have stored up will be exhausted prematurely. Where will you turn, withered ones, at the threshold of death? Truly, I say, you do not know the spiritual shields, and cover yourselves with the sundry tatters of Maya!

631. We welcome all who approach to be of use to the Teaching, but We rejoice at those who have made the Teaching their life.

Those who strike at the Teaching will be stricken in return. But how can harm and defeat be distinguished from usefulness and offering? You cannot know the dividing lines of all the ways of thinking in the world.

Bearer of happiness, where is thy distinguishing garment of happiness? What light kindles the rainbow of radiance? Only in the Chalice are collected the kernels of true knowledge.

Furious attacks will only strengthen you on your path.

632. Our Teaching does not accept vacillation in the disciple. A true disciple is steadfast, knowing there is no end. The fire of striving is the impeller of events. The attainment is wondrous when the disciple can say, "Master, I want to drink to the full of the chalice of labor."

633. What I told you yesterday about the vision above the Chalice has a scientific explanation. Saturating space with intensified thought, we clothe aspects of our striving with a particular image. Thus, out of elemental matter we create a desired image, which remains near the place where it was created, fortified by our thoughts. The eye of a child or a refined consciousness can perceive this formation. Similar observations are useful in studying creativity of thought. Of course, to be successful one must preserve the aura of the place and unceasingly add layer upon layer to the transmissions. The hour before dawn and the rhythm of chant will be helpful.

As you have heard, one can observe the growth of hair in a similar way. It is instructive to observe the capillary structure of the hair, as a conductor of consciousness. Also, study of the pores of the skin will provide some very important observations.

634. Tell those who find the trials cruel that the goal-fitness of those trials is demonstrated by the fact that without them the spirit would not progress. The spirit's experience comes from the accumulations of former incarnations, but the spirit also wants food from the realities of its present life. Labor is available for all who desire to progress. But one should not think of the spirit as the sole producer of the experience of conscious achievement. A portion of the knowledge accumulated in the Chalice must also be applied.

635. It could be asked, if things do occur such as those heard of in the Tibetan monastery, then why are such manifestations not heard of in the West? Of course, the West also has many cases of the same order, but often the true nature of the phenomena is over-looked. The way of thinking in the East is more refined in some aspects. Therefore I advise you to notice and evaluate all facts. We despise superstition. All prejudice must be left behind.

636. The influence of Our rays is like the illumination of torches; they open the consciousness when the spirit, propelled to the heights, desires to open the gates of Truth. It is very difficult to illumine the dark consciousness.

You, conceited ones, accept Our advice: To blow the trumpet of self-satisfaction forever is unwise. Remember the dark side, and do not reject the Hand that points to the better destiny!

637. I do not say it is easy, I do not say it is impossible, but I point out the path on which the comforts of earthly life are justly granted, yet the highest is not rejected. But, of course, the hour is not easy. The Teaching will proceed by unexpected ways, but one may rejoice.

638. Every condition is revealed more clearly by its opposite. Light exposes darkness. What, then, is the opposite to the light of psychic energy? Of course, absolute darkness. This emanation of deadliness, emptiness, and valuelessness is the shadow cast by the Fire of highest energy. If we know the crystal of psychic energy, then we know the deposits of darkness. The highest ascent of Teros is echoed by the lowest descent of Tamas.

639. You noticed correctly that in receiving distant transmissions a special kind of vigilant receptivity is needed. Not vacant receptivity, but a keenness of the centers. One must be able to distinguish between will-fulness and the refining of perception. Thus we shall gradually discern our inner forces.

640. I shall say that you can become participants in the evolution of Cosmos. You can master the inheritance of the ages. You can manifest understanding of Infinity. You can improve the fate of the planet. But let the fires be set aflame! Do not extinguish the sacred fire of spirit. Do not reject the Hand.

Illumined by the radiance of the Mother of the World, our physical existence is seen to be but a grain of sand. But the cumulation in the Chalice is like a radiant mountain!

641. You noticed the vibration of objects after you had touched them. This is one of the manifestations of either your own or an external psychic energy. You also observed how the personal disappeared from daily life with the growth of psychic energy. Likewise, one should be reminded that the psychic energy is responsible for the shaping of circumstances.

642. One of the most difficult requirements of the Teaching is learning to speak appropriately—to speak so as to properly direct the thinking of the listener, but without intruding upon his karma. To tell all is to enchain. But to awaken striving and indicate a direction is the true task of the Teaching. Protective care will invisibly watch over the growth of consciousness. As a hand leads in the dark along winding streets, so does the Teacher place His Hand upon the shoulder of the disciple. Not vacuum but vigilance is proper for guidance. The Indication fills space, but does not hit the student on the head. Not for any one person, but for the general evolution is the Teaching given. It is as a ray of the sun. Blessed is the one who acts as a hunter of light!

643. Once a Yogi was asked how he shaped space psychologically. He answered, "The emanations of psychic energy are like the fragrance of flowers. Why strain that which ascends to the highest Aum? The finest ether absorbs the currents of psychic energy, and people inhale it; thus the effects occur."

There are four ways of perfectment: acceptance of the gift of the Teaching; liberation from the ego; manifestation of courage, knowing all dangers; learning to make the enemies work for the General Good.

644. You submit to examination by physicians of different kinds. You allow your body to be cut by the scalpel. You permit physical experiments. But when you are spiritually ill and your consciousness is dim and you do not perceive the light of the coming future, still you reject any thought about the shield of regeneration. I have said that your shield is in recognizing Our existence. Accept this advice—heal your consciousness! You who complain about your liver, examine your thoughts!

645. Some ask how one should regard daily routine. Most people are quite afraid of it. It is considered to be the death of creativity, and the demeaning of dignity. But We say that you should learn to see in each day's labor the *pranayama* that uplifts your consciousness. Prana descends from the higher spheres; but any labor produces energy, which in its essence is similar to the spatial energy. Thus, the one who knows the common essence of energies can sew shoes, or beat rhythms on a drum, or gather fruit. In all these the higher energy is generated, since it is born out of the rhythm of Cosmos. Only a low consciousness dreads the rhythm of labor and thus builds its own prison. It is difficult for humanity to understand that a king and a shoemaker are comparable in every respect.

646. Many words are spoken about the Teaching of Life, but few are put into action. There is little value in those who repeat the Teaching without applying it. We are not speaking about those who lack understanding, but those who have approached the Teaching are responsible for their thoughts and actions.

647. The full understanding of Our Precepts must be expressed by immediate, undeferrable action. The disciple must not in his good intentions find an excuse for a bad result. Light-mindedness, negligence, and the demeaning of Our Instructions weigh heavily on the scales. Even the disciple will examine himself three times and say, "I see no mistakes in my actions."

"Do not lower your eyes to the lowlands, but turn to the heights of the Mother of the World, and thus judge your actions by the measures of the Infinite."

648. When you plant *balu* and rhododendron in the plains, when you plant apples on the mountains, can you expect immediate results? Likewise, in the mastering of psychic energy sufficient time must be allowed for transformation of the essential nature of the energy. A forced application of tension will not bring expected results. Often people expect results in one dimension, though they occur in a completely different one. Therefore, know the time needed for the growth of energy.

Certainly, one may deepen one's understanding of the Teaching of Agni Yoga in all directions. But this is accomplished only in accord with one's assimilation of what has been given.

649. A disciple who has responded to the call of the Teaching and is aflame with all fires of devotion is truly a co-worker of the Cosmic forces. Having increased by his own actions the forces of Cosmos, having adorned spatial thought with his thoughts, is he not then a creator? And is not the wisdom of the ages his best adornment?

The vastness of the spatial Fire of Cosmos offers the best destiny to searching humanity.

650. Even your physicians admit that during nervous exaltation one's strength increases tenfold. Thus they acknowledge psychic energy. But they see that such states are brief and are followed by a loss of energy. Precisely for this reason is the Yoga needed, so that while increasing the ascent, one is kept from falling. Collapses are brought on by a lack of realization and by failure to apply one's psychic energy. The ignoramus limps as if lame, but the one who knows can conquer the most unattainable heights.

The power of authority is not demonstrated by a flow of instructions that are pleasing to both the one who gives them and those who receive. The Teacher must be sure that the actions taken lead in the right direction—though they may take manifold forms. Just as a courageous captain can save his ship by jettisoning the cargo, or by cutting down the masts, so does the Teacher with full power of authority lead his disciples to victory.

Is it possible to avoid the burdensome currents? Of course it is better to face them head-on in battle than to zigzag to evade them. But the decision to engage in battle is the responsibility of the leader. The joy of battle is known to those who are aware of its purpose, to those who know the necessity of victory.

Now you know that the battlefield is rife with possibilities. It is there that the visible and invisible worlds are in contact and affect each other. This is not magic, just as walking on water is not magic—not by command but out of necessity. How can one reach the goal, if one is without faith? Straight-knowledge needs both direction and goal. Not knowing the goal leads to a piling-up of confusion. Fallen leaves nourish the black soil, but each seed brings an explosion of energy into the world.

651. Attentiveness can be tested in a simple way. Move an object to a new place; if it remains unnoticed, do the same with a larger object and observe what "elephant" finally attracts the "sharp" eye. Test yourself and others. Test for fear, for irritation, and for laziness—and for all failings that cause the litmus paper to blush with shame. There is no need of complicated invocations, since simple attentiveness moves one many steps further. Thus one should begin to develop the "eagle-eye."

One yogi gained the reputation of being a practical joker because unnoticeably he moved various objects in people's houses, and when asked why, answered, "I am checking to see if you have become blind." Truly, there are few who notice changes in their surroundings. But the first sign of an "eagle-eye" is the ability to notice the smallest changes, since on them depends the vibration of the whole.

652. Harmonious sendings bring much usefulness, especially when one dominant tone can be followed, as for a musical key. A primary note may even be struck with a tuning fork. A magnet, a tuning fork, a ring, and many common devices easily enter into the daily life of the young yogis. The clearing away of accumulations of debris requires the use of shovel and broom. One should not fear everyday objects—as below, so above.

It is wise to become accustomed to there being no rest or end. But the realization alone of Hierarchy and Our Brotherhood already directs the traveler along the shortest path in the Infinite.

653. The thought of obedience to a Teacher is foreign to humanity. But how can a spirit not succeed when the Teacher is the Leading Beacon? How can the disciple lose his fire when the Teacher is the kindler of all fires? How can the Shield of the Teacher be an obstacle to the disciple when it is the Teacher who impels his fiery striving? In the consciousness of humanity lives a germinal desire to strive for a common work that leads all forward, in unity. But humanity must learn independent action, and must implement the affirmed thoughts of the Teacher. Thus does human evolution achieve harmony with Cosmic Reason. Humanity must learn to create by the higher way.

Truly, emulation of the Teacher is the taking of the Image of the Teacher into one's heart.

654. How can one come close to the Source? How will the higher understanding be affirmed? Only by the law of Hierarchy. The Guiding Hand is the Uplifting Hand. The Indicating Hand is the Hand revealing the path to the Highest Law. Thus is created the great step of the law of Hierarchy. Truly!

655. How do people understand the law of Hierarchy? How do they fulfill its laws in life? How do they intensify the best striving in themselves? Truly the law of Hierarchy is mistakenly understood as an individual's right; it is forgotten that a Hierarch is a

Link in a Chain, and One who fulfills the Will of an even Higher One. Only by knowing this is it possible to properly respond to the higher mission. Only thus can one validate the Trust and build the fiery accumulations in the Chalice.

656. Remember the laws of gravitation and repulsion, action and counteraction. Steadfastness results from attraction, and tension from repulsion. Attraction along the line of Hierarchy leads to Me, and repulsion from the enemy to glorification. Thus, the Teacher and the enemy are cornerstones.

The trainer of wild animals must first excite their rage before he succeeds in taming them. No motion is possible without tension; therefore, every progressive Teaching needs its enemies and its Teacher. One must keep in mind the physical law in order to understand the immutability of the law of the spirit. My Advice is that the significance of the Teacher and the need for enemies must be understood. Certainly, only the Teacher will lead the enemy to fury. The full measure of evil must be manifested before one may rise regenerated out of the flames of wrath. It is impossible to avoid the obstacles of the path, but know that no obstructive tensions will occur without being of benefit. Indeed they may be of service to entire nations!

If a hermit is able with his thought alone to destroy a stronghold of evil, then the tensity that is allowed by the Higher Forces will be like a battering ram against the hostile forces.

I vouch for success, but only if unity is achieved, and Hierarchy is accepted. Many things can undermine good results, but decisiveness brings relief.

One should not reject the invisible world; one should demand of oneself cooperation with it.

657. In fulfilling My Will you offer Me the opportunity to fulfill your will. Where is the boundary between wills that together strive toward Light? One may remember that We lead those who have entrusted themselves to Us along the paths of well-tested magnets. One can trust a Helmsman who has already sailed the oceans.

"Cross the bridge. Test thyself. But My Star has known the ages."

Fear will not touch the well-tested heart.

658. The quality of action is forged by striving. When words are turned into action, the higher energy is affirmed. Only in life can one manifest the higher energies. Not words but actions are considered to be the affirmation of the higher energies. Only when the potential of the spirit is manifested in action can concordance with the Highest be affirmed.

Thus, a striving quest provides the key to the Infinite.

659. Our Teaching is so powerful because Our Words enter into life as wondrous affirmations. Thus do Our Words live, for the creative impulse is saturated by the power of Fire. Only when Our Advice is applied in life can the higher step be taken.

Why is your mission so effective? Because it carries within it Our pledge of Cooperation. Thus We affirm Hierarchy based upon the law of succession. When the Cosmic Law is realized, a true understanding of the Chain of Hierarchy is established. Thus, the one who better fulfills his tasks will be closer to Hierarchy. The Hierarchy of Service is but the manifestation of the fulfillment of an even Higher Will. Only in this way do We affirm the Law of Hierarchy. And thus does Cosmic Law enter life.

660. Through what means is the spirit transformed? Through the impulse of creative work.

Through what does the spirit ascend? By the creativeness of striving. How, then, can the spirit fail to be saturated with fire if only thus is one able to join the Cosmic Magnet? But the consciousness of the Higher Spirit indeed is saturated fire! Therefore only the realization of the Higher Will can lead the spirit toward its goal. Thus each consciously-taken step lends beauty to action. Creative labor that adheres to the affirmed fire is magnetized through conscious fulfillment of the Higher Will.

661. Each thought put into action is a contribution to the fiery creativeness. Each fulfilled thought is linked to Our actions. How carefully must the disciples examine the quality of their thoughts! Has not the worm of egoism, or conceit, or the manifestation of self-love hidden somewhere? The ability to admit this honestly is something that each spirit must develop within himself. Only thus can one fulfill one's mission in the Plan of the Lords.

The Chain of Hierarchy is built by fulfillment of the Higher Will.

662. Certainly the power of Hierarchy is the most vital, and only by this bridge can one build. Thus, in the foundation of each great beginning is laid the energy imbued by the law of Hierarchy. Only upon the principle of harmony and unification can one build. Only upon the basis of affirmation of the principle of Hierarchy can higher possibilities be affirmed. The Creative Will proclaims that a united consciousness leads to harmonious decisions.

663. Who, then, creates by the power of the spirit? The Bearer of Fire, the keen servitor of evolution, the creator of men, the one who gives all his fires for the growth of humanity. Humanity must be like these Light-Bearers in its quests.

How, then, does the Hierarch create on Earth? By uplifting all the surroundings. Thus, all spheres are uplifted by the pure flame of the Hierarch.

664. Certainly creative thought will regenerate the world. He who masters thought creates evolution. Thus We can move human consciousness toward progress. We create by thought.

Humanity, truly, must realize the significance of thought! The Teaching, truly, must be embraced by sensitive thoughts! Each striving thought can impel the spirit to achievement. Hence We value so highly the ability to shape one's thoughts. Each great thought is joined to the Chain of Hierarchy. Thus is evolution built.

665. Subtlety of receptivity is necessary for an understanding of the Teacher. In the realization that the Teacher imbues the disciple's spirit with higher understanding is contained the entire progress of the disciple. The creativeness of the spirit can be impelled upward only when thought ascends. The link between the Teacher and disciple is forged by spiritual striving. Truly, who will uplift the spirit of the disciple if not his Teacher? Only the Higher can uplift the lower. Without this understanding it is impossible to advance. Thus, let us conclude by stressing the refinement of receptivity.

666. Hierarchy is affirmed in the Universe by cosmic law. The Cosmic Magnet has placed the Highest Might above everything; thus this law is based on cosmic affirmation. How, then, can one fail to join the Highest Might, which guides the planet? Only Reason can direct the Cosmic Magnet. Therefore, Cosmic Reason, which permeates everything, brings tension to everything. The energies that differ in potentiality take their proper place in Cosmos, affirming their role according to the level of their developing power. Thus, the degree of potentiality of the energy determines its position on a higher or lower step. Similarly is the evolutionary step of the human spirit determined; the Cosmic Magnet intensifies the quality of the spirit, leading it into the Infinite.

667. In Cosmos the center of striving rests upon the principle of Hierarchy. Cosmos acts by means of attraction to the manifested powerful center. Thus the cosmic seed is manifested in each action of Hierarchy by the quality of the striving, which ascends through realization of the predominant principle. Cosmic creativeness brings together the harmonious energies. This principle is so important that it is an undeniable necessity, which is truly affirmed by the principle of Hierarchy. The entire Universe is saturated with this principle. This spirit, which imbues all cosmic manifestations on the planet, is affirmed by the Highest Reason. Therefore, man, being a part of Cosmos, cannot separate himself from this principle. When cosmic creativeness is imbued with Reason, each manifestation of the Infinite is affirmed by the same principle.

668. Of all principles leading to the broadening of consciousness, the principle of Hierarchy is the most powerful. Each manifested change is based upon it. Whither can the spirit direct itself without the Guiding Hand? Where can the eye and the heart turn without Hierarchy, when the Giving Hand of the Hierarch affirms the flow of destiny, and when the Hand of the Hierarch directs one to the best manifested date, and one becomes familiar with even the highest energies? Therefore, the seed of the spirit becomes imbued with the Cosmic Ray of the Hierarch. Since the most powerful principle contains in itself the potentiality of fire, the pure Fire of the spirit of the Hierarch is affirmed as

the highest principle. Thus shall we remember our spiritual Leaders. Thus shall we revere the Law of Hierarchy.

669. "How, then, O Lord, to spread Thy Teaching? How, then, O Lord, to find those for whom it is predestined to apply Thy Word for fulfillment?"

And the Lord said in reminder, "A hermit searched for one to whom to entrust the Revelation. And he took the scroll and placed it at the crossroad, 'Let the Supreme One Himself point out who should find His Teaching.'

"And a little girl came and wrapped her bread in the scroll of Scriptures. But the hermit prepared another scroll and again placed it at the crossroad.

"And a merchant passed and wrote over the scroll with his calculations of his profits. But the hermit did not tire, and once more placed another scroll there. And thus until the very end of his labors and his days.

"But when the Higher One asked the hermit how he had spread the Teaching, he answered, 'It is not given unto me to judge which bird will build the best nest out of these Teachings.'

"Truly, we never know who will use the scroll to torment, who will leave it for oblivion, and who will place it under his pillow in order to affirm it as his own foundation.

"I do not consider that thou hast acted wrongly in offering thy labor for the use of people unknown to thee."

Thus the Lord affirmed the spreading of the Teaching impersonally, without impatience, without irritation, and without expectation.

Thus, give you also to all—without prejudice, without judging.

Carry, O bird, the Teaching; and in thy flight deliver it into the hearth of those who live in expectation of receiving it.

Carry the Teaching to the crossroad!

670. Give these notes anonymously, lest someone, from some dark corner, make accusations about a self-interested motive. We shall continue Agni Yoga when the Indications already offered have been applied.

Many means and possibilities follow the mastering of the fires.

The element of fire is as unlimited as Infinity. The study of its properties will constitute the joy of life.

A life imbued with the qualities of Fire is a life of *podvig*.

Agni Yoga is ended. There will be additions to the next part, and there will be experiences, and observations upon the seeding and growth of the Fiery Flower.

Apply pure striving!

Given in the Valley of the Brahmaputra, which finds its source in the Lake of the Great Nagas, the Guardians of the Teaching of the *Rig-Veda:*

"I have set down the foundation of Agni Yoga in four directions, like the pistil of a flower.

"I affirmed Agni Yoga as the pillar of My Steps, and received into My Hands the fire of the Stone.

"I now have given the fiery Stone to her, who by Our decision shall be named the Mother of Agni Yoga, because she consecrated herself to the test of the Fire of Space.

"The streams of this fire were seared upon the Stone in its great flight before the image of the sun.

"A veil of sparks covered the summits of the Protectress of the Snows when the Stone made its fiery passage from south to north into the Guarded Valley."

AGNI YOGA SERIES

Agni Yoga Society
www.agniyoga.org

CPSIA information can be obtained
at www.ICGtesting.com
Printed in the USA
BVHW050950270223
659303BV00011B/176